THE DEATH AND LIFE OF THE SINGLE-FAMILY HOUSE

In the series *Urban Life, Landscape, and Policy*,
edited by ZANE L. MILLER, DAVID STRADLING, AND LARRY BENNETT

ALSO IN THIS SERIES:

NATHANAEL LAUSTER

THE DEATH AND LIFE OF THE SINGLE-FAMILY HOUSE

Lessons from Vancouver on Building a Livable City

TEMPLE UNIVERSITY PRESS
Philadelphia • Rome • Tokyo

TEMPLE UNIVERSITY PRESS
Philadelphia, Pennsylvania 19122
www.temple.edu/tempress

Library of Congress Cataloging-in-Publication Data

Names: Lauster, Nathanael Thomas, 1972– author.
Title: The death and life of the single-family house : lessons from Vancouver
  on building a livable city / Nathanael Lauster.
Description: Philadelphia : Temple University Press, [2016] | Series: Urban
  life, landscape, and policy series | Includes bibliographical references
  and index.
Identifiers: LCCN 2016018608 (print) | LCCN 2016029774 (ebook) | ISBN
  9781439913932 (cloth : alk. paper) | ISBN 9781439913949
  (paper : alk. paper) | ISBN 9781439913956 (E-Book)
Subjects: LCSH: Housing, Single family—British Columbia—Vancouver—History.
  | Dwellings—British Columbia—Vancouver—History. | City and town
  life—British Columbia—Vancouver—History. | City planning—British
  Columbia—Vancouver—History.
Classification: LCC HD7305.V3 L38 2016 (print) | LCC HD7305.V3 (ebook) | DDC
  333.33/80971133—dc23
LC record available at https://lccn.loc.gov/2016018608

Printed in the United States of America

9 8 7 6 5 4 3 2

To Ron and Cindy Lauster,
Teachers, Conservationists, and Book Lovers

CONTENTS

LIST OF FIGURES AND TABLES

Figures

Tables

ACKNOWLEDGMENTS

Vancouver's #14 bus runs along an electrified trolley line. Up toward the University of British Columbia, the line makes a funny one-block jump. Then it climbs a steep hill. One day, somewhere around that hill, my four-year-old said to me, "This is the house habitat!" Sure enough, for the next five blocks of our ride, we were surrounded by detached houses, leaving behind a long strip of low-rise apartments and commerce. Maybe his comment should not have surprised me, especially given his love of nature documentaries. But I really liked the idea of "house habitat," and it quickly became an organizing principle of the present book project. And so my first acknowledgment and thanks go to my always insightful oldest son, Ezra.

A host of others have also earned my deep appreciation for all they have contributed to this book. Grants from the University of British Columbia and the Social Science and Humanities Research Council (SSHRC) of Canada supported the data-collection projects undergirding the book and paid for the work of my two research assistants, Mia Chung and Amanda Watson. Both were extraordinarily important in getting the data collection up and running. Mia, in particular, took an active part in both the coordination and the interviewing process, eliciting many of the most insightful comments from our research participants. Another research assistant, Joseph Tohill, provided help with a key graphic.

My colleagues at the University of British Columbia have been extraordinarily supportive, especially within the Sociology Department. Neil Guppy and Rima Wilkes provided constructive reads of a lengthy early draft—an extremely generous act. Other colleagues and friends, including (but not limited to) Gillian Creese, Francesco Duina, Stephanie Gee, Amin Ghaziani, Neil Gross, Sara Harris, Sean Lauer, Isaac Martin, Alina McKay, Kevin McKouen, Hilary Silver, Gerry Veenstra, Jim White, Elvin Wyly, Carrie Yodanis, and Jing Zhao, encouraged me in my writing, provided publishing advice, and/or participated in lengthy conversations with me about my study. Many thanks, as well, go out to my students over the years. They have often provided helpful feedback about what did and did not work in early drafts, especially in my courses "Urban Sociology" and "Built Environments."

I owe a deep debt of gratitude to David Stradling, series editor, for providing a warm welcome to my early manuscript and for guiding me through the process of making it a much better work. Temple University Press editor Aaron Javsicas also provided invaluable guidance. I could not have asked for a better editorial team to shepherd me through. Series editor Zane Miller also provided encouraging feedback. Three anonymous external reviewers deserve my thanks for their close reads of early drafts. They offered many insights and recommendations, nearly all of which went into improving the book.

Finally, I thank my family, both extended and local. Completing this book would have been inconceivable without the support of Amy Hanser, who discussed initial ideas with me, read my work, encouraged me with generous praise, and provided exceptional insight into how to make my writing better. What a lucky human being I am to have Amy in my life. Having begun by expressing gratitude to my oldest son, I close by offering thanks to my youngest, Darragh, for reminding me regularly of what a joy it is to dwell within this world.

THE DEATH AND LIFE OF THE
SINGLE-FAMILY HOUSE

INTRODUCTION

> It's not even a starter home; it's just a start.
>
> —JASON LASERRE, VANCOUVERITE

Jason Laserre grew up in a large, single-family house. Moving from the suburban outskirts of metropolitan Vancouver in toward the core, the newlywed spoke somewhat disparagingly of the modest rental apartment he shared with his wife. It offered not a home, but "just a start." Where would this start take him? Jason drew on a widespread cultural script as well as his parents' experiences in describing the most obvious destination: "[You] get married, then you move out to the suburbs, and you get a two-layer house, and it's like, however many bedrooms and a backyard and a dog." For Jason, as for many others, a house was expected as part of the package deal of adulthood. Houses have become the standard habitat for North American humanity.[1]

But Vancouver does not work that way anymore. As a local headline would have it, "In the city, single-family homes are a dying breed."[2] Houses, it seems, are not simply habitats for people. Houses have habitats of their own. Across most of North America, these habitats remain protected by law. But Vancouver is tinkering with the legal protections afforded its houses and has largely prevented the expansion of suburban sprawl into its remaining agricultural hinterland. Scarcity amid growth has produced speculation. The

---

[1] See Townsend 2002 for more on cultural scripts and package deals. Here and throughout the book, I use "North America" as shorthand for the United States and Canada, following Population Reference Bureau convention (www.prb.org), with no slight intended toward Mexico or any of the countries of Central America and the Caribbean. Quotes from Jason come from interview data, as discussed below and in the Appendix.

[2] Bellett 2013.

benchmark price of a detached house across Metro Vancouver now tops a million dollars, and few can afford even the worn-looking bungalows that remain.[3] Instead, most people now live in the various urban alternatives, low-rise and high-rise, increasingly springing up across the metropolitan area.

These transformations would seem to directly challenge cultural expectations about the good life. What a surprise, then, that Vancouver is frequently touted as the "most livable" city in North America.[4] How should we make sense of this remarkable discrepancy? How do people like Jason Laserre cope with the steadily increasing likelihood they will never acquire a house of their own?

As it turns out, Jason seems to be coping fairly well. A house, he noted mildly, is "just not feasible for some people." Along with the exorbitant cost of reproducing his parents' lifestyle, Jason considered the hardship of his father's daily commute: "Watching him come home tired every day, and having to sit through all those extra hours—wasted hours—in the car. . . . I mean, it just doesn't seem very enjoyable." Living in his apartment near downtown, it took Jason ten minutes to walk to work: "And when I finish working, I'm tired, and I can be home ten minutes later—it's . . . it's great!" Though he initially seemed to reject the notion that the little apartment he shared with his wife constituted anything but a "start," he later contradicted himself, noting that he is making no plans to move. Even imagining raising a baby there, Jason suggested, "We would make do." As he put it, "This is our first home together, you know, it feels great!"

In this book, I describe the dramatic transformation in Vancouver's built environment and provide tools for analyzing how it came about. I also explore how most residents of Vancouver attempt to make themselves at home without a house. Sometimes they fail. Single-family detached houses do things for their inhabitants that are hard to replace, providing meaning and structure to everyday life. Nevertheless, most Vancouverites succeed in assembling a home, both for themselves and their families, and many even find that local lifestyles improve on what a house might have to offer. There are lessons here for the rest of North America. We can start building our cities differently without sacrificing their livability. We can rethink the extraordinary legal protections that support the single-family detached house. Maybe they are no longer necessary. Maybe we can let them die away. This raises an important question: how did they come alive in the first place?

As I argue, the death and life of the single-family house cannot be disentangled from the notion of habitat. In this book, I move back and forth

---

[3] See the popular Internet game *Crack Shack or Mansion*, available at http://www.crackshack ormansion.com/. Dollar figures here in Canadian currency.

[4] Canadian Press 2011; *The Economist* Intelligence Unit 2015.

between two conceptions of what I call "house habitat": the first is concerned with the habitat houses create for people, and the second with the habitat people create for houses.[5] Investigating the former sort of house habitat requires detailing the experiences of urban residents. Looking into the latter—the habitat people create for houses—means taking history seriously. The past informs the future of the "Great American Cities" that U.S.-Canadian urbanist Jane Jacobs wrote about so passionately a half-century ago.[6] During the early decades of the twentieth century, houses were molded into important social positions and turned into regulations to be set loose within the expansive and interconnected urban ecologies of North America. From there, newly defined "single-family detached" houses took on a life of their own, grew wild, and overran the landscape. What do we get by taking houses seriously as creatures built, defined, and protected by our regulations? For one thing, we can better figure out how to get them under control. But why would we want to?

The metaphor of the invasive species may be useful here. Consider, for a moment, the mountain pine beetle. The pine beetle is a small insect, less than five millimeters in length. Nevertheless, it has been blamed for enormous losses within the coniferous forests of western North America. The sticky sap in pine trees usually works to repel insects and larvae looking for a meal. But the mountain pine beetle has developed a symbiotic relationship with a sort of fungus, commonly known as blue stain fungus, that stops pine trees from producing resin. The mountain pine beetle carries spores of the fungus from tree to tree on a special structure in its head.[7] In exchange, fungal infection stops the pine tree from being able to kill or expel pine beetle larvae with sap. Together, feeding larvae and fungal infection tend to kill off trees within a few weeks of an attack. Pine beetle infections occur most readily among older or weakened trees. Healthy trees are more resistant. But something, possibly linked to climate change (pine beetles do not weather very cold winters well), has allowed the pine beetle to devastate vast swaths of western forests in recent years, killing weakened and otherwise healthy trees alike. As the pine forests die off, many scientists worry about their loss as a carbon sink leading in turn to further global warming.

There is a direct relationship between the spread of the beetle and the supply of housing, insofar as much of the lumber used to build houses

---

[5] As noted in the Acknowledgments, my son coined this term. See Gieryn 2002 on the structured and structuring roles of buildings.

[6] Jacobs 1961.

[7] Fungi are actually carried as spores in mycangia, structures located near the mouth parts of the beetle that are specialized for the purpose. Six and Bentz (2007) and Rice and Langor (2009) provide fascinating insights into the complexity of the various species of blue stain fungi often simultaneously carried around by pine beetles, furthering its ability to sustain a destructive march across northwestern forests.

around the world is harvested from the mountainous forests of western North America. But more intriguingly, there is the unsettling relationship between the pine beetle and blue stain fungus to consider. While the pine beetle most often takes the blame for the destruction of these forests, we could just as easily imagine the blue stain fungus as the primary villain. Or, even more accurately, we could think of the symbiotic relationship between pine beetle and blue stain fungus as the true culprit. Break the relationship and we could save the forest. This is a thought worth holding on to.

As people spread outward from North American cities, so too do detached houses. The house makes all sorts of environments inhabitable for people, and is especially linked to family formation and reproduction. People seem to carry around favorable ideas about houses, regularly identifying them in surveys as the places they want to live. This is especially the case for parents with children. The sprawl associated with the outward progress of the house displaces existing ecosystems, one habitat for another. The use of carbon-intensive energy to heat and cool houses, as well as to get from the house to other places in the city, further contributes to climate change, disrupting ever more habitats. Arguably, the relationship between houses and people is to the world as the relationship between fungi and pine beetles is to the forest: trouble. Maybe we should break the relationship.

Transforming a Troublesome Habitat

Habitat and invasion: these ecological concepts are worth taking back to the city. They were first brought there with the founding of urban sociology. Once upon a time, the industrial and commercial Urban Core of the city, rather than the single-family house, was viewed as invasive. Urban Cores were problematically understood as sprawling outward, deluging nearby neighborhoods with wave after wave of ethnic minorities and members of the lower classes along the way. Neighborhood succession from one habitat to the next was viewed as "naturally" accompanying urban growth.[8]

A central argument of this book is that the regulations defining the single-family house were hammered into the shape of a white picket fence capable of halting this process. Our forebears set in place a Great House Reserve around the Urban Cores of North America, and to this day not much else can get in there. Even in the City of Vancouver, where this reserve is arguably under the most sustained attack, it still covers some 80 percent of

---

[8] The Chicago School founding the field of urban sociology within North America relied heavily on ecological metaphors (Abbott 1997; Wachsmuth 2012). See Burgess 1928 for a few lasting examples.

the residential land base, while accommodating substantially less than 40 percent of the population.[9]

The Great House Reserve was built as a wall to contain the market-governed city, taming it for human inhabitation. Once built, the regulatory framework mostly faded into the background, so that most of us do not see the lines drawn between Urban Core and house reserve unless we happen to peruse the technical maps appended to local zoning bylaws.[10] Only then do the stark limitations placed on urban development across most of North America become clear. Only then does the house take shape as a creature of land-use standards: the single-family detached dwelling. Though this regulatory form of the house is a relatively recent invention—just about a century old—the house written down on paper has been quite successful at defending and expanding the domain of the house in concrete.

Highlighting the regulatory construction of the house offers a different story from those more commonly told about the shape of North American cities. Both detractors and apologists of sprawl tend to treat the house as little more than an extension of human nature or North American culture, enacting a morality play across the metropolitan landscape. For apologists, house life epitomizes that which is best in humanity: market freedom coupled with family values. This is a position championed, for instance, by works like Robert Bruegmann's *Sprawl: A Compact History*, which points, quite correctly, to the many problems houses seem to solve for us.[11] Read this way, the suburban spread of houses represents not an invasive and destructive plague on the land but a monument to continental contentment. For detractors, the vision turns darker, focusing—also quite correctly—on the many problems associated with house living, but ultimately attributing these problems to the rapaciousness of our culture or lifestyles: "We have met the enemy, and he is us."[12] This is the theme of a long line of books, most recently *The Housing Bomb*, whose central metaphor concerns North America's "house addiction."[13] The case for change seems either depraved or futile. By contrast,

---

[9] Rough figures are drawn from Metro Vancouver Policy and Planning Department (2008) land-use estimates for 2006 for the City of Vancouver, combined with 2006 census figures for households by structure. Importantly, houses here include semidetached and duplex structures to match land-use categories, making these numbers more inclusive than census categories alone—see Chapter 1 for further detail.

[10] Or, in other cases, the deed restrictions systematically imposed on lots.

[11] Bruegmann 2005; see also less scholarly illustrations by Kotkin (2012).

[12] The quote is from various iterations of Walt Kelly's environmentalism message in his comic strip *Pogo*.

[13] Peterson, Peterson, and Liu 2013. See also Beauregard 2006, 6, for a more Freudian interpretation of futility: "Life in the suburbs was a mark of American exceptionalism. . . . [N]eglect of the cities has deep roots in the American consciousness." Despite their dark outlooks, both books still have much to offer analysts.

if we start from a position where we can clearly separate ourselves from our houses—we are not our houses; they offer just one of many possible habitats—then the case for change does not look quite so scary or grim.

The metaphor of pine beetle and blue stain fails us here. If we have become symbiotically related to our houses, then any attack on the house—our coevolved partner in crime—remains an attack on humanity. But what if our relationship to the house is not symbiotic after all? What if it is more parasitic? Let's set aside all the farms, fields, and forests displaced by houses. Let's set aside even the associated warming of the planet: devastation of habitat on a massive scale. Putting things in a more human perspective, are houses even good for people?

Conversations with a diverse collection of Vancouverites provide insights into how houses mold our thinking and shape our routines. Houses definitely seem like solutions to many problems of everyday urban living, maximizing control over space, but ultimately they cause more trouble than they are worth. In terms of everyday life, they take a great deal of work to maintain, they can be boring and isolating, and they tend to reduce our adaptability. More broadly, houses fail to support our health, our families, our communities, and our systems of democratic governance. This book offers a close study of the "life" of the house, spanning its historical evolution and present inhabitance. Through this research, I suggest that we could do better for ourselves, our cities, and our world by letting the house as a regulatory creature die away.

Situating the Study

Vancouver, the third largest metropolitan area in Canada and twenty-fifth largest in North America, provides a useful illustration of an urban habitat in transition. As demonstrated by archival research, Vancouver was an early adopter of house-oriented zoning bylaws in North America, producing by the middle of the twentieth century one of the most house-dominated metropolises on the continent. But since the 1960s, Vancouver has rapidly broken with the single-family detached house, in a fashion more complete than any other urban area on the continent. In a challenge to the idea that consumers demand houses, Vancouver's dramatic transformation has left it recognized as one of the most livable cities in the world as well as an international model for sustainability and urbanism. Indeed, Vancouver has rebranded itself as the world's "Greenest City," and its downtown planning principles have been spread around the globe as Vancouverism. But Vancouver's story as planning icon remains incomplete without investigating its turn away from the single-family detached house.[14]

---

[14] See Boddy 2003, 2005; Peck 2010; and Punter 2003 on the rise of Vancouverism.

By virtue of its startling trajectory, Vancouver offers an ideal case study. In its early similarity to cities across the United States, Vancouver's history challenges strong arguments about American exceptionalism in urban form.[15] Sprawl readily crossed the U.S. border, and explanations for the rise of the house need to do the same. Shared history provides fertile ground for drawing lessons from Vancouver's subsequent transformation. What changed? As I argue, Vancouver's transformation, though unique, was never predestined by geography or demography. Instead, regulatory transformations enabled Vancouver to renovate, build over, and build around the house. Could this process work elsewhere? How are Vancouver's residents coping with their new environs? Could others cope as well?

I am one of Vancouver's residents. As a local, I have tracked media stories about housing as they develop. Donning the cap of the historian, I have similarly explored the archival records and policy documents defining housing types and promoting their spread. As a housing researcher and demographer, I have worked extensively with census and survey data concerning people's relationships with their dwellings. I return to these data sources in the pages ahead, paying special attention to how they might be used to document Vancouver's history with the house and, through this history, speak to North American patterns as a whole.

Through the years from 2008 to 2010, I also worked with my talented research assistant, Mia Chung, to gather in-depth interview data from over fifty residents of the Vancouver metropolitan area. At first we sought to gather information on the moral connections people made between their housing and family situations. But increasingly it became clear that the practical elements of everyday life occupied at least as central a role in residents' narratives of how they "fit" with their housing. Most members of our sample did not live in houses, but a few did, especially as we ventured out into surrounding suburban municipalities. We asked residents probing questions about their experiences with housing, their problems, their desires, and their plans. We followed up by interviewing realtors and other professionals about their experiences working with clients. In order to both encourage openness and honor the privacy of those who spoke with us, interviewees were granted confidentiality and are identified here only pseudonymously. But many of our recorded discussions are recounted in this book, often circling back to how and why people feel connected to houses, and what might prompt them to accept dwelling in a different fashion.[16]

---

[15] See, e.g., Hirt's (2014) *Zoned in the USA* and Beauregard's (2006) *When America Became Suburban.*

[16] More details on the method of recruitment, sample characteristics, and procedures followed are provided in the Appendix.

Since so many people generously volunteered their stories to help me understand the relationship between people and houses, it seems only fitting that I should share a little of my own. During most of the writing of this book, I lived with my common-law spouse, Amy, in the two-bedroom apartment she owned on the eastern border of the Kitsilano neighborhood in Vancouver. We shared her 734-square-foot apartment, on the top floor of a low-rise building, with two cats and our young son. He took over one of the bedrooms (our former office) when he was born. The cats took over the rest. As I began to revise this manuscript for publication, we had a second child and moved to a townhouse that more than doubled the size of our former space. We now border Vancouver's Great House Reserve. We are surrounded by the green of trees here, and the townhouse is nice, but the green of "real house" envy starts just across the street.

As children, Amy and I both grew up mostly in the suburbs of the United States. We got used to living in houses. To be sure, we both experienced alternative housing situations as we moved out, including dormitories in college and apartments in our graduate school and early working days. Now we are both relatively well-paid employees of the University of British Columbia.[17] It seems natural that we should be living in a house at least as magnificent as those of our parents. Our employer even offers a generous program to help out with down payments on mortgages. Nevertheless, we consider buying a decent house to be well out of our financial reach. On our side of Vancouver, houses tend to start at around two million dollars.[18]

Our inability to afford the exorbitant cost of a detached house in and around Vancouver clashes with the expectations we held in our younger days. The role a house played in our youthful imaginings of the future, even if often implicitly, intrigues me now that I seem unlikely to own one. What I find even more interesting, as a sociologist, is that so many other people have or had similar expectations. Indeed, many of us seem to carry houses around with us, even if we do not live in them. This is the personal history of expectation and dismay, redirected toward curiosity, that I bring to the present research project. Am I okay with never owning a house? All things considered, I think I am, and I would like to encourage other people to think they would be, too.

---

[17] Our earnings are estimated to be in the top 5 percent of Vancouver households, though it is likely that many households underreport income.

[18] The May 2014 Real Estate Board of Greater Vancouver (2016) benchmark price (i.e., what you could expect to pay) for a detached house in Vancouver's West Side was C$2,229,800. As seen from BC Assessments data from the City of Vancouver's "VanMap" application, available at http://vancouver.ca/your-government/vanmap.aspx, the modest ranch house across the street from us was assessed around C$2.5 million in 2014, while its newer and larger neighbor was assessed at C$3 million.

In the work ahead, I draw on a set of ideological lenses that offer keen insight into housing, especially those derived from pragmatist and actor-network theoretical traditions, as well as feminism and political economy. These lenses inform both my empirical view of what cities *are* doing and my normative vision of what cities *should be* doing. I circle back to this normative vision, concerned with the promotion of justice and diversity within a democratic tradition, toward the end of the book. As I suggest there, habitat thinking and social justice thinking go hand in hand in offering ways to better understand our history, our housing, and what our cities should be doing for us.

Chapters Ahead

The text that follows is divided into eight chapters, with the first half focused on the history of how cities created so much habitat for houses, and the second on the sort of habitat that houses create for people. Chapter 1 defines what a house is and why it might matter. I argue that the house was unfolded into multiple forms—a concrete thing, a fuzzy cultural idea, a market commodity, and a regulatory creature. I focus on laying out this last and generally least familiar form of the house, providing a brief and sociologically informed history of how the house was written into local bylaws all across the continent. From there I argue that once the regulatory creature went to work, it structured much that followed. Culturally, people generally came to understand the house as a flexible sort of package deal associated with family, a concept pulling together plentiful space, ownership, and a yard.

In Chapter 2, I lay out the case for labeling the house an urban parasite. I draw on a variety of data as well as diverse literatures bridging the fields of anthropology, ecology, economics, engineering, geography, planning, political science, public health, sociology, and urban studies. Ecological ramifications, including habitat loss and climate change, take center stage, but I also note the trouble created by houses for urban vitality, the poor, democracy, family, and human health.

The next two chapters chart the rise and fall of the house within the history of Vancouver. Together they describe how the house as a regulatory creature was brought to life, put into service, and ultimately put in its place. Chapter 3 reveals Vancouver's early story, as a young metropolis rapidly sprawling out from its center and leaving ordered rows of houses in its wake. In the first part of the chapter, I examine Vancouver's frontier past, exploring the problems associated with its settlement and dramatic market-led growth. In the second part, I detail how the City of Vancouver took up the international fad of town planning as a solution to its diverse problems, initiating the formation of its Great House Reserve. The detached house became just about the only thing people could build outside Vancouver's older urbanized core. The metropolis seemed destined for house domination, just like most of the rest of the continent.

In Chapter 4, I describe how, during the 1960s, the character of the region began to change in dramatic ways. First the modernization of planning drew Vancouver into the same trajectory as other North American metropolises. Then it rather spectacularly unraveled. Both what was built and what went unbuilt matter for the recent history of Vancouver. Ultimately Vancouver built around the house, built over the house, and renovated its very nature as a regulatory creature. Its rapidly developing regulatory ecology made the denser city a more desirable place to live. The chapter charts the amazingly precipitous decline of the house as the dominant technology for dwelling in Vancouver, and provides a sense of the contingency involved.

In the remaining chapters of the book, I populate Vancouver's urban landscape by interviewing its contemporary residents. What do they think of the death of the single-family house as an accessible way of life? In Chapter 5, I draw out the implications of this question by considering whether Vancouver has become uninhabitable for everyone save the ridiculously wealthy. One question leads to others concerning the relationship between habits and habitats. How hard is it for people to change the lifestyles to which they have grown accustomed? What distinguishes a lifestyle from a living standard? Ultimately, it seems, Vancouver provides the cultural scaffolding for many people to reinterpret their lives as success stories even when they do not own houses.

In Chapter 6, I take seriously the notion that on an everyday basis, the house still provides the most inhabitable of living environments. What gets in the way of establishing decent working routines for all of those Vancouverites who cannot afford houses? I investigate the difficulties associated with lacking control over enough space. The problems apartment dwellers and their like encounter with their living spaces are embedded in their relationships with one another, as well as in their attempts to fully inhabit the world around them. The house, as a package, often seems a ready solution to the problems associated with making city life livable.

In Chapter 7, I chart alternative visions of the good life, derived from urban inhabitants who reject the single-family house. Urban residents describe how apartments, townhouses, and the like both remain more accessible than detached homes and require far less maintenance work. Moreover, they remain surprisingly good places to raise children. A different version of home and inhabitability ultimately emerges from conversations with Vancouverites. Urban living provides excitement and promotes adaptability. It permits access to more communal space, and encourages people to more fully share and engage with others as they occupy the diverse land-scapes around them.

In Chapter 8, I build on earlier chapters in describing how habitat think-ing and social justice thinking complement one another. I also suggest direc-tions for better city building. Vancouver provides valuable lessons about how to diversify cities. At the same time, it has many lessons to learn in order to better promote social justice. I argue for tearing down the walls separating the Great House Reserve from the rest of the city. But mostly that is because these barriers are getting in the way of what we should be doing: building more and building better.

WHAT'S A HOUSE?

A building that people, usually one family, live in.

—*Cambridge Free English Dictionary*

What is a house? As it turns out, providing an adequate answer to this deceptively simple question requires tracing the unfolding of the house across multiple domains into at least four noteworthy forms: as concrete thing, as cultural idea, as market commodity, and as regulatory creature. The last of these plays a particularly important role in the story ahead, but each form speaks to a different way in which the house operates as a social actor.[1]

First, a house is a very physical thing. The typical North American house is literally set in nineteen tons of concrete, and hence made up of a substance we commonly employ as an adjective to describe the very notion of solid reality.[2] We can build houses and we can tear them down. We can see, feel, and at times even hear them (when the wind is just right, or where the floor creaks in time to our steps). Artist Lynda Barry memorably evokes their aromas, from "mint, tangerines, and library books" to "the cat pee smell of the house next door."[3] When we consider our sensory experiences of houses as physical entities, we also get a glimpse of all the ways they act on us.

---

[1] Law and Singleton (2005) speak to the importance of objects' flickering forms in social analysis.

[2] U.S. Department of Energy 2012, table 2.5.7. By comparison, typically three to four truckloads of logs are required for framing materials. See, for instance, the "How Much Wood Goes into a House?" estimates from the Idaho Forest Products Commission, http://www.idahoforests.org/woodhous.htm.

[3] Barry 2002, 52–53.

They have been constructed to do so—to constrain and enable our actions in particular ways. Walls limit our movements, but also keep out strangers and noises. Ceilings keep out the rain. Doors reenable movement, and help distinguish "indoors" from "outdoors."

These are just some of the more obvious appendages of the house, made visible by the work they do on our behalf. As highlighted by sociologist Bruno Latour, it is relatively easy to argue that built things do this work far better and more faithfully than human replacements (e.g., bodyguards and umbrella-bearing servants) could accomplish without them.[4] Yet houses remain underappreciated actors. By and large, and especially if we inhabit a house in decent repair, we tend to take all their work for granted. To complicate matters further, houses are not easy to define in a collective sense. Since our experiences with them remain rooted in direct and uniquely placed sensory interaction, houses resist easy generalization. This is the first form taken by the house—as a concrete and individually substantial thing, a unique sensory experience, a pervasive but unremarkable agent at work within our everyday lives, a habitat.

Even if our experiences with individual houses remain unique, we still have ways of speaking about houses collectively, in symbolic form. Indeed, I suspect most North Americans carry around a rough mental picture of what a house generally looks like, thereby conveying some sort of transportable house ideal. If asked to depict one, I could readily draw a rectangular base, add a triangle for the roof, sketch in a door and a window, and maybe put a chimney up on top—something like a two-dimensional version of a house from the game *Monopoly*.[5] In the appropriate neighborhood, I could also simply point to the houses around me, following the same logic laid out by U.S. Supreme Court Justice Potter Stewart's definition of pornography: "I know it when I see it."[6] Nevertheless, if asked to describe a house in words, I find it surprisingly difficult to get beyond the sort of misleading and incomplete answers I might provide when my son asks (e.g., "It's where people live"). This may be because we are sloppy with the word *house*. It is an old and well-worn word. We use it as both verb and noun, in correspondingly general and restrictive senses, and we seldom bracket it with technical definitions. This ambiguity is important to keep in mind when talking to people and writing about their thoughts on houses. As far as most people

---

[4] Latour 1992.

[5] The City of Vancouver used a *Monopoly*-style house image as a logo for its "Home, Property, and Development" website hub until December 2013: https://web.archive.org/web/20131205181104/http://vancouver.ca/home-property-development.aspx.

[6] Quote from *Jacobellis v. Ohio* (No. 11) 378 U.S. 184 (1964) accessed via the Legal Information Institute (Cornell University) at https://www.law.cornell.edu/supremecourt/text/378/184.

are concerned, the house as an idea remains at least somewhat flexible and transportable.

This is the second form of the house we may encounter: the cultural idea of the house. Even though it remains fuzzy, the house as an idea acquires power by association. It becomes part of our cognitive habitat, structuring our understanding of the world. As we will see, the association of the house with success, adulthood, and moral correctness lends it some weight in people's deliberations about where they would feel most at home.

Speaking to the fuzziness of the house as an idea is the fact that as a consumer good within the context of real estate markets, it seems to take on only slightly sharper definition. For instance, as prospective buyers browse residential market websites, like realtylink.org, they are quickly directed to the "house" as a distinct (and often default) "property type." Here the house is contrasted with an alternative set of property types, including (among others) apartments, townhouses, duplexes, farms or ranches, mobile homes, and multiplexes. Within my neighborhood, searching on "house" pulls up a wide range of properties, including those further described as coach houses, duplexes, and triplexes—each for sale as a single residential property. I am also able to search by characteristics including price, bathrooms, bedrooms, and age range.

Looking further—for example, within the market reports issued by the Real Estate Board of Greater Vancouver—the term "house" disappears, but I can find tallies of properties recently sold as divided into categories of detached, attached, and apartment. I can also retrieve the average, median, and "typical" home index price for properties within these categories. Both the terms "detached" and "house" remain mostly undefined within market reports and search functions. As these terms enter into more arcane financial tools, such as when linked to mortgage-backed securities, they undergo further categorical shifts in meaning. For instance, within one ratings agency report on mortgage securitization, "detached single-family homes" are considered the same as "semi-detached houses, row houses, and freehold townhomes," but fundamentally different from "2–4 family" and "condo" alternatives.[7]

This is the third form of the house: market object, commodity, or consumer good. Here the mutability of houses allows them to retain a fair amount of the ambiguity they carry through common usage. This flexibility is useful in making a deal. Here is what you want, and here is what I have: it is pretty much the same, right? The measure of the agency possessed by a

---

[7] See The Real Estate Board of Greater Vancouver website for "News + Statistics," www.rebgv .org, and DBRS (2011) report, p. 16. While "2–4 family unit" and "condominium" are both defined (or at least sketched) in the glossary (p. 32), no other property types are provided a definition. Both Glaeser and Kallal (1997) and Simkovic (2013) suggest, though for different reasons, that a general lack of transparency in the securitization of mortgages is not accidental.

house here is usually in what it costs. The potency of the house grows in relation to its market position, as acted on by buyers, sellers, landlords, renters, builders, and realtors.

If defining houses as physical entities, cultural ideas, and consumer goods remains somewhat elusive, there is at least one form in which the flickering nature of the house can be pinned down. In the halls of local government, the single-family detached house takes a carefully codified shape within bylaws and other assorted regulatory practices. In this sense, we may speak of the house as regulatory creature. The elaborate definitions of the house in law are what make it distinct from other structures as a technology for dwelling. In codifying these distinctions, technical definitions both rely on the guidance of existing regulations and legislation and enable further regulatory frameworks to develop around their encoded categories. The house both acquires a definite shape and takes on agency as an actor, directing what people should be doing and how cities should be built.

So where do the four forms of the house come from? To make a long story short, they were unfolded into their present configuration as an experimental solution to the myriad problems associated with inhabiting a city governed by markets. The house as a regulatory entity proved crucial in this endeavor, enabling the expansion of the house as both a physical entity and a commodity while transforming its character as an idea. Let's unpack this a little bit.

Unfolding the House

To envision a house in its primordial form, imagine a building constructed by its inhabitants as an extension of their dwelling practices. Indeed, linguistically and philosophically, Martin Heidegger argued that building and dwelling were once one and the same, rooted in human existence and unified as both activities and nouns. "Building as dwelling, that is, as being on the earth . . . remains for man's everyday experience that which from the outset is 'habitual'—we inhabit it, as our language says so beautifully." Similarly, in its early usage, the word *house* brought together "a building for habitation" with "the inhabitants or affairs of a house . . . a family and its retainers." The house spoke to the unity of idea and form, family and structure, building and dwelling, habitat and inhabitant.[8]

Today, very few people live in structures they build for themselves. Instead, people mostly purchase or rent their housing through real estate markets. Feeding those markets, builders are contracted by developers to

---

[8] Quotes are from Heidegger 1971, 145, and *Oxford English Dictionary* (online ed., accessed January 21, 2016) definitions. See also Bourdieu 2005 and Coontz 2005; of note, Bourdieu's earliest (1973) work extended on this idea for the Kabyle.

construct on appropriately zoned lots houses they never expect to live in, according to building codes and architectural designs they had no hand in creating. Today, as demonstrated all too poignantly during the United States' foreclosure crisis, houses remain eminently detachable from families.[9]

Across North America, the unfolding of the house from its primordial materials into its present four forms (concrete, culture, commodity, and creature) occurred primarily during the late nineteenth and early twentieth centuries, a particularly momentous period in history. A great transformation was afoot— a transformation meant to unleash on the world governance by market. Built on the operating principles of the factories sprouting up across the industrializing urban landscape, markets were viewed as models for reorganizing the city as well as the countryside and, more broadly, social life as a whole.

Karl Polanyi studied this process intently, but also argued that the transformation could never be complete. Social life resisted commodification. In particular, labor, land, and money constituted essential elements of a market economy, but these things remained socially embedded and could never be treated as more than "fictitious commodities." They required enormous amounts of regulation both to sustain them and to even partially transform them from the circumstances of their production—outside the market—into something seemingly governable within a market context. In short, "regulation and markets . . . grew up together," and all attempts at governing by market ultimately required the installation of new regulations to protect aspects of social life, constituting the "double movement" of market liberalization.[10]

At the very heart of the Great Transformation, the rapidly growing industrial cities of the Victorian Age beckoned to migrants displaced from the countryside. Landed interests within and around cities profited greatly from the influx of people and money, organizing themselves into real estate–based "growth machines." They refashioned land into a form mimicking other commodities, but it always remained uniquely located and intimately connected to the parcels around it, hence embedded in social relations and resistant to commodification. The treatment of urban land as a market-governed commodity, combined with the rent and sale of lots to the highest bidder, threatened social life with constant displacement. The free market city could not be sustained, and a host of urban ills were quickly observed by a rising and reform-minded middle class.[11]

---

[9] Richard Harris (2004) chronicles the decline in self-building and the rise of corporate suburbs. See Martin and Niedt 2015 on the impact of widespread foreclosure.

[10] Polanyi 1957, 68.

[11] See Molotch 1976 and Logan and Molotch 2007 on growth machines and the mismatch between the socially embedded "use value" of land and its "exchange value." See Storper and Manville 2006 for one of many critiques of treating land like a commodity deriving from perspectives beyond Polanyi's.

From the perspective of reformers, early industrial cities appeared as monstrous threats to decency, domesticity, and orderliness. Neighbors rented out their rooms and opened shop fronts during hard times. Factories, taverns, and tenements sprang up next to private homes during boom times. Streets first stank of horse manure, then filled with clamorous trolleys and dangerous cars. As unstable work arrangements mixed with readily available amusements, loud and hostile drunkards from the working classes littered those same streets. Culturally suspect immigrants provided a further threat to decency.[12]

As noted by social historians, the metastasizing chaos of the market-governed city posed a special problem for the ascendant middle classes, who looked to their housing as both stage and sanctuary. They needed a decent stage to demonstrate their moral superiority, distinguishing themselves from the working classes and (in Europe at least) the landed aristocracy. A related problem involved the need of business owners and managers to circumscribe their social ties, enabling the market, rather than historically embedded social obligations, to govern relationships with their workers. The middle class required a refuge from the ties that bound them to less fortunate members of society. But as long as the primacy of private property rights could be taken for granted within the market-governed city, housing could not be relied on to provide either a decent stage or a lasting sanctuary. There were simply too many unruly neighbors.[13]

A variety of creative protective actions were attempted—banning nuisances, licensing problematic businesses, retreating into protective enclaves—until, finally and experimentally, the idea of the single-family house was written into use-based zoning bylaws. From these tentative beginnings, a Great House Reserve was rapidly set up, blocking the outward expansion of North America's Urban Cores. The reactive nature of this transformation was aptly summarized by mid-twentieth-century zoning lawyer Richard Babcock, who echoed Polanyi's broader analysis in noting that the enactment of this Great House Reserve worked like a "double movement" solving two competing cultural objectives:

> These objectives are protection of the single-family home, and protection of the free market place. In land-use policy, the first objective requires that government take positive action, the second demands that the government refuse to take positive action.[14]

---

[12] See Addams 1910, Anderson 1991, Burgess 1928, Fogelson 2005, Hirt 2014, and Mawani 2009.

[13] See Coontz 2005, Fogelson 2005, Gillis 1996, and Wright 1981. Frykman and Löfgren (1987) provide similar insights from Sweden, and I borrow the terms "stage" and "sanctuary" from their analysis.

[14] Babcock 1966, 79. On planners, see Perin 1977 and Grant and Scott's (2011) Canadian update.

Writing Down the House

The use-based zoning bylaws that provided the formative matter for the house began as experimental regulatory innovations. They followed and built on powers established in fire codes and public health laws. In North America, they seem to have been invented in Los Angeles in 1909 and refined in Berkeley and New York City in 1916, from whence they quickly spread. Their diffusion was aided by the Standard State Zoning Enabling Act, developed and promoted by the U.S. Department of Commerce in 1924 as a model for state legislatures. The spread of zoning laws to Canada was facilitated by the rise of an international town planning profession and a generally shared reliance on common law.[15]

Underlining their experimental nature is the fact that use-based zoning bylaws very nearly failed their first major test as legal technologies, much as race-based zoning bylaws had failed in previous years.[16] After a series of conflicting lower-court cases, the U.S. Supreme Court took up the legality of use-based zoning in 1926. Though initially deadlocking, the justices legitimized zoning as law in the case of *Euclid v. Ambler*. Despite the contestation and contingency surrounding the case, the decision ultimately established the robustness of use-based zoning in the United States and likely helped pave the way for its spread into Canada during the same time period.[17]

A few relevant sections of the court decision establish how the legal technology of use-based zoning works and describe its codification of the single-family detached house. The most exclusive use district in Euclid, Ohio (the suburb of Cleveland at the heart of the case), was the U-1 district, limiting land uses to "single-family dwellings" consisting of "a basement and not less than three rooms and a bathroom." Other use districts also allowed single-family dwellings but progressively expanded the range of options possible to

---

[15] See Baar 1992, Hirt 2014, Perrin 1977, Talen 2012, and Wright 1981, with Jackson 1985 and Taylor 2009 expanding mostly on New York (where, unusually, houses were not initially distinguished from apartment buildings). Sewell (1994) suggests that Kitchener, Ontario, was the first Canadian city to adopt comprehensive zoning in 1924. But, as discussed in the next chapter, the municipality of Point Grey may have a better claim, though it amalgamated with Vancouver shortly after it passed zoning legislation in 1922. While most of Canada adheres to common law, Quebec also follows civil law.

[16] See Bauer 1945 and Taylor 2009. Race-based covenants and deed restrictions would last far longer, though they too eventually became unenforceable.

[17] See Baar 1992, G. Power 1989, Talen 2012, and Valverde 2011 for histories leading up to *Euclid v. Ambler*. Though they suggest slightly different trajectories and rationales, all note the narrowness of the victory and the contingency of the case. The Court vacillated before settling on the constitutionality of use-based zoning as legitimate based on the prevention of nuisance.

include "two-family dwellings" (U-2), "apartment houses [and] hotels" (U-3), and a range of other commercial and industrial uses. As the court noted:

> The serious question in the case arises over the provisions of the ordinance excluding from residential districts apartment houses, business houses, retail stores and shops, and other like establishments. This question involves the validity of what is really the crux of the more recent zoning legislation, namely, the creation and maintenance of residential districts, from which business and trade of every sort, including hotels and apartment houses, are excluded.[18]

Both "apartment houses" and "business houses" were still provided the label *house* in the language of the early twentieth-century decision, much like the *townhouse* of today, underlining the flexibility of the term in its historical usage. At the same time, and rather crucially, apartment houses were not considered primarily residential. Instead, they were classified as business and trade, and thereby made akin to hotels, with which they shared a contractual nature and an ability to generate profit for landlords. In what was, in effect, a dramatic intrusion into free market–governed property rights, the Court sided with the city's rights to create and maintain residential districts built around the house.[19]

Much rested on the Court's narrow reading of "residential." The backdrop of this reading was the rise of a middle-class "cult of domesticity." The cult celebrated a discourse of family values that bestowed on the middle class a unique moral worth relative to both the working class and the landed aristocracy. Indeed, Justice Louis Brandeis, who offered a decisive vote in favor of the legality of zoning, had earlier in his career cemented his legal reputation by arguing for a new right to privacy protecting the domesticity of home life, noting, "The intensity and complexity of life, attendant upon advancing civilization, have rendered necessary some retreat from the world." Protecting residential districts provided a space for retreat—sanctuary at last.[20]

The Court's decision valorized the sanctity of private home life as a realm carved out against the commercial interests of the marketplace. In

---

[18] *Euclid v. Ambler* refers to *Village of Euclid v. Ambler Realty Co.* (No. 31) 72 U.S. 365 (1926), available via the Legal Information Institute (Cornell University) at https://www.law.cornell.edu/supremecourt/text/272/365, accessed August 1, 2015.

[19] This distinction is preserved in the way mortgages are packaged into mortgage-backed securities, with those obtained for developing purpose-built rental apartments packaged into "commercial" mortgage-backed securities instead of "residential" mortgage-backed securities.

[20] See Coontz 2005, Frykman and Löfgren 1987, Gillis 1996, and Wright 1981. The quote is from Warren and Brandeis 1890, 196.

so doing, it wrote into law the general view of home championed by the rising middle class. Outside the boundaries of home, the market ruled. Inside the boundaries of home, families—especially women—preserved a "separate sphere" characterized by obligation, intimacy, and a form of companionate equality.[21] In short, the home internalized and bounded all the social ties increasingly banished from the public sphere by the rise of market governance. So it was that the Supreme Court decision largely justified use-based zoning by emphasizing the family's importance. Expert reports involving "painstaking consideration" were viewed as concurring

> in the view that the segregation of residential, business and industrial buildings . . . will increase the safety and security of home life, greatly tend to prevent street accidents, especially to children, by reducing the traffic and resulting confusion in residential sections, decrease noise and other conditions which produce or intensify nervous disorders, preserve a more favorable environment in which to rear children, etc.[22]

The protection of children was a central concern. But only middle-class children mattered. The many children living in apartments were henceforth to be considered as engaged in business transactions with their landlords rather than entitled to residential protections. The court continued to view apartments as a challenge to the "private" and "residential" character of detached house neighborhoods:

> With particular reference to apartment houses, it is pointed out that the development of detached house sections is greatly retarded by the coming of apartment houses, which has sometimes resulted in destroying the entire section for private house purposes; that in such sections very often the apartment house is a mere parasite, constructed in order to take advantage of the open spaces and attractive surroundings created by the residential character of the district.

Apartment houses were viewed as insidiously taking over neighborhoods formerly composed of single, detached houses, "until, finally, the residential character of the neighborhood and its desirability as a place of detached

---

[21] See Ferree 1990 and Laslett and Brenner 1989 on the rise of separate spheres, an underexplored aspect of Polanyi's (1957) idea of the "double movement" accompanying market governance.

[22] *Euclid v. Ambler.* Notably, the establishment of appropriate fire protection was also cited as a key justification for zoning.

residences are utterly destroyed." They blocked out light, prevented airflow, and brought noise and traffic, forcing children out of the streets where they might otherwise play. "Under these circumstances," the Court noted, "apartment houses, which in a different environment would be not only entirely unobjectionable but highly desirable, come very near to being nuisances."[23]

The characterization of apartment houses as "very near" to nuisances is important. Charting a middle ground relative to broader discourse, the Supreme Court did not view apartment houses as things altogether bad to encourage. But they needed to be kept to their proper place, or, as the Court more colorfully noted in its decision, "A nuisance may be merely a right thing in the wrong place, like a pig in the parlor instead of the barnyard." With this metaphor of animal husbandry, the Supreme Court reinforced a distinction between the working "barnyard" of the Urban Core, including commercial, apartment house, and industrial districts, and the "parlor" of the Great House Reserve.[24]

Reassembling House and Family

The Supreme Court's focus on children both implied and reinforced the overlap of house and family, an overlap with deep cultural and linguistic roots. But the process of writing the single-family house down on paper necessarily recast and clarified the proper interrelationships. Crisp, separable definitions were needed for both *house* and *family*.

The house as a regulatory creature acquired definition at the same time as it acquired the power to regulate. Prior to its legal manifestations, the shape of the house seemed especially vague. According to North American architectural manuals of the mid-nineteenth century, the defining characteristics of the house included merely "chimneys, the windows, and the porch," with the chimneys singled out as "essential" in order to "distinguish apartments destined for human beings from those designed for lodging cattle."[25] Here the term *apartments* was used to designate a broad set of accommodations, including houses and their interiors, and the important distinction was between building for people versus building for cows. This vague definition developed contemporaneously with at least one regulatory circumstance where the distinction was of real legal importance: homesteading. The homesteader claiming preemption rights had to construct at least "a little cabin or shanty

---

[23] Ibid.

[24] Ibid. See also Baar 1992 on the Court's opinions of apartment houses.

[25] Downing 1842, 20–21, quoting an earlier edition of Loudon 1846, 15.

as one of the conditions on which he is to make his claim good." Building a barn was not good enough.[26]

Through the twentieth century, zoning defined the house in increasingly cohesive and comprehensive fashion, incorporating shape, height, square footage, lot coverage, internal subdivision, and, of course, use. As in earlier homesteading, the presence of a house was viewed as demonstrating the "residential use" of land. But with the invention of use-based zoning, the rapidly growing towns and cities of North America began to set aside large tracts of land for "residential use" alone. Beyond the outskirts of town, suburban tract developers wrote the same regulations into deed restrictions and the bylaws of homeowners' associations. And so the house, narrowly defined, became in many places the *only* thing one was allowed to build, and it could *only* be used in support of the nonmarket *residential activities* sustaining families.[27]

Restrictions placed on the use of houses left *family* defined largely along the lines of blood, marriage, and adoption. As a result, family became at least theoretically separable from house and household. The single-family detached house, then, could be defined with reference to both its separation from built structures around it and its containment of a single family, where all members' relationships could be independently verified by lineage or legal document. The work they did for one another remained, by definition, noncommercial. The two terms, *house* and *family*, were legally pulled apart only to be put back together again, but in the process they were modified and clarified so that each became more exclusive.

Middle-class housing reformers played a large role in defining the terms of the day. Social historians demonstrate early twentieth-century reformers' concerns with working-class practices of subdividing houses and taking in lodgers and boarders. In demarcating their moral superiority, the middle classes viewed these activities as detrimental to children and the sanctity of the family. These concerns made their way into government reports and regulations, so that a U.S. labor report from 1910 suggested that the nation's daughters were especially at risk when families shared their dwellings with paying guests, because "[this] cannot help but blunt a girl's sense of proper relations with the other sex and foster standards which are not acceptable in this country."[28]

Defining families along strict lines and placing them in structurally distinct houses provided the family with solid-seeming boundaries: borders against boarders. Regulating the use of houses, so they could be occupied by

---

[26] Jacques 1859, 56.

[27] McKenzie 2005.

[28] As reported by Modell and Hareven (1973, 468).

no more than one family at a time, helped ensure that the boundaries of the house remained more or less in place against the threat of internal subdivision. As an added bonus for some, the new regulations worked to keep out immigrants and preserved single-family neighborhoods as more exclusively middle class.[29]

North American courts have been alternately wary and gracious in assigning municipalities the right to define family. In 1979, the Supreme Court of Canada (*Bell v. Her Majesty the Queen*) struck down such rights as beyond the power granted to municipalities by provincial enabling acts. Similar debates have been raised in U.S. courts at least as early as 1974, and it seems that the issue remains far from settled there. Despite these battles, bylaws continue to define families in the process of defining appropriate use of residential properties. Moreover, they place strict limits on how many boarders or lodgers might live in a dwelling unit. For instance, in the City of Vancouver, the Zoning and Development By-law (10.21.1) states: "No dwelling unit shall be used or occupied by more than one family, but it may also be used to keep a maximum of two boarders or lodgers, or five foster or eight daycare children." Vancouver codes go on to define a family as "(a) one or more individuals all related to one another by blood, marriage [including common-law], or adoption or (b) a maximum of three unrelated individuals living together as a household," with option (b) signifying at least a nod to court-enforced limits on municipal powers.[30]

Vancouver bylaws also define structural aspects of dwellings, mandating a minimum size (thirty-seven square meters or about four hundred square feet), and the availability of a complete bathroom unit, containing "one water-closet, one hand wash-basin and one bathtub or shower." Somewhat strikingly, while a minimum of one bathroom is required, a maximum of one kitchen is allowed per dwelling unit. This latter regulation tends to reinforce the one-family-per-dwelling-unit bylaw, ensuring that everyone

---

[29] Babcock (1966) and Perin (1977) provide multiple examples of this process.

[30] The successful plaintiff in *Belle v. HMTQ* was initially determined to be in violation of local bylaws for having two unrelated roommates in a duplex-zoned area. Dwellings in the area were allowed to be shared by only individuals or families, where families were defined as bound by "consanguinity, marriage, or legal adoption." The Vancouver bylaw now allows exactly three roommates to be considered a family for bylaw purposes. For a full decision, see *Bell v. R* under Lexum's collection of "Judgments of the Supreme Court of Canada," available at http://scc.lexum.org/en/1979/1979scr2-212/1979scr2-212.html. See Perin 1977 and Dunski 2005 on U.S. debates, with quotes from the Vancouver Zoning and Development By-law, archived by the City of Vancouver and available via its bylaw website: "Section 10—General Regulations" (p. 8), available at http://former.vancouver.ca/commsvcs/BYLAWS/zoning/sec10.pdf, and "Definitions" (pp. 5–6), available at http://former.vancouver.ca/commsvcs/BYLAWS/zoning/sec02.pdf.

living in a dwelling is using the same kitchen and hence part of the same household.[31]

Municipal bylaws placed a straitjacket around Heidegger's vision unifying dwelling and building, strictly limiting acceptable versions of "being" within the world even down to defining who could lawfully share the same kitchen. Single-family detached houses were enshrined by local legislation as the ideal form of "dwelling unit," and their construction was enabled nearly everywhere people were allowed to live. More importantly, vast tracts of land became set aside to support *only* single-family houses.[32]

Seeing the House

Since single-family houses were encoded within local rather than federal law, the state (and housing researchers) initially had few ways of "seeing" their spread. Technical and legal details varied across diverse municipalities, zoning districts, and land covenants. As a result, there is no singular North American version of the regulatory form of the house. But locally, where land parcels are regulated, the single-family detached house tends to be quite crisply (and often elaborately) defined in law. And that is where the single-family house as a regulatory creature does most of its work.

Despite the specificity of local definitions of single-family detached houses, it is not difficult to build on the similarities between them in order to come up with a more or less common definition that works across North America. Such a common definition may be found in both Canadian and U.S. census categories, going back at least to 1960. Table 1.1 lays out the structural categories used in Canada and the United States. In Canada, enumerators are asked to identify by type the "dwelling unit" they are examining. In the United States, respondents are asked to identify by type the "building" they live in. For the detached house, dwelling-unit type and building type are one and the same. Elaborating on detachment in the Canadian context, the census instructions explain that a single-detached house is "a single dwelling not attached to any other dwelling or structure (except its own garage or shed). A single-detached house has open space on all sides, and has no dwellings either above it or below it."[33] In the United States, detachment is

---

[31] Vancouver Zoning and Development By-law, "Section 10—General Regulations" (pp. 8-10), archived by the City of Vancouver and available at http://former.vancouver.ca/commsvcs/ BYLAWS/zoning/sec10.pdf. Note that housekeeping units (containing cooking facilities, but not necessarily a bathroom unit) and sleeping units (containing neither bathrooms nor cooking facilities) are regulated separately, especially through lodging house bylaws.

[32] See, e.g., Sewell 1994 for Canada and Levine 2006 and Perin 1977 for the United States.

[33] A detailed discussion of "structural type" within the Canadian census, including the section quoted here, may be found at the Statistics Canada website. Recent definitions from "Structural Type of Dwelling and Collectives Reference Guide, 2011 Census" are available at http://

TABLE 1.1 CENSUS DESCRIPTIONS OF DWELLING STRUCTURES OR TYPES IN
CANADA AND THE UNITED STATES

Canada	United States
To be coded by enumerator *for occupied private dwellings, unoccupied private dwellings, and dwellings occupied solely by foreign and/or temporary residents.*	**As asked of respondent: Which best describes this building?** *Include all apartments, flats, etc., even if vacant.*
[ ] single detached house	[ ] A mobile home
[ ] semi-detached house	[ ] A one-family house detached from any other
[ ] row house	house
[ ] apartment or flat in duplex	[ ] A one-family house attached to one or more
[ ] apartment in a building that has 5 or	houses
more stories	[ ] A building with 2 apartments
[ ] apartment in a building that has fewer	[ ] A building with 3 or 4 apartments
than 5 stories	[ ] A building with 5 to 9 apartments
[ ] single attached house	[ ] A building with 10 to 19 apartments
[ ] mobile home	[ ] A building with 20 to 49 apartments
[ ] other movable dwelling	[ ] A building with 50 or more apartments
	[ ] Boat, RV, van, etc.

similarly defined in terms of "open space on all sides" or where "the house
is joined only to a shed or garage." These terms fit broadly with local bylaws
defining single-family houses, but they also point out complications. For
instance, both the U.S. and Canadian census forms detail the alchemical
ingredients required to turn *mobile homes* into *detached houses*. It takes the
construction of an extra room in the United States, but just permanent attachment to a foundation in Canada.[34]

From here, the criteria distinguishing detached houses from alternatives
become even more arcane. In the U.S. case, *attached* is described as meaning "that the house is joined to another house or building by at least one
wall that goes from ground to roof," including townhouses and row houses.
In Canada, the various forms of attachment that enumerators are asked to
choose from are somewhat more complex. Row houses include townhouses,
but remain distinguished from semidetached dwellings (side by side or front
to back), and apartments in duplexes (one on top of the other). Leftover
dwelling structures (with more than two units) are categorized by stories in

---

www12.statcan.gc.ca/census-recensement/2011/ref/guides/98-313-x/98-313-x2011001-eng
.cfm; with historical variations under "More Information on Structural Type of Dwelling" at
http://www12.statcan.ca/census-recensement/2006/ref/dict/dwelling-logements013a-eng.cfm.
A variety of other bodies also impose coding schemes, which tend to be variations enabled and
encouraged by the census categorization. See also Bowker and Star 1999 for a relevant discussion of categorization.

[34] Questionnaire texts and instructions for the U.S. census are kept by the IPUMS project,
spanning all years by question. For "units in structure," see the detailed information for
years provided here, explaining the "Units in Structure" variable: http://usa.ipums.org/usa
-action/variables/UNITSSTR#questionnaire_text_tab.

Figure 1.1 House-shaped triplex in Vancouver. (*Photograph by the author.*)

Canada, distinguishing high-rises from low-rises, and by number of units (two and above) in the United States.[35]

From a broader perspective, the categories for types of dwellings in the United States and Canada are remarkably similar. Elsewhere the definition of what counts as a "house" varies widely, and in many countries, as in Iran and Malawi, there is no attempt to distinguish this type of structure. In other countries, like Mali, the definition of a "house" is attached to modernity and remains distinct from living in a more traditional "compound," while in Thailand, compound and traditional forms of living are considered equivalent to living within a detached house.[36]

Even if North American census enumerators work with a limited and relatively well-defined range of options, the picture in Figure 1.1 illustrates why they still have a difficult job to do. A casual passerby might name this

---

[35] Ibid.

[36] International categorizations from IPUMS-International archived census questionnaire text descriptions for unharmonized variables in Iran (IR2006A_DWTYPE), Malawi (MW2008A _STRUCT), Mali (ML2009A_DWTYPE), and Thailand (TH2000A_DWELLTYP), available from IPUMS-International website's variable menu: https://international.ipums.org/inter national-action/variables/group/h-other?variableType=UNHARMONIZED.

structure a house (I can make out the rough shape from the game *Monopoly*, in addition to a door, window, and chimney, as nineteenth-century architects thought were required). Nevertheless, it functions as a triplex, containing three separate dwelling units, though only one door faces the street. Equipped with this knowledge, a Canadian census enumerator would likely place this structure into the "apartment in a building that has fewer than five stories" category. One from the United States would likely choose "a building with three or more apartments." But a unit inside was marketed via real estate listings as a "row/townhouse," a common designation for any unit with a door to the outside. Of course, were all the units owned by the same landlord and rented out at the time of sale (instead of owned separately as condos), then the building might well have been marketed as a "house," plain and simple, speaking to the flexibility of market terminology.

Commodity, Concrete, and Culture

Overall, the writing of the single-family detached house into law gave it a more sharply defined shape, one that could be tracked by census takers. More importantly, it also created a new actor capable of shaping North American cities. The house was set loose within the regulatory landscape. The expansion of zoning bylaws, together with deed restrictions, building codes, fire codes, and related bylaws, set standards for the infrastructural technology used to define and create dwellings of all sorts—but all were placed in relation to the protected standard for single-family houses. From municipal bylaws and deed restrictions, the house expanded its range into the set of regulations informing eligibility for mortgage insurance and became inextricable from broader calls to support home ownership, often with sizable tax benefits. The house in law structured the way the house as a market object could be constructed and sold. The house began to unfold. In this way, the detached house as regulatory creature lent a crisp new definition (a sort of replicable and mutable DNA) to the other forms taken by the house—as commodity, concrete, and culture.[37]

After World War II, developers quickly found it advantageous to restrict their lots to single-family houses in order to qualify their properties for the mortgage financing required by their emerging customer base. Observing firsthand the developers of the "fifties and sixties," zoning lawyer Richard Babcock noted a shift from earlier eras, whereby builders became "more at home with the intricacies of double entry bookkeeping than with joists and

---

[37] Both the United States and Canada offer capital-gains tax breaks on primary residence, but only the United States enables mortgage payments to be deducted from income tax, of enormous and regressive benefit to homeowners. See Lasner 2012 on occasional experiments in financing home ownership within multiunit buildings.

rafters," a useful preparation for comprehending "the mysteries of federal mortgage policy." Babcock continued:

> In spite of his new sophistication, the housebuilder is essentially a cautious animal. He should be, faced as he has been with substantial and complicated risks in financing, inadequate market analyses, quixotic twists in government housing programs, and a public image that would make a Jay Gould cringe.[38]

If the complexity of dealing with the federal policies shaping the commodity form of the house increasingly absorbed developers' attention, builders also began to realize that their alternative construction options within municipalities were growing more and more constrained. As Babcock noted:

> The same man who ten years ago was pouring foundations of bungalows with built-in barbecues and unfinished recreation rooms now is howling mad because a bunch of reluctant village trustees look suspiciously at his color slides which show what the Swedes have done with mixtures of row houses, high-rises and garden apartments.[39]

Zoning regulations required developers to stand before suspicious and reluctant "village trustees" if they had any hope of building something besides houses, houses, and more houses. As the process of developing anything new grew more uncertain, the concrete form of houses built to code filled up the urban and suburban landscape. When surveyed today, developers continue to indicate that they would like to build more densely but remain prohibited from doing so by the regulatory regimes they face, coupled with neighborhood suspicion and opposition to change.[40]

As a key symbol embedded within the interactions of newly emerging collectivities, the house took on new cultural associations following its marketability as a commodity, its encoding within law, and its growing physical ubiquity across the urban landscape. Some new associations predictably arose from marketing to the general population; the house was increasingly sold as a nationally specific dream of the good life, both in the United States and Canada and across large parts of Europe. After World War II the house was even marshaled by salesmen, like William Levitt, in the war against communism: "No man who owns his own house and lot can be a Communist. He has too much

---

[38] Babcock 1966, 44.

[39] Ibid., 47.

[40] See Fleischmann and Pierannunzi 1990, Green and Schreuder 2008, Kimelberg 2010, and Kimelberg 2011 on development barriers. See also Perin 1977 on developer uncertainty. Hirt 2014, Levine and Inam 2004, and Levine 2006 offer evidence of developer wishes.

to do." Some developers, like Levitt, came to identify themselves explicitly as house builders, never venturing into more heavily regulated and financially complicated alternatives. For others, house development often represented simply the least complicated and lowest risk of multiple investment opportunities.[41]

Increasingly, planners and policymakers viewed houses as the top rung in a heteronormative "ladder of life" that they frequently imagined at work distributing people across various urban dwelling options. They protected the house as the endpoint of the singular life course they projected onto the population at large—a life course that often looked much like their own. As a result, the house became the keeper at the gates to the good life, segregated from the city's commercial, industrial, and apartment-oriented Urban Core. Planners and policymakers typically worked to shore up the invisible wall surrounding the house habitat even as they enabled and encouraged more diverse development within the confines of the Urban Core. Districts zoned for houses became "sacred land" while the rest of the city proceeded with business as usual. In turn, a growing concern for planners became how to transport people across the boundary distinguishing Core from Reserve, linking the house to the rise of the automobile.[42]

The House Repackaged

How have regular urban residents come to understand the house as a symbol? On one hand, it appears that houses retain their fuzzy flexibility in everyday conceptualizations. On the other, houses frequently become categorized by people in ways that make them even more exclusive than rigidly interpreted bylaws or census categories would suggest.

Multiple people with whom my research assistant and I spoke over the course of our research affixed their cultural ideas about the house to physical structures that failed to meet official definitions. For instance, several respondents considered their residences to be "detached houses," even though the buildings actually contained two separate apartments (including separate kitchens and bathroom facilities), one over the other, making their housing units officially apartments in duplexes in Canadian census terms. Risako Tagami, a married professional who grew up in Vancouver and still lived there, described her entire neighborhood this way, stating, "It's all detached housing," which she followed immediately with, "There are a lot of suites." Indeed, people were especially likely to apply the term "house" to anything

---

[41] See Bourdieu 2005 on Europe. Levitt is quoted in Jackson 1985, 231. See Ball 2003, Buzzelli 2001, Buzzelli and Harris 2006, and Somerville 1999 on the organization of the house-building industry in cross-national comparison.

[42] On the housing ladder, see Perin 1977 and Grant and Scott's (2011) Canadian update. On sacred single-family zoning, see Babcock 1966, Steele 1987, Warner and Molotch 2000, and Weaver 1979.

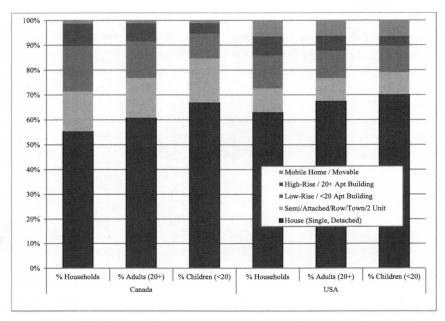

Figure 1.2 Households, adults, and children, by country and dwelling type. *(Based on Canada Census 2006 and U.S. American Community Survey 2006 data. Graphic prepared by the author.)*

that looked vaguely like the *Monopoly* game piece. Structures that plausibly might once have been single-family houses tended to retain the "house" title for people. Even after they were later subdivided into separate units or suites, such "houses" were often contrasted with apartment "buildings" in places where census workers would make no such distinctions.

The flexibility with which people approach defining a house may have something to do with its normative character. Even in the delimited way the census categorizes physical structures, it is clear that detached houses outnumber all other residential buildings across North America. As of 2006, over 55 percent of occupied dwellings in Canada were detached houses, compared with an even larger 63 percent of dwellings in the United States. Houses contain more people than other types of dwellings, both per unit and across the population as a whole, as displayed by Figure 1.2.[43]

The ubiquity of the house, as a roughly sketched idea that people apply in expansive and inclusive ways, may contribute to its normative power.

---

[43] This analysis uses 2006 census figures from Statistics Canada (community profiles and CHASS analysis), and 2006 American Community Survey data for the United States, weighted by households. Data may be analyzed online courtesy of the IPUMS (Integrated Public Use Microdata Series) project at www.ipums.org, housed at the Minnesota Population Center (see Ruggles et al. 2010). See further details in Appendix.

Many things might be considered houses, until they reach a point where they clearly need to be moved to some other cognitive category. According to the census, children are even more likely to live in detached houses than adults, and the vast majority of North Americans grow up in them, underscoring the connection between house and family and further explaining its "naturalness" for most adults. In short, the house is the first form of dwelling that *most* children come to recognize. But if the legible ubiquity of the house lends it a certain flexibility, people also tend to conceptualize the house in more restrictive senses than we find in the census.[44]

In our interviews, not only were houses (at least sometimes) detached structures erected around a singular household-oriented dwelling space (as per census definitions), but they also came with plenty of room inside, yards outside, and home ownership. For instance, Kathy Martin and Ted Demarest, a thoughtful professional couple living with a newborn in a rented single-bedroom apartment, discussed their ambivalence about buying a place together. For Ted, buying seemed to imply purchasing a detached house. When questioned about this implication, Ted first disclaimed it but then reasserted that for him, the notion of ownership did go together with the notion of a house:

> TED: [Kathy's] done a lot to sort of . . . talk me out of this . . . but it's . . . almost like a sort of a panic, sort of. . . . Not panic, but, like: if we don't have a house what happens if, if we . . . lose our jobs, everything goes bad and we don't, we don't have a place to live? If we got a house, at least you've got a place to live when you're older, or whatever. And we sort of talked through that and thought through that. But that's sort of at the bottom of some of my thinking about having a house is that security. But I mean, you think about it, it isn't, though, because we're going to be paying a mortgage for twenty-five to thirty years anyway, and if [the] worst happens—you can't afford the mortgage—you lose the house anyways. So . . .
>
> NATHAN: And when you say a house, in this sense, do you actually mean, like, a detached structure? Or do you mean just an owner-occupied [dwelling]?
>
> TED: Owner-occupied. I don't necessarily mean a detached structure, but . . . I don't know . . . having something that's not strata [i.e., a condominium], that's freehold, that you actually own the land, does sort of appeal to me as well, because it's actual land you're owning, not beholden to a strata council or other co-owners and

---

[44] Over 70 percent of U.S. children growing up in the 1970s and 1980s were also living in detached houses, according to census data from the IPUMS project (see Ruggles et al. 2010).

stuff like that. You're your own little piece of property that nobody . . . well, except the government, of course, can tell you what
to do with it.

Ted made explicit what had been implicitly packaged together for him. A
house meant ownership, and ownership meant a house. He asserted the coherence of this package, even when pressed on the detachability of its components. The partially shared nature of condominium ownership meant that
it was not, in some fundamental way, real ownership to Ted. By contrast,
owning a house provided a type of security he found intuitively appealing.
Even though he continuously provided thoughtful qualifications to this appeal (e.g., the tenuous meaning of ownership with a mortgage and the government's right to direct his land use), Ted kept circling back to it.

Ted's cultural understanding of the meaning of a house echoed the logic
of the U.S. Supreme Court as it broadly equated the house—in its single,
detached form—with residential life free of the business interests associated
with rental contracts. In fact, many houses at the time of the 1926 *Euclid v.
Ambler* decision were rented, and many still are today. But fewer ownership
opportunities, in both the United States and Canada, have been provided
for alternative dwellings. Various mortgage financing regulations limited
early forms of federally guaranteed mortgage insurance to detached houses.
Even today, those purchasing detached houses face fewer limitations in their
mortgage options than other buyers. Moreover, prior to the mid-twentieth
century, regulatory regimes were generally ill-prepared to adjudicate more
complex ownership claims associated with structural attachment, at least
beyond the establishment of early cooperatives and joint obligations for the
"party walls" separating townhouses. Legislation enabling condominium (or
strata) ownership remains a relatively recent phenomenon, developed and
spread mostly in the 1960s. The complicated legal implications of related
forms of joint ownership are still being worked out. Ownership of a detached
house *seems* at least a little simpler.[45]

It is not unusual to see tenure (i.e., distinctions between owning and
renting) distinguished from structure or building type in housing analyses, but for most people, the conceptual packaging of the house erases this

---

[45] On mortgage differences, see Central Mortgage and Housing Corporation 2013 regulations
concerning the maximum loan-to-value ratios deemed acceptable for mortgage insurance,
allowing detached-house buyers to take on more credit. See D. Harris 2011, Hulchanski
1993, and Lasner 2012 for discussions of the spread of condominium legislation, allowing
individuals to divide up their stake in a building or development between jointly owned
and managed common areas, and separately owned, titled, and managed units within common areas. Here condos supplanted the ambiguity often associated with cooperatives. See
Navarro 2013 on reports of the discriminatory treatment faced by cooperatives in qualifying for federal disaster relief after New York City's Hurricane Sandy. Bula 2012 provides
examples of concerns in Vancouver.

TABLE 1.2 PERCENTAGE OF OWNER-OCCUPIED HOUSEHOLDS, BY DWELLING
TYPE AND OVERALL

Dwelling type	Canada	United States
House (single, detached)	91.8%	86.8%
Semi/attached/row/town	61.5%	51.0%
Low-rise/<20 apt. building	22.0%	11.9%
High-rise/20+ apt. building	25.5%	15.9%
Mobile home/movable	83.6%	74.5%
Overall	67.4%	67.3%

Source: Canada Census 2006, U.S. American Community Survey 2006 data.

distinction. The distinction is also somewhat tenuous in practical terms. Employing census tenure definitions indicates that an astounding 91.8 percent of Canadian houses were owner-occupied in 2006, as revealed in Table 1.2. The figure for that year for the United States is a similar, if slightly less impressive, 86.8 percent, dropping to 82 percent by 2010 after the housing bust and resulting foreclosures took their toll. Note that ownership is more common in Canada for every type of dwelling; however, the figures for ownership overall are roughly similar between the United States and Canada due to the different distribution of Canadians across dwelling types.

Turning these figures around, it is also clear that most owner-occupiers own houses rather than, say, condominium apartments or mobile homes. In Canada, 74.3 percent of all owner-occupiers lived in houses in 2006. In the United States, where condominiums have not proven quite as popular among developers, ownership is more tightly bound to the house, with more than 84 percent of owners living in houses.[46]

Overall, houses are very likely to be owner-occupied, and owners are very likely to live in houses. Yet the package of features culturally connected to houses both incorporates and goes well beyond ownership. For instance, my research assistant (Mia) followed up on comments by Vicky Chenowith, a married professional renting a two-bedroom apartment in Kitsilano, about how her purchasing plans were closer after the birth of her new child:

> MIA: So . . . why is . . . buying closer than it was before?
> VICKY: Because we need more space. Right, so, a house will give us more space, and I've always wanted a house, but I wanted a house when we have a family. Like, that's my dream, a house with a family. So if we didn't have the family part, then we don't need the house. So that's why it kinda became closer.
> MIA: Right, I see. So the two parts sort of come together?
> VICKY: Yeah. That's what it is. Yeah.

---

[46] Author's analysis of 2006 census data from Statistics Canada and ACS data from the United States, weighted by household (see IPUMS details in note 43).

MIA: I see, I see. And why is it that you feel like you need a house
with children?

VICKY: I grew up in a house with—like, you know, part of it is really
emotional, I think, wanting a house—and I grew up in a house
with a family, and there's more space, like a backyard, and just
[a sense of] ownership. I've never owned a house, and you know,
I just want that sense of home more, you know?

Here Vicky quickly moved from ownership to roominess to house to yard
and back again, tying together for us a coherent house package in her answers. This package was what she was looking for, and what had grown closer
after the birth of her daughter, rather than, for instance, simply moving to
a rental apartment with more space. The way the package was bound together with her childhood helped explain its coherence to Vicky as well as
its appeal, especially as she contemplated raising a child of her own. Vicky's
"package deal" brought several features common to houses together into a
vision of what a house should entail, and also brought the house together
with family in a vision of what a home should entail.[47]

On average, houses really are larger than other dwelling types, and recently they have been getting even bigger, averaging 2,000 square feet in
Canada and 2,505 square feet in the United States. Even before this growth
in size, detached houses in Canada were already nearly 25 percent larger
than attached alternatives, and over 80 percent larger than apartment units.
In the United States, the disparity in size tends to be even bigger.[48]

Another way to think about roominess is in terms of the number of
rooms. Figure 1.3 provides recent estimates of the number of rooms by dwelling type in the United States and Canada. Houses tend to have both more
rooms overall and more bedrooms than other types of dwellings. Perhaps
not surprisingly, differences in roominess are particularly large between detached houses and dwellings in apartment buildings, with various forms of
townhouses, attached houses, and duplexes offering a middle ground.[49]

---

[47] I borrow the "Package Deal" concept from Nicholas Townsend's (2002) book, which inves-
tigates how Californian men come to construct successful masculinity—including fatherhood, ownership of a house, a good job, and a wife—all as part of an internally coherent and
also at times contradictory package.

[48] Canadian average from Canadian Home Builder's Association (2013) poll. U.S. average from
census data for new construction in 2012 available under "Median and Average Square Feet
of Floor Area in New Single-Family Houses Completed by Location" at http://www.census
.gov/construction/chars/pdf/medavgsqft.pdf. See Canada Mortgage and Housing Corporation 2006, 45, for a comparison of change in size over time in Canada. For comparative data
by structure type, see Natural Resources Canada 2013, 21, and the U.S. Energy Information
Administration's Residential Energy Consumption Survey (RECS) data for 2009 from table
HC10.1, available at http://www.eia.gov/consumption/residential/data/2009/#undefined.

[49] Slight differences in the way people are asked about how many rooms they have and what

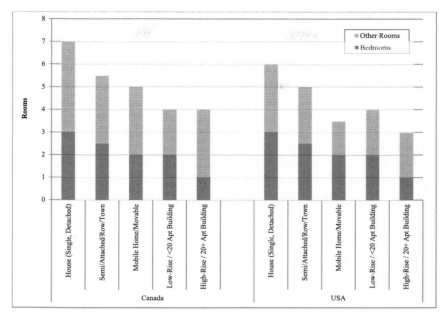

Figure 1.3 Median number of bedrooms and other rooms, by dwelling type and country. (*Based on Canada Census 2006 and U.S. American Community Survey 2006 data. Graphic prepared by the author.*)

Houses are also much more likely to have yards, as Vicky imagined. In many cases, yard dimensions are even mandated by law. For instance, in Vancouver's single-family-zoned areas (designated "RS" in zoning regulations), houses are legally required to be accompanied by yards, including front yards, side yards, and backyards of specified dimensions. For the RS-1 zone, front yards are set at a minimum of 20 percent of the total lot depth, except where this might make a new house dramatically out of character with surrounding properties. Backyards are set at 45 percent of lot depth, with similar attention to houses on either side. Minimum side yards are set through a complicated formula, but should never be less than 10 percent of the lot width, and need never be more than 20 percent of the width. Similar regulations elsewhere encouraging ever larger lot sizes, along with the ubiquity of single-family residential zoning, help ensure that an estimated 23 percent of North America's urban land base remains planted in turf grass.[50]

---

counts as floor space mean that figures for the United States and Canada are not entirely comparable.

[50] Robbins 2007, 30. Talen (2012) also speaks to the ubiquity of yard regulations and Foote et al. (1960) to the quick post–World War II rise in lot sizes.

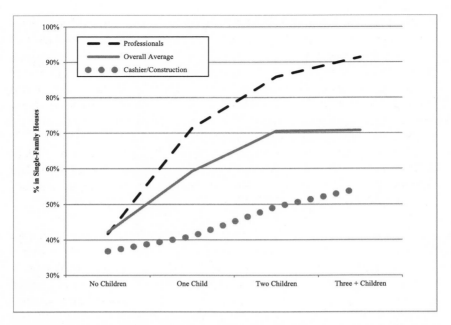

Figure 1.4 Percentage of householders in the United States living in a detached house, by number of children and occupation, household heads ages twenty-five to forty-four, 2008–2010. (*Based on U.S. American Community Survey 2008–2010 data. Graphic prepared by the author.*)

Finally, there is the association between houses and families to consider, especially as it pertains to childrearing. Just how often do houses come with children? As revealed in Figure 1.4, well under half of all adult householders age twenty-five to forty-five without children live in detached houses.[51] But the addition of a child catapults about 60 percent of parents into houses. Adding another child leaves 70 percent of parents in houses—small wonder that most North American children grow up in houses. Historically, the rapid spread of houses across the post–World War II metropolitan landscape went hand in hand with the Baby Boom. Research suggests that during this era, more houses encouraged more babies, a suggestion also made by contemporaneous observers. It seems similarly likely that the desire of parents for houses—a desire they could increasingly afford to satiate with the help of mortgage financing—helped inform the success of house builders.[52]

---

[51] Data from the collected 2008–2010 American Community Survey sample, housed by IPUMS (Ruggles et al. 2010). See details in Appendix. Occupational codes included for cashiers and construction workers (4720, 6260) and accountants, doctors, engineers, and lawyers (800, 2100, 3060, and 1320–1530). See Ruggles et al. 2010. Canadian data, for various reasons, are more difficult to tabulate in a comparative fashion.

[52] See Lauster 2010a, 2010b, 2012. Wright (1981) provides media examples. Ström (2010) and

Nevertheless Figure 1.4 also outlines some striking disparities. Houses usually become accessible only through the market, and as commodities they often remain priced out of the reach of many parents. Differences in the wage structures and stability of various occupations lead to differences in access to houses. As a result, the children of construction workers and cashiers are much less likely to live in houses than the children of accountants, doctors, lawyers, and engineers. The market distribution of houses demarcates a dividing line between the parental haves and have nots.[53]

There is good reason to believe that the house resonates as a symbol, at least in part, in terms of its ubiquity and association with inequality. The successful live in houses. By these terms, most North Americans seem successful. But what of those left out? They will have more to say soon.

Distinguishing between the different forms taken by the house (concrete, culture, commodity, and creature) enables a study of how these forms unfolded and became influenced by one another. My central argument is that from its primordial form, combining culture with concrete (or timber and sod), the house became sharpened into an idea and then into a solution to urban woes by early twentieth-century reformers. It was written into law as a regulatory creature largely in order to tame the market-governed and chaotically growing industrial cities of the era and make them more inhabitable for the growing middle class. The regulatory creature, in turn, produced and structured the commodification of the house and crucially informed its subsequent appearance in culture and concrete.

Through zoning and related ordinances, large swathes of land were legally reserved as habitat for houses. From there, the house as a regulatory creature invaded general urban planning—especially concerns over transportation—and proceeded to jump into the realm of mortgage finance policy. As the house unfolded into the form of bylaws, building codes, and mortgage regulations, it also demarcated a new position for a tightly segregated commodity. The character of houses could be preserved through market interactions only by regulating what could be done with land nearby. Houses in concrete were built to code and bylaw, as well as with reference to policy-structured mortgage financing and capital flows.

Given the formative role of regulation, I generally avoid speaking about the rise of house dominance in simplistic terms of supply and demand. This is not to suggest that cultural support for the house was unimportant, but

---

Mulder and Billari (2010) offer related discussions of the relationship between housing and childbearing in Europe. See Mankiw and Weil 1989 for a prominent, if somewhat questionable, housing-demand story treating the Baby Boom as an exogenous influence.

[53] Lauster 2012 provides further discussion of comparisons by occupation, and Lauster 2010a indicates that similar results obtain when distinguishing by household income, nested within the metropolitan area.

rather that it quickly became contingent on regulatory processes. These same processes attenuated any straightforward relationship between supply and demand. I fully acknowledge widespread desire for the house across the twentieth century, and elaborate in later chapters on similar desires today. These speak to how cultural associations constructing the meaning and importance of the house shifted in subtle ways and across multiple domains after its regulatory codification, incorporating a singularly defined family and also adding desires for and expectations about ownership, roominess, and a yard to the mix.[54]

Nevertheless, as noted by researchers even at the time, mid-twentieth-century consumers remained "relatively impotent" in determining the regulatory environments and urban forms that shaped the housing they had to choose from.[55] As they made choices based on limited selections, consumers—especially young families—often lacked the means to express their desires through the market. On the other side, though a variety of consumer surveys were launched, developers often failed to find available (or to act on) any reliable guides for consumer demand save for their own instincts, opinions, and heteronormative guiding heuristics.[56] By contrast, obscure financial regulations often overruled consumer demand in determining developer profits. On the whole, regulatory and financial constraints on developers became increasingly pressing through the twentieth century, guiding transformations in urban form.[57]

This argument both elaborates on and refutes many previous works. Some of these, including John Archer's *Architecture and Suburbia*, Robert Beauregard's *When America Became Suburban*, and Peter Ward's *A History of Domestic Space*, masterfully trace the transmutations of the house as an influential idea and cultural icon. Others, like Witold Rybczynski's *Home* or Bruegmann's *Sprawl*, build on this basis to assert that the culture

---

[54] Bourdieu (2005) also speaks to the limits of discourse concerning supply and demand. A reading of R. Harris 2004 suggests that the house followed the suburbs more generally in increasingly conforming to a singular, prepackaged corporate model.

[55] Abu-Lughod and Foley 1960, 262.

[56] Wright (1981) notes the surveys. See Grant and Scott 2011, Mohamed 2006, and Perin 1977 for discussions of the "housing ladder of life" and various examples of developer heuristics as well as frank acknowledgments of their limitations.

[57] On regulatory and financial demands, see Fleischmann and Pierannunzi 1990, Green and Schreuder 1991, Hirt 2014, and Kimelberg 2010 and 2011. Kripner (2011) speaks especially to the unheralded role of Regulation Q in limiting the interest rates that could be paid for mortgages relative to alternative investments, which often resulted in the complete drying up of funds available to support mortgages. The lifting of Regulation Q enabled money to flow into mortgage markets, but destabilized interest rates there, shifting more risk onto debtors and leaving all parties carefully watching Fed policies. Similar policy changes occurred in Canada, progressively lifting the interests that could be paid on mortgages over time to entice more capital into the housing market.

of the house or its commodification as ideal solution to everyday living has more or less determined its spread in concrete across North America. These works suggest both too much and too little, blending together the house in concrete, culture, and commodity. In addition to downplaying the role of regulation, they downplay the mutability of culture and the variously articulated processes by which housing increasingly became built and financed across the early twentieth century. That a culture valuing the house developed and took root in the middle class remains an insufficient explanation for urban form, as might be suggested by similar cultural histories written in England, France, and Sweden, where fewer than half of residents live in detached houses. A better explanation can be constructed by examining the intervening role of the house as regulatory creature in North America.[58]

A few studies, including Sonia Hirt's *Zoned in the USA*, Jonathan Levine's *Zoned Out*, and Emily Talen's *City Rules*, all speak directly to the importance of zoning in determining urban form. Others, like Kenneth Jackson's *Crabgrass Frontier*, speak eloquently to the role of financing and mortgage policies. Sometimes these authors overemphasize American exceptionalism. Other times, they underemphasize the particular power of the single-family detached house, a crafty little regulatory creature that rapidly extended its range across diverse policy domains. Nevertheless, their research on regulation remains foundational to the book ahead. Altogether, in clarifying, elaborating on, and refuting the works above, I herald the birth of the single-family detached house and its subsequent invasion of North American landscapes and everyday lives. I also speak to the most potent possibilities for effecting change.[59]

---

[58] See Archer 2005, Beauregard 2006, Bruegmann 2005, Rybczynski 1987, and Ward 1999. Social histories by Gillis (1996) on England, Bourdieu (2005) on France, and Frykman and Löfgren (1987) on Sweden, as well as Hirt's (2014) work, provide insights into the general value of cross-Atlantic comparison. See Eurostat website on "Housing Statistics," available at http://ec.europa.eu/eurostat/statistics-explained/index.php/Housing_statistics#Type_of_dwelling, for comparative figures for detached-house living, though actual definitions of what constitutes a "detached house" may vary markedly by country.

[59] Hirt 2014; Jackson 1985; Levine 2006; Talen 2012. See R. Harris 2004 on the perils of ignoring Canadian similarity to the United States and McKenzie 1994 on deed restrictions and HOAs.

WHAT'S THE PROBLEM?

Man is . . . plagued by external parasites.

—**CHARLES DARWIN**, *THE DESCENT OF MAN*

To put the case in its strongest terms, the house as a regulatory creature is an invasive parasite evolved from the maelstrom of the twentieth century's rapid, market-led urban growth. Just a metaphor, perhaps, but an important one: though our ancestors built the thing, the spread of the single-family detached house now looks very much like an urban infestation. It threatens the health of our families, our cities, our democracy, and our world. So why do we continue to reserve most of our urban land as exclusive "house habitat"?

In this chapter, I provide a sketch of the damage wrought by preserving habitat for houses. The trouble comes in two primary forms: first, the clearing of other habitats for houses, and second, the kind of habitat produced by the house. I document how the spread of the house has led to the local destruction and displacement of alternative habitats. I explore the symbiotic relationship between houses and cars, and the way they work together to transform habitat on a global scale. Houses also provide poor habitat for humanity. The habits they inculcate tend toward the unhealthy and antisocial. They crowd out the public sphere, reinforce inequality and challenge democracy, and divide people rather than bringing them together.

Habitat Lost: Local Displacement

A friend in urban planning once cynically noted to me that suburban developments tend to be named after the landscapes they displace: "Rippling Brook Way" for the paved-over stream, "Cottonwood Court" for the trees torn down. If there are too few subdivisions named "Cornfield Lane" or

"Dairy Barn Circle" to make this observation entirely true, it still speaks to the hunger of houses for land. The spread of floor space and expansive yards (again, often mandated by municipal codes and specific development practices) leads directly to the occupation and transformation of more and more of North America's landscape. The ecological communities previously supported on a given plot of land (e.g., forested or agricultural) are often directly displaced by the arrival of houses, lawns, and the roads and utility lines connecting them all together.[1]

Even when displacement remains incomplete, a sort of hybrid ecology is created at the point of "wildland-urban interface," a term used by scientists to group together areas where houses are plunked down in the middle of undeveloped vegetation. While they may not entirely displace existing habitats, houses at the interface bring along infrastructure and introduce risks associated with the fragmentation of habitat, the arrival of exotic species, and the decline of biodiversity. By contrast, loss of agricultural land may seem like the simple substitution of one human-managed ecosystem for another. But loss of agriculture close to the city may mean its expansion elsewhere, displacing wilder ecosystems further afield. Disappearing habitat for farms also raises a host of concerns about our wider food systems, such as where the most productive land is likely to be located (often near the cities) and how much energy we should be using to transport our food around.[2]

Figure 2.1 tracks what was lost through the development of 3,361 square kilometers of land across southern Canada between 2000 and 2011.[3] Crop land took by far the largest hit, but a diverse set of other habitats were also displaced by development. How much of this is driven by houses? While alternative forms of development—including multiunit housing, office parks, factories, and the like—also advance the reach of urban infrastructure, it is clear that houses both serve in the vanguard of most urban expansion and fill out the ranks. Because of their low density, houses also quicken the pace of development faster than would be expected by population growth figures alone. Using satellite imagery, analyses estimate that the land consumed by the fifteen largest Canadian urban areas (including some ninety municipalities) grew in size by an average of 123 percent between 1966 and 2001. By contrast, the total population of Canada grew by only about 50 percent during this time period. Patterns of rapid growth in developed land were similar in the continental United States, where estimates suggest that the amount of

---

[1] See also Rome 2001 on displacement and Robbins 2007 for an insightful look at all of the chemical inputs and resultant toxicity the new ecology entails.

[2] See Radeloff et al. 2005 and Theobald 2005 on the wildlife-urban interface, with the former noting the resulting greater risks attached to wildfires.

[3] Data from Statistics Canada 2013, 26, table 3.2. Note that estimates here, based on a finer resolution than earlier estimates, correspondingly tend to suggest greater overall loss of land.

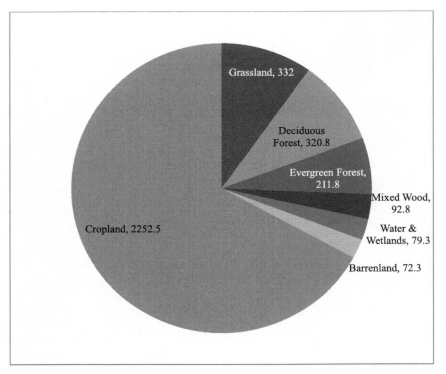

Figure 2.1 Land lost (km²) to expansion of the built environment across southern Canada between 2000 and 2011, by type of ecosystem formerly supported. (*Based on data from Statistics Canada 2013, table 3.2. Graphic prepared by the author.*)

land developed at urban or suburban densities increased from 95,635 square kilometers in 1980 to 125,729 in 2000.[4]

To be sure, both Canada and the United States are large countries with a great deal of land relative to the number of people they contain. Nevertheless, a careful estimate including the low-density exurbs that ring most metropolitan areas suggests that about 13.3 percent of the land base in the continental United States was already developed for predominantly residential use by 2000 (up from 10.1 percent in 1980). That is an area nearly the size of Texas and California combined, containing mostly house-oriented forms of suburban and ex-urban sprawl and growing fast. With respect to habitat displacement, it is not growth in the number of North Americans that matters, but growth in the number of houses.[5]

---

[4] See Zhang, Guindon, and Sun 2010 on Canada, and see Theobald 2005 on the United States, using about 0.6 units per acre as a cutoff defining suburban or urban development. See also Brown et al. 2005 for a similar set of estimates using different criteria and data.

[5] Theobald's (2005) estimates are based on fine-grained (1–4 ha) models combining census

Habitat Found: For Cars

Returning to the metaphor provided by the pine beetle and blue stain fungus, one parasite often works with another. In similar form, houses cultivate cars. Integrated through planning, they displace vastly more habitat than either could manage alone. Because houses consume space and tend to surround themselves with other houses, which also consume space, people often cannot walk to where they need to go. Because all that space results in a relatively low population density, it is also not very efficient to run public transit lines to areas with many houses. Low-density areas tend to end up with very few riders for what are often very expensive systems to maintain. In short, public transit loves density. The relationship between urban density and public transit use is exceptionally strong, with some suggestion of a cutoff—perhaps around twelve persons per acre (or about three thousand per square kilometer)—below which ridership drops off and expense per user makes transit impractical. By contrast, cars love the sprawl associated with houses, and houses love cars back.[6]

How much do houses love cars? The vast majority of people who work in North America drive a car to get to their jobs, but house dwellers are far more likely to drive to work than others. Figure 2.2 compares census journey-to-work data to figures on housing structure for all of those reporting some sort of commute in 2006. Looking at how many people reported driving to work, the differences by housing type are stark for both Canada and the United States. House dwellers, along with those living in mobile homes, were by far the most likely to drive to work. In Canada, over 85 percent took private motor vehicles to work; in the United States, approximately 95 percent.

Trips to work taken by drivers and passengers in Canada also tended to be longer for those who lived in detached houses and mobile homes. Nearly half of house dwellers had commutes over ten kilometers in length, compared to just over a third for those in other forms of permanent dwelling. Of course, not all trips are to work. Houses, because they tend to be surrounded

---

data on housing units at the block level (incorporating block size) and mapping data (e.g., road networks), with "exurban" defined as more than 0.69 hectares per housing unit (or less than 0.6 units per acre), but less than 16.18 hectares per unit, with the latter boundary considered a low enough density to support agricultural households. Theobald acknowledges that some forms of agriculture (e.g., orchards, but also certain organic farms) might be feasible below 16.18 hectares per housing unit.

[6] In studies from 1996 and 1999, Kenworthy and Laub use international data from urban areas to estimate relationships between urban form and costs. The strongest relationships they find are the inverse relationship between urban density and auto dependency and the positive relationship between urban density and transit use, with R2 exceeding 0.65 in both cases (interpretable as >65 percent of variance explained). Estimates like these (originally produced in P. Newman and Kenworthy 1989) are used to arrive at the twelve-person-per-acre figure cited by Northwest Environment Watch's 2002 report on sprawl and its implications in the Pacific Northwest. See also Hirt 2014.

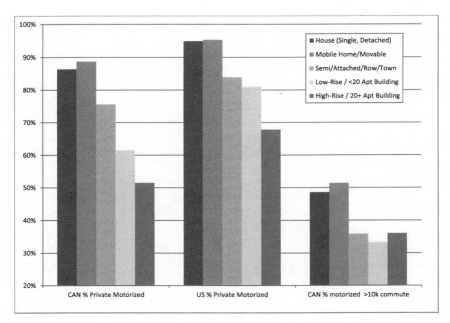

Figure 2.2 Journey-to-work data: percentage traveling by private motor vehicle and distance traveled, by dwelling type for Canada and the United States. (*Based on Canada Census 2006 and U.S. American Community Survey 2006 data. Graphic prepared by the author.*)

by other houses, are also farther from stores and other places people need to go, resulting in extra driving for non-work trips as well. Overall, no other form of dwelling comes close to supporting so many cars, even though all buildings are often *mandated* by municipal codes to reserve parking spaces for them. Reserving land for cars, including roads and parking, contributes enormously to loss of habitat, both directly and by opening adjacent land parcels to development. In the process, cars often introduce toxic materials and hazards to local ecosystems, including both air pollution and chemical runoff.[7]

Habitat Lost: Global Displacement

Together, cars and houses also present a larger problem for ecosystems all over the world insofar as they emit an enormous proportion of the pollution associated with global warming. On a trips-per-capita basis, cars create

[7] See Dowling 2000 for an especially nice discussion of the role cars play in suburban mothering and the City of Vancouver's archived "Section 4: Off Street Parking Space Regulations" component of Parking By-law 6059, available at http://former.vancouver.ca/commsvcs/BYLAWS/parking/Sec04.pdf, for just one example of mandated parking.

far more greenhouse gases than most forms of public transportation, to say nothing of walking or biking. Added all together, fuel combustion by cars produced over 12 percent of Canada's total greenhouse gas emissions in 2011 and nearly 17 percent of those from the United States. Of course, Canada is also a major producer of the sort of fossil fuels that get combusted by automobiles. This is not all consumed in Canada, and a great deal of it goes to the United States. Adding in all of its oil and gas extraction and processing activities contributes another 23 percent of Canada's total emissions. Altogether, expansion of car use (including the rise of SUVs) and associated oil production have been dragging Canada and the United States away from meeting their commitments to greenhouse gas reductions, accounting for a large portion of the sizeable rise in emissions since 1990.[8]

Cars are not the only things consuming fuel. In addition to their voraciousness with respect to land, houses also hunger for energy. Because houses share no common walls, floors, or ceilings with any other dwellings, they waste energy relative to most urban alternatives. As detailed in the previous chapter, houses also tend to be much larger than other forms of dwellings. This means they need to work much harder to keep the amount of space they contain at a controlled temperature. Such climate control (heating and cooling) accounts for over half of total residential energy consumption.[9]

As revealed in Table 2.1, a Canadian energy survey from 2007 estimated that houses use over 50 percent more energy from all sources than attached dwellings (e.g., duplexes or townhouses), and over 200 percent more energy than apartments: low-rise and high-rise alike.[10] Strikingly, the outsize energy consumption of houses does not seem to be explained by the larger households they tend to contain, since energy use patterns remained roughly the same even when dwelling types were compared for only households of the same size. This household survey did not include the common areas of apartment buildings, which often drain extra energy for climate control, lighting, elevators, and the like, especially if further luxury features such as gyms, spas, and pools are included. Nor did the survey include "embodied energy," like the energy that goes into producing the cement holding many buildings together (which also gives off its own greenhouse gases in the mixing process). But the evidence is relatively robust that even accounting for these factors,

---

[8] Estimates are calculated by the author using UN FCCC (United Nations Framework Convention on Climate Change) reports from Environment Canada 2013—table 2.13—and the U.S. Environmental Protection Agency 2013: table ES-8 for total; table 2.15 for passenger cars, light trucks, and motorcycles.

[9] U.S. Department of Energy 2012.

[10] Natural Resources Canada 2010, table 11.2. U.S. Department of Energy (2012) figures from its 2005 household survey provide substantively similar results by housing type, but using a different typology and without controlling for household size (table 2.1.11).

TABLE 2.1 ENERGY CONSUMPTION (GIGAJOULES PER HOUSEHOLD), BY
DWELLING TYPE AND HOUSEHOLD SIZE

	All households	Household size 1	Household size 2	Household size 3	Household size 4+
Single, detached house	137.9	116.4	134.4	143.6	148.1
Double/row house	87.2	73.4	85.5	91.6	99.8
Low-rise apartment	43.9	40.1	45.2	42.9	77.1
High-rise apartment	43.8	38.8	42.2	—	—
Mobile home	98.1	80.6	100.4	—	—

Source: 2007 data from Canadian Energy Use Survey.

townhouses, low-rises, and mid-rise apartments, at least, tend to be more efficient.[11]

Economists Edward Glaeser and Matthew Kahn followed these studies, but at a metropolitan level, in attempting to model the effects of urban form and location on holistic energy use in the United States. They proceeded to link energy consumption to CO_2 production.[12] Their study estimated standardized household emissions from driving, public transit, home heating, and electricity for different metropolitan areas in the United States, and different locations (central vs. peripheral) within each metro area. The findings? Controlling for climate, bigger and denser metropolitan areas produced less CO_2 per household than sprawling ones, and living in the city center, as opposed to the suburbs, helped. This tends to confirm at the metropolitan level the findings of other studies at the neighborhood and household level. Dense urban living produces less greenhouse gas.

In Figure 2.3, I draw on recent Canadian and U.S. national reports submitted to the UN Framework Convention on Climate Change. Just over a third of greenhouse gas production in the United States was associated with the combined impacts of residential energy use and cars. In Canada, these sectors made up a smaller proportion of overall emissions, running closer to 23 percent of total output. As noted previously, the discrepancy between the two countries may be partially explained by the larger proportion of total emissions produced by Canada's fossil fuel production industries. Without these emissions, the proportions of greenhouse gas output devoted to residential and travel uses look quite similar. But closer consideration of the emissions from fuel production in Canada provides a more holistic portrait of the total effects of burning up so much fuel in our cars and houses,

---

[11] See Gray, Gleeson, and Burke 2010 and Rickwood, Glazebrook, and Searle 2007 for reviews and discussions of evidence from Australia; Holden and Norland 2005 from Norway; and Jonathan Rose Companies 2011 for the United States. Of note, buildings of the same general type (e.g., house, townhouse, low-rise, high-rise) vary widely in energy use depending on their materials of construction and various features, and this is especially true for high-rises.

[12] Glaeser and Kahn 2010.

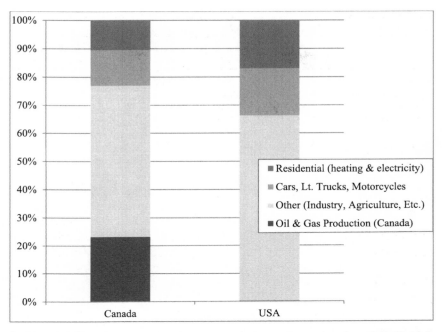

Figure 2.3 Greenhouse gas emissions, by contributing sector in Canada and the United States. (*Based on 2013 submissions to the UN Framework Convention on Climate Change. Graphic prepared by the author.*)

especially since nearly all the fuel Canada produces is ultimately consumed within North America.[13]

Even without considering where the fuel to power it all comes from, the energy consumed by North American passenger vehicles and residences alone accounted for some 2,421,200,000 metric tons of CO_2-equivalent greenhouse gas in 2013. Placing this number in context, energy consumption by North American housing and driving alone produces nearly the same amount of greenhouse gas as recently estimated *total* emissions of India and all of sub-Saharan Africa *combined*. In short, moving North Americans out of their houses and cars and into more efficient alternative dwellings spaced

---

[13] Estimates are calculated by the author using UN FCCC reports from Environment Canada 2013, table 2.13, and the U.S. Environmental Protection Agency 2013, table ES-8 (for residential total, including electricity) and table 2.15 (for passenger cars, light trucks, and motorcycles). Emissions from residential electricity use in Canada was not calculated separately in the report, but was estimated here as 31.8 percent of the total for electricity, based on residential demand data from Statistics Canada 2012—table 8.7.1. This is similar to, though somewhat lower than, the proportion of electricity emissions accorded to residential use in U.S. reporting (36.9 percent—see table 2.5), likely reflecting real differences in factors like air conditioning usage.

closer to where they need to travel could really have an impact on global warming. The alternative is continued habitat destruction on a global scale.[14]

Habitat Lost: Urbanity

Let's return to the city. What implications does reserving so much room for houses have for our broader urban habitats? Perhaps the largest issue is the way houses crowd out alternative land uses, dramatically narrowing the range of possible habitats that a city can support. A sterile, carefully bounded monoculture sharply limits the growth of a thriving urban ecosystem.[15]

The freestanding walls and moat-like lawns of houses separate us from one another more effectively than other forms of dwellings. Houses tend to preserve and expand private space at the cost of public space. Their low density means that even when alternative land uses find a foothold (not always easy given zoning restrictions), they are not likely to draw many users. This is a problem for any stores without the broadest of customer bases, a dynamic favoring big-box general retailers and malls over street shops. It is also a problem for public amenities such as parks, pools, and the arts. These thrive where they receive a financial base from taxes and visitors. But people are less likely to visit amenities the farther they live away from them, and less likely to support paying for them if they never visit. The density at which houses tend to thrive simply does not support much of a scene.[16]

The boringness of the suburbs is one of the oldest and most persistent critical themes. In contrast, the kinds of engagement that a higher-density city can provide have been eloquently described by observers ranging from committed urbanists, like Jane Jacobs, to libertarian economists, like Edward Glaeser, to political theorists of justice, like Iris Marion Young. Jacobs, in particular, finds a dynamic urbanism in well-traveled and -surveilled sidewalks, championing the interactive spaces of what might be termed the urban village. Glaeser looks more to the innovation-enhancing possibilities provided by the freewheeling sharing of ideas and talent pools encouraged

---

[14] Estimated at 2,494,600,000 metric tons, using data from UN Framework Convention on Climate Change 2005, table 1—excluding Land Use Change and Forestry; author calculations. Though they provide a nice comparison, estimates for India and Sub-Saharan Africa remain rough and should be treated with a great deal of caution, both for reasons of outdated data and due to the measurement difficulties involved in gathering data for non–Annex I countries (i.e., countries where reporting is not required by the UN). Other measures than those suggested could also help, of course, without greatly altering housing patterns. Moving away from power plants fired by fossil fuel (especially coal), for instance, would significantly reduce emissions, especially in conjunction with the widespread adoption of electric cars.

[15] However, see Archer 2005 and R. Harris 2004 on the diversity contained by the term *suburbs*.

[16] Of course, it is not clear that suburban residents want a scene. See, e.g., Dowling 1998.

by urban life. Young speaks to the variety and eroticism of the city as a place where the "other" is made attractive.[17]

Visions of urban vitality are similarly peddled by Richard Florida through his ideas about the "creative class," attracted by the cultural amenities of city life. While houses promote a certain residential homogeneity, alternative denser housing forms tend to share space with museums, galleries, concert houses, clubs, cafes, and other cultural venues as well as boutiques for specialty shopping. The density of the city also provides space for subcultural communities, especially gay enclaves—a key draw for the creative class as he conceptualizes it. Overall, alternatives to the house both exemplify and support greater variety in the built environment, drawing in those who appreciate the artistic potential of the city and its diversity of scenes.[18]

Habitat Lost: For the Poor

Promoting urban vitality is wonderful, but there is a catch. As noted by critical scholars, processes of gentrification are driven by various elements of the creative class Florida describes, along with the New Urbanist ideas most associated with Jacobs. As the privileged return from their sojourn to the suburbs, they tend to displace those they initially left behind, undermining the urban habitat left to the poorer denizens of the inner city. From this perspective, the sprawling detached houses of the suburbs look like just the lure needed to keep the middle class from competing with the poor for limited space within the Urban Core. But the house is no friend of the poor: quite the opposite. Consequently, curtailing its spread need not lead to gentrification. Two related points demonstrate the important but often overlooked part the house plays in restricting living options for those of lesser means: (1) houses tend to be more expensive than other types of dwellings, and (2) the house in law was built to keep poor people out, constraining their options to the mutable Urban Core.[19]

Of these two points, the simplest to establish is that houses tend to be expensive ways of housing people. This is especially true in cities, where the land required to support houses is much more expensive than elsewhere. The expense of houses is further boosted by the building codes, servicing requirements, and regulatory aspects of constructing the house into law.

---

[17] Sennett (1970) revived boringness as a critique of suburbia right after Gans (1967) noted its aged character. See also Jacobs 1961, Glaeser 2011, and Young 1990.

[18] See Florida 2002, Fischer 1995, and Silver and Clark 2015.

[19] See Peck 2005, which carefully summarizes and sharpens a number of critiques of Florida's work. Freeman and Braconi 2004 notes that displacement may not be as severe as imagined, based on a study of New York. See K. Newman and Wyly 2006 for a response and more critical reanalysis.

TABLE 2.2 AFFORDABILITY ESTIMATES FOR STANDARD TWO-STORY HOUSES
AND STANDARD CONDOMINIUMS

	Price	Price/sq. ft.	Minimum qualifying income	Percentage median household income on housing
Canadian std. house	C$410,600	C$274	C$87,800	47.8%
Canadian std. condo	C$237,600	C$264	C$51,400	28.0%
Vancouver std. house	C$832,800	C$555	C$157,200	87.8%
Vancouver std. condo	C$388,900	C$432	C$74,800	41.8%

Source: Royal Bank of Canada estimates for 2013.

Self-building has become increasingly onerous, and corporate construction costs tend to be higher for single-family houses than other forms of dwellings. In Canada, recent affordability estimates for ownership were calculated by the Royal Bank of Canada (RBC), summarized in Table 2.2.[20] These model "standard" forms of housing and allow a comparison between prices for standardized 1,500-square-foot two-story houses and 900-square-foot condominium units. As demonstrated, the price differences are stark, with houses costing some 73 percent more than condos. Differences are even more pronounced in expensive metropolises, like the Vancouver area, where houses cost over 114 percent more than condos. The greater size of houses accounts for some of the difference, but even on a price-per-square-foot basis, houses just cost more.[21]

RBC also calculated the minimum income required to qualify for a mortgage to buy a house or condominium. The figure for houses lies well beyond the median household income, for both Vancouver and Canada as a whole. The last column denotes the percentage of the median household income from 2013 that would need to be devoted to housing payments in order to afford purchasing the standard house or condo. Ownership of a house always requires more household income to maintain than condo alternatives, and related figures demonstrate that houses have grown increasingly voracious and exclusive over time. Middle-income households generally cannot afford to purchase the standard 1,500-square-foot house.[22]

Renting households, in particular, usually find barriers to buying houses insurmountable. A study by the U.S. Census Bureau estimated that in 2004, before the Great Recession, the median new single-family house in the

---

[20] Royal Bank of Canada 2013.

[21] See Quigley and Raphael 2004 on land prices, R. Harris 2004 on the decline in self-building, and Bertaud 2010 on construction cost estimates.

[22] RBC calculations assume buyers are able to come up with a 25 percent down payment and to secure standard twenty-five-year mortgages at prevailing five-year fixed interest rates, with no more than 32 percent of pre-tax income going toward mortgage costs, property tax, and heating as well as maintenance fees for condos.

United States was beyond the reach of 96 percent of those families currently renting. The median condominium was more affordable than either the median or modest version of the detached house, though 84 percent of renting families still found it inaccessible. In general, the affordability of modest home ownership for all families only got worse through the Recession, dropping to an all-time low since the census began keeping track.[23]

Houses are not only too expensive to support lower-income households; they also, as regulatory creatures, work to wall in the Urban Core. This constrains the space available for building cheaper alternatives to the house. Put slightly differently, we can divide the developed portions of metropolitan areas into their Urban Cores and their house reserves. The Great House Reserve keeps the poor out, which was, for many of those involved in its creation, a feature and not a bug. The protections built around the house ensure that multiunit developers cannot move into the reserve lands. Nor can existing houses be subdivided. At best, multiunit developers are enabled to move into leftover and poorly planned lots along arterials nearby. Only within the Urban Core do developers have more room to maneuver. There they can cater to either poorer households, constrained to the Core, or the middle class, drawn to the amenities of urban life. This dynamic pits one constituency against the other and lies at the heart of the gentrification debate.[24]

Doing away with the house in a more comprehensive fashion means dissolving the strong boundary erected against expansion of the Urban Core. Reenabling the succession of house-dominated neighborhoods would open more space both for urban redevelopment by the middle class and for the repurposing and subdividing of existing single-family detached houses to support multiple lower-income households. In short, limitations on housing options for the poor are fundamentally connected to the constraints placed on expansion of the Urban Core.

To be certain, the house as a regulatory creature is not the only problem facing the poor. The more that markets are left to distribute housing, the less say the poor will have over their living circumstances anywhere. As discussed toward the end of the book, other sorts of protection might usefully be put to work to look after their interests. Regardless, the house (1) remains inaccessible to the poor and (2) further constrains their living options by hemming in the Urban Core. The latter point ensures that gentrification can

---

[23] See Savage 2009 on 2004 and E. Wilson and Callis 2013 for a 2009 follow-up.

[24] On zoning keeping out the poor, see Babcock 1966, Hirt 2014, and Perin 1977. See Ley 1996 and Lees 2000 on gentrification, with the latter calling for more examination of its regulatory context. See Hess 2005 on poorly planned garden apartment development and Glaeser and Ward 2009, Gyourko 2009, Levine 2006, and Shlay and Rossi 1981 on general unaffordability issues. On mobile homes as alternative housing for the poor, often placed in the hinterlands beyond Core and Reserve, see Kusenbach 2013 and Sullivan 2014.

best be avoided by pairing new constraints on the outward sprawl of houses to the lifting restrictions on the outward expansion of the Urban Core. Want to help the poor? Then tear down the wall separating the house habitat from the rest of the city.

Poor Habitat for Democracy

Houses are not just unaffordable for most people; they are ultimately unaffordable for cities, too. The fiscal situation of cities varies from place to place, but overall, houses tend to create a drain on municipal coffers. They are often taxed at lower rates than other properties, reflecting zoning restrictions on what can be built on single-family lots and how they can be used. But houses are more expensive to service on a per-unit basis, both in terms of basic utilities infrastructure and, as previously noted, in terms of transit and transportation infrastructure. This can mean that my modestly wealthy neighbors and I, living in low-rises and townhouses, end up supporting the very wealthy house owner nearby by paying more property tax relative to the amount of urban land and services we receive. The disparity becomes more notable as one crosses municipal boundaries into nearby house-dominated suburbs, where residents frequently enjoy the services (e.g., roads, commerce, employment opportunities) provided by the city without paying into the municipal tax base at all.[25]

Setting aside so much urban and suburban land for houses alone seems fundamentally unjust given that so many people cannot afford them and yet end up paying for them through their taxes anyway. To the extent that social inequality erodes democracy, then, houses contribute to this erosion. But there are additional reasons to be concerned about the rise of the house, having to do with the habits they reinforce. By nature and design, with moats of lawn and free-standing walls, houses insulate people from broader social ties. They curtail and privatize democratic impulses. As recounted in Chapter 1, this circumscription of social ties was often considered by the rising managerial classes of the industrial age to be a feature of the single-family house rather than a bug. For many people, it seems to remain that way. The house provides material form to middle-class withdrawal from public life. In so doing, it fosters political disengagement, favoring privatized rather than collective solutions to social problems.[26]

The tendency to surround houses with other houses, typically of similar configuration, only adds insult to democratic injury. Critics have often derided the social homogeneity of the suburbs. In this, they often overlooked

---

[25] See Brueckner 2000 on servicing costs and R. Harris 2004 in noting that tax starvation and collapse were also common for many suburban municipalities.

[26] Dowling 1998; Pratt 1986.

the differences between suburbs, even as they correctly perceived the so-cial similarities across households within given neighborhoods. In many cases, surrounding themselves with similar people may not have been the in-tent of suburbanites—housing conditions and search for more private space typically top the motivations driving movers—but selection effects still tend to produce a homogenous internal character. Political theorists suggest this is important insofar as "who we 'happen' to see regularly as we move through the world has an influence on who we think of as citizens and who we think to engage with as citizens—in other words, whose perspectives must be taken into account when making political decisions."[27]

Even for those who do not intend it, the withdrawal afforded by the detached house together with the homogeneity experienced within neigh-borhoods tends to reduce the diversity experienced by residents overall. By contrast, through exposure to difference and encouragement of frequent negotiation over how best to live together, urban neighborhoods tend to promote greater tolerance and more political engagement. To be certain, difference and negotiation can also produce disagreements, at times eroding trust. But domination by houses offers a poor solution, tending to channel disagreement into intolerance, avoidance and disengagement, and diminish-ing the habitat for democracy.[28]

These concerns mirror those of a long line of progressive urbanists—especially women—invested in the potential for city life to draw people into one another's orbits, from Jane Addams to Catherine Bauer to Jane Jacobs to Iris Marion Young. The latter argued, perhaps most forcefully, that cities, rather than suburbs or villages, offered the best hope for sustaining a so-cially just and engaged vision of democracy. The domination of metropolitan landscapes by houses undermines the potential of the city to draw people together. Furthermore, suburban developments often cleave away from cit-ies, incorporating, if at all, in ways that cut off broader civic obligations.[29]

Poor Habitat for Families

Does the house not give as it takes away? In reinforcing the separation of spheres, houses could contribute to creating a protective haven for families,

---

[27] See R. Harris 2004 on suburban diversity and Bruegmann 2005, Foote et al. 1960, Gans 1967, and Rossi 1980 on intent. The quote is from Bickford 2000, 363, though Bauer 1945 and Brooks 2002 make the same point.

[28] See T. Williamson 2010, T. Wilson 1985, and Wirth 1938 on urban promotion of tolerance. Fischer (1981) and Sennett (1970) explore the problems that can be produced by negotiations over living together, while Dunn and Singh (2014) make links to broader democratic theory. Thad Williamson (2008) finds that when they do engage, the house dwellers of the suburbs tend to skew conservative, a finding mirrored in Canadian research (e.g., Pratt 1986).

[29] Addams 1902; Bauer 1945; Jacobs 1961; Young 1990.

where they could work out egalitarian relationships on their own, safe from the sorts of discrimination and power imbalances present in broader society. In so doing, it seems at least plausible that single-family houses could promote tiny contented democracies in place of vast and unhappy ones. But feminists have long cried foul on this supposition. For one thing, only some types of family meet the accepted definition of "single family," emphasizing ties of blood, adoption, and (often heterosexist) marriage. Others across the full range of diverse human living situations remain excluded from the world of single-family residential neighborhoods, reinforcing the idea of a singular "Standard North American Family."[30]

Within the standardized home, though it is generally imagined as an egalitarian space where family members look after one another, the work that goes into maintaining the home and keeping it contented remains decidedly feminized. Relative to alternatives, houses increase the maintenance work required of homemakers, both inside and outside. Moreover, the exclusive homogeneity of house-dominant suburbs has the potential to create real problems for those tasked with housekeeping work. Detached houses can be isolating for those left behind to tend to them, providing sparser community support further removed from shared community services. Isolation places a special burden on women, unequally tasked with most childcare and housekeeping work. In providing space and limiting women's alternative options, the rise of the house may have accommodated and encouraged more childbearing. But the overburdening of women may be one reason why some research has documented a negative relationship between the development of detached houses and local couple stability. Where women manage to avoid shouldering the lion's share of the burdens of housework and childcare, they often do so by hiring domestic labor and inadvertently reinforcing racialized inequality.[31]

The maintenance of home as a "private" sphere, shielded from society, can also lead to shielding from public scrutiny. To the extent that detached houses foster isolation, they can prevent women and children—in particular—from accessing the protections afforded by broader social ties. This can become a serious problem for vulnerable members of households when they find home to be a source of violence and instability rather than a haven from a heartless world.[32]

---

[30] Dowling 1998; Ferree 1990; Hartmann 1981; Laslett and Brenner 1989; Wright 1981. See Lauster and Easterbrook 2011, Pyke 2000, and Smith 1993 on standardized families.

[31] On housework, see Coltrane 2000, Fava 1975, Garey 1999, R. Harris 2004, Hayden 2002, Hirt 2014, Hochschild and Machung 1989, Shlay 1995, and Wright 1981. On fertility, see Lauster 2010a, 2010b, and 2012 and Mulder and Billari 2010. On couple stability, see Lauster 2008. On hired help, see Glenn 1992 and Pratt 2012.

[32] Blunt and Dowling 2006; Tomas and Dittmar 1995; Wardhaugh 1999. For more on the complicated relationships between social isolation and domestic violence, see Beyer, Wallis, and Hamberger 2015 and Lanier and Maume 2009.

Outside the home, house dominance furthers social exclusion and reduces opportunities to encounter diversity. Together with the unaffordability of houses, this creates real problems for making constitutional democracy work. Within the standardized home, the habitat created by house dominance can reinforce traditional inequalities and power imbalances. Trading big interconnected democracies for little detached household ones can make both forms of governance less just.

Poor Habitat for Human Health

Aside from the implications for urbanity, the poor, democracy, and family, researchers increasingly suggest that a human habitat structured by cars and houses is just plain bad for us in terms of human health. Motor vehicles, of course, have many ways of killing people. According to the CDC, an astonishing 36,000 people died from motor vehicle accidents in the United States in 2009 alone (a normal year), with the greatest toll exacted on those in their late teens and twenties. A study in Canada estimated a more modest but similarly troubling 2,875 deaths due to motor vehicle accidents in 2004, with somewhere around 14 percent of those deaths involving struck pedestrians or cyclists. Cars and their ilk also contribute toxic particulate matter influencing air quality. This is most obvious, of course, in the poisonous haze that often hangs over North American cities.[33]

Less obviously, cars and houses together foster more sedentary habits, contributing to health risks such as obesity. Dense urban neighborhoods support more walking, as people run errands on their own two feet instead of in a car. The more houses in an area, and the larger the lots separating them, the more likely people are to have to take a car to get anywhere. Romantic images of the effort that goes into maintaining the country estate may persist (for instance, George W. Bush's vigorous bushwhacking), and some maintenance is certainly required. But most maintenance work is dull and sedentary, especially when carried out in conjunction with energy-intensive technologies such as riding lawn mowers and power vacuums. Living in walkable cities remains more physically engaging.[34]

On a related note, higher-density areas also tend to make healthier food options more readily accessible to people. In a study measuring distances to fresh food stores in the province of British Columbia, the proportion of a neighborhood's housing stock made up of detached, single-family houses was the strongest predictor of lacking a healthy source of sustenance nearby.

---

[33] On the United States, see CDC (Center for Disease Control) data release, as described and analyzed in Kochanek et al. 2011. On Canada, see Ramage-Morin 2008. On air quality, see Frank et al. 2006.

[34] Saelens et al. 2003; Frank, Andresen, and Schmid 2004.

The sort of exclusive zoning that supports houses also tends to keep out alternatives, like places that sell fresh food. Homogenous habitat potentially makes for unhealthy eating habits.[35]

None of this is to suggest that house dwellers will always look worse off than those living in denser urban forms of housing when compared side by side. House dwellers are often wealthier, with access to more resources, more status, and more health care. But the driving, the sedentary behavior, and related bad habits associated with living in a house increase the health risks of residents even as inequality and poverty often increase the risks for those excluded from single-family residential neighborhoods.[36]

Altogether, house habitat displaces alternatives. The establishment of a Great House Reserve has protected house habitat even as it continues to expand in size. Agricultural and wild lands suffer in an immediate sense, as do the more urban habitats prevented from expanding beyond a constrained Urban Core. The house allies itself with the car at the same time as both contribute to global warming, potentially risking the displacement of everyone and everything. The house habitat excludes the poor. But even for those who can afford to live there, the Great House Reserve is a troublesome place to live. By its nature it leads to disengagement, contributes to inequality, and encourages a sedentary, unhealthy lifestyle.

In short, the house is a parasite. So why do so many people want to live in houses? And why do our cities continue to protect so much house habitat? Even if we can agree that houses constitute a clear and present danger, can we really succeed in separating ourselves from them? The chapters ahead tackle these topics, first by investigating the rise and fall of the single-family house in Vancouver—one of the few North American metropolitan areas to seriously challenge the invasive spread of the house.

---

[35] Black et al. 2011.

[36] See Parks, Housemann, and Brownson 2003 for one attempt at controlling for wealth and environment (though not housing type) in assessing exercise across rural, urban, and suburban contexts.

BRINGING THE HOUSE TO LIFE IN VANCOUVER

The city passed through the various stages common
to all young and lusty infants.

—ARTHUR G. SMITH, CHAIRMAN,
VANCOUVER TOWN PLANNING COMMISSION, 1928,
QUOTED IN HARLAND BARTHOLOMEW,
*A PLAN FOR THE CITY OF VANCOUVER,
BRITISH COLUMBIA*

At the southwest corner of British Columbia, the City of Vancouver extends westward like an open hand proffered in greeting toward the Pacific Rim. Stanley Park and Pacific Spirit Park, home to the University
of British Columbia, form the damp green thumb and fingertips of the city.
Vancouver's high-rise downtown core occupies the base of the thumb, separated by an inlet known as False Creek from the swanky neighborhoods of
the city's West Side. Eastward of the thumb, the port of Vancouver meets
the railroad, extending up Vancouver's sleeve into the neighboring municipalities of Burnaby and Port Moody. Across the water of Burrard Inlet to
the North Shore, an imposing set of mountain peaks signifies the start of
the Canadian wild, just above the suburbs of North Vancouver and West
Vancouver clinging to their lower slopes. To the south of Burnaby lies the
tiny city of New Westminster, former capital of the mainland portion of the
province. The suburb of Richmond sits on the flat islands in the Fraser River
along Vancouver's southern border. Beyond these near suburbs, the south-
eastern city of Surrey dominates the settlements at the edge of Vancouver's
metropolitan bounds. The far suburbs join together the likes of Delta, White
Rock, and Langley to the south and Coquitlam, Port Coquitlam, Pitt Mead-
ows, and Maple Ridge to the east, up the long arm of the Fraser River Valley.

Altogether, the collected municipalities including and surrounding the
City of Vancouver go by a variety of names, including Metro Vancouver, the
Lower Mainland, the Greater Vancouver Regional District, and sometimes, in
the careless fashion of metropolitan collectives, just Vancouver. While there
is often a surprising degree of variation in weather across the municipalities

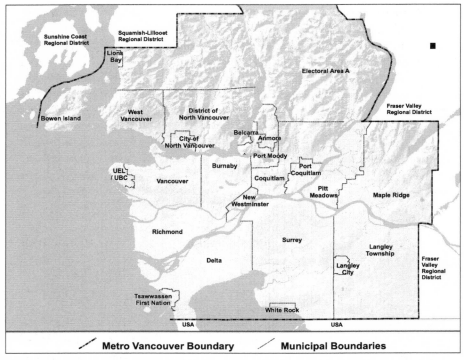

Figure 3.1 The municipalities of Metro Vancouver, as reported within the Regional Growth Strategy from 2010 (map 1), Greater Vancouver Regional District By-law 1136. (*Reproduced with the permission of Metro Vancouver.*)

contained here, they all tend to experience a rainy but otherwise mild climate. Metro Vancouver is protected from the stormier weather of the Pacific Ocean by the large island an hour and a half's ferry ride off its coast, somewhat confusingly known as Vancouver Island. The body of water sheltered by the island is called both the Salish Sea and the Georgia Strait, reflecting respectively aboriginal and colonial histories. The Sea extends south to Puget Sound, surrounding Vancouver's sister in the United States, the city of Seattle. The Fraser Delta forming much of the arm behind Vancouver's Pacific handshake is bisected by Canada's border with the United States at the 49th parallel, creating, by default, the southern boundary of the metropolitan area, as mapped in Figure 3.1.[1]

---

[1] Each title, save for the careless "Vancouver," has at various times been associated with some form of regional governance. When speaking of Vancouver as a municipality, rather than as the metro area, I refer to it as "the City" or by its full name as the "City of Vancouver." Vancouverites suspect that confusion over the distinction between the City and the Island was behind a recent drop in the City's ranking as "most livable," since traffic on Vancouver Island was cited by *The Economist* [magazine's] Intelligence Unit as a reason for reducing the livability on the Mainland (Canadian Press 2011).

At nearly 2.5 million residents, the metropolitan area of Vancouver is the third largest in Canada, after Toronto and Montreal, and ranks within the twenty-five largest in North America, fitting roughly between Denver and Pittsburgh. International immigration has accounted for much of the area's growth, and about 40 percent of residents were born in another country. The Lower Mainland is also quite multicultural, in ways that defy ready categorization. But drawing solely from Canada's definition of its "non-white" population, the census lists over half the residents of the municipalities of Vancouver, Richmond, and Burnaby as "visible minorities." Especially large portions of the population identify as Chinese in these cities, with another large portion identifying as South Asian in the city of Surrey.[2]

Vancouver is famed for its semi-tamed natural beauty: the snowy peaks turned ski resorts to the north, generally visible throughout the Lower Mainland; the temperate rainforests occupying its larger parks; the seals and occasional whales spotted in its waters; and the bears foraging around the slopes of its northern suburbs. It has frequently been lauded as the most livable of the world's cities, a place where urban comforts meet breathtaking wilderness views. It has also become identified with a particular planning movement, broadly oriented toward New Urbanist sustainability, "EcoDensity," and/or "tall, skinny high-rise towers set on townhouse podiums." Increasingly, such planning ideas have been spread around the globe as *Vancouverism*. Finally, of course, it has been highlighted as the second-least affordable place in the world to buy a house, just after Hong Kong. All this makes Vancouver a particularly interesting case study for detailing the history of how the house was first brought to life.[3]

Frontier City on the Salish Sea

A crucial part of any settlement history involves the acknowledgment that the Fraser Delta was inhabited long before it became a part of the colonial frontier, as established by archaeological remains estimated to be over two thousand years old. The Coast Salish bands living around the Vancouver area seem to have settled largely within permanent multifamily longhouses through the winter, spreading out into more decentralized and temporary

---

[2] Data on immigration and visible minority status from Statistics Canada National Household Survey (NHS) profiles for 2011: https://www12.statcan.gc.ca/nhs-enm/2011/dp-pd/prof/index.cfm?Lang=E.

[3] Livability as per Mercer Ratings (Punter 2003) and *The Economist* [magazine's] Intelligence Unit (2015). More recently, Vancouver was lauded as having the world's best reputation by the Reputation Institute (Stueck 2012). The quote is from Boddy 2003, 14. On Vancouverism, see Berelowitz 2005, Boddy 2005, Peck and Theodore 2010, and Punter 2003. On affordability, see Demographia 2013. All extant reports highlight Vancouver's unaffordability.

camps during much of the summer. Relevant descriptions of Coast Salish housing were first recorded in detail by Simon Fraser, traveling in an 1808 exploratory expedition for the North West Company down the river that would come to bear his name. Fraser's journal entries made clear the size of the longhouses common to the villages he passed through:[4]

> The whole range, which is 640 feet long by 60 broad, is under one roof. The front is 18 feet high, and the covering is slanting. All the apartments, which are separated in portions, are square, excepting the Chief's which is 90 feet long.[5]

While there is no precise equivalent, a present-day census taker would perhaps have characterized these indigenous structures as low-rise apartment buildings, a potent reminder that there is little "natural" about the detached house in Vancouver. Ironically, Fraser frequently accused the locals of thievery during his travels, though he pardoned as a necessity his own forcible acquisition of a chief's canoe. He somewhat sheepishly noted that he left behind a blanket for it. The North West Company would eventually merge with the Hudson's Bay Company (HBC)—renowned for such blanket diplomacy—and would successfully establish a fortified trading post in the area, named Fort Langley, in 1827.[6]

From the trading monopoly granted to the company by British royal charter would eventually emerge the makings of a form of colonial governance. The company's charter established it as both a corporate body, beholden to shareholders, and a more publicly accountable governing body. The transition toward more formal governance through the nineteenth century was sped along by British concerns over territorial encroachment by the United States, so that in 1858 British Columbia became an official colony of the British Empire, with its capital in New Westminster.[7]

The second official proclamation of the newly installed governor was a warning that all real estate was claimed by the crown—a theft from the natives of such magnitude as to put Simon Fraser to shame. Anyone attempting to sell lots along the Fraser River without royal authorization would henceforth be prosecuted for fraud. The lands surrounding the new capital were promptly surveyed by the Royal Engineers, who set up government reserves

---

[4] On archaeology, see Coupland 1991 and Moss and Erlandson 1995.

[5] Quoted in Lamb 2007, 123.

[6] Lamb 2007, 124–128. Hudson's Bay Company merged with the North West Company, its chief rival and Simon Fraser's erstwhile employer, in 1821, under pressure from the British government.

[7] The provincial government began as a private trade corporation, following the same trajectory that Valverde 2012 suggests characterizes cities as municipal corporations.

Figure 3.2 Photograph of Granville town site (which would soon be renamed the City of Vancouver) in 1886, looking west from Westminster Avenue and Oppenheimer Street (now Main and Cordova Streets), enhanced and with a key by noted Vancouver archivist Major Matthews. *(Reproduced from Vancouver Archives.)*

in a number of strategically important locations. Small blankets of land were also set aside as Indian reserves around local villages. The rest of the land was gradually subdivided and offered up for sale and settlement by the crown through a series of royal acts. Speculators purchased and held many lots from afar, in what would prove a persistent theme through Vancouver's history. But gold prospectors, lumbermen, fishing interests, and a scattering of farmers joined the Royal Engineers who remained, tending to the generous 150-acre land grants earned by their service. Saloons, lumber mills, and canneries would form the nuclei for small towns as the new locals began to look eastward toward the railway promised them in return for becoming Canadian.[8]

In 1884, the Canadian Pacific Railway (CPR) company chose the village of Granville over nearby Port Moody as the western terminus of the transcontinental railroad. Figure 3.2 shows the Granville site in preparation for its impending incorporation as the newly renamed City of Vancouver (the name

---

[8] The first official proclamation was a ban on sales of liquor to the Indians. See also Hayes 2005 on engineers and their maps.

change was a CPR suggestion).[9] At least two hotels and a variety of relatively undifferentiated houses, stores, and shacks huddled together beyond the burnt stumps of newly cleared land, capped with a "for sale" sign. The rail-road's decision cemented the soon-to-be city's rapid growth at the center of a burgeoning West Coast metropolis. In exchange for its choice of Granville as a final destination, the CPR received vast land grants around the new city, placing real estate deals at the heart of the Vancouver project from the start.

The enforced transferability of land did not go unprotested. Settler Sam Greer infamously defended his claim to Kitsilano Beach against the railroad by shooting the sheriff sent to evict him in 1887. But he lost his land anyway, and spent time in jail for the shooting. First Nations groups also failed to make much headway in pressing their claims, especially against the CPR, through Vancouver's early years. Nevertheless, long battles in the courts have more successfully kept First Nations–related ownership questions from being fully settled, and large tracts of land around the city have at least nominally been returned to tribal ownership. Other local landowners would cooperate with the railroad, including the trio of Englishmen who preempted the lands now known as the West End neighborhood of Vancouver, located near Stanley Park. They provided the CPR every third lot from their subdivided claim, thinking the nearby location of the railroad terminus would more than make up for the value of land lost. Overall, the railroad itself was both the most contested and the most important driver of the early City of Vancouver's "growth machine," hard at work transforming the land into something resembling a commodity.[10]

Growing Pains

Sociologist Harvey Molotch was the first to describe the city as a "growth machine." In so doing, he captured the pattern whereby a class of people with interests in a city's real estate becomes heavily invested in manipulat-ing local politics to promote growth. Most municipal politics is organized around bringing more people and more capital to the city, benefiting landed interests by raising the price of land. The broad outlines of this narrative are generally supported by a summary reading of Vancouver's history. It is no surprise that many mayors and city councilors had their hands in real estate deals before, during, and after their time in office.[11]

---

[9] This version of the photo may be found at the Vancouver Archives website at http://search archives.vancouver.ca/index.php/view-of-granville-looking-west-from-westminster-avenue -main-street-and-oppenheimer-cordova-street-3.

[10] See Blomley 2004 on overlapping ownership claims and Molotch 1976 on the idea of the growth machine.

[11] Molotch 1976; Logan and Molotch 2007. Harvey (1973) ultimately developed many over-lapping ideas. Galois (1980, 252n55) lists early mayors in real estate and development.

Yet Vancouver's rapid growth was necessarily coupled with attempts to transform nature into Polanyi's "fictitious commodity" of land. Regulation necessarily accompanied the move to govern cities by markets. Most often it was deployed in reactive fashion, in response to the host of problems that rapid market-led growth created for Vancouver's earliest residents, even the wealthiest and best connected among them. As friendly critics of the "growth machine" paradigm have pointed out, the really interesting devils were less in the overall support of local coalitions for growth than in the details of how they proposed to manage it. A short discussion of Vancouver's governance amid its growing pains provides a foundation for understanding the role the house would come to play as a manufactured solution to a host of woes.[12]

The principles that growth should be promoted and should benefit local landholders were written into the city's documents of incorporation. These stipulated a corporate governance structure—not so different from the Hudson's Bay Company. Only the control of real property, through ownership or lease, entitled city residents to vote, and the property needed to have an assessed value of at least C$300 for each voter it contained. Entry into local property-assessment rolls enabled voting, except if residents found themselves in an officially excluded category (e.g., being a married woman or Chinese). In lacking a lease to a property, lodgers and boarders were also disenfranchised. As noted by historian Jean Barman, until 1921, "property owners could vote in as many city wards as they held property." On the whole, real estate constituted something like a share in Vancouver's stock.[13]

The city's governance powers largely reflected its administration of property contracts and control over the use of public space. The first bylaw, passed in May 1886, merely appointed city officers, including a city clerk, an assessment commissioner, an engineer, and a police magistrate. The second bylaw, passed only a week later, set restrictions on liquor sales and outlawed vagrants, mendicants, and houses of ill repute, suggesting the kinds of growth the frontier city wanted to avoid while also protecting some of its earliest businesses. Bylaw 3, passed the next week, divided the city into wards. Bylaw 4 set the terms for assessing property tax, as passed the following week. A week after that, the newly incorporated city burned down to the ground.[14]

MacDonald (1973) notes that ten of sixteen members of the 1912 council of aldermen were in real estate or local business. More recently, Tom Campbell (1967–1972) and Gordon Campbell (1986–1993) were also noted developer mayors.

[12] Gill 2000; Kimelberg 2011; Surborg, VanWynsberghe, and Wyly 2008.

[13] Renters with leases could also be deemed eligible if they paid more than C$50 a year in rent. See An Act to incorporate the City of Vancouver 1886, esp. sec. 6–8, and Barman 1986, 121.

[14] Full text from Vancouver Archives website, with summaries available at http://app.vancou ver.ca/bylaw_net/. Gassy Jack's Saloon was one of the founding businesses of Vancouver.

The Great Fire that ravaged the city within the first months of its founding began as a brush-clearing fire, of the sort seen prominently smoldering in Figure 3.2. The blaze destroyed most of the buildings then in existence and suggested the need for a fire bylaw, passed promptly thereafter. This was the first bylaw to subject new buildings to city inspection and approval. Rounding out the first ten bylaws were two licensing acts for the regulation (respectively) of liquor sales and horse-drawn cabs, two acts enabling the city to raise funds for itself via loans, and the city's first public health bylaw. This last, the public health bylaw, instituted regulation of boarding and lodging houses and laid down conditions restricting the occupation of houses or parts of houses wherein a sick person had once resided, subject to inspection.

Slaughterhouses also came in for special licensing through the city's first health bylaw, as a potential nuisance. The repulsive sights, smells, and sounds of slaughterhouses were to be kept away from those who might be offended by them. In these and similar ways, the city began to adopt powers to combat urban problems of the day, with vice, fire, illness, and smell topping the list. These were all problems in which one person's use of property could be deemed harmful to the public at large, and especially those living nearby. Based on the logic of nuisance, a key facet of English common law, the city began to curtail private property rights in order to promote the public good. Yet as historian Norbert MacDonald has observed, early Vancouver politicians were quite wary of this interference. Their inclinations likely stemmed from their belief in free markets, coupled with their own sizable property interests. Licensing, as demonstrated with respect to slaughterhouses (as well as liquor sales and taxis), provided a small-scale and targeted solution for the city in regulating potentially troublesome industries. Once the city took up licensing powers, it could build on these powers to regulate where certain types of property uses could be located within the city—at least by exclusion, as with slaughterhouses.[15]

The city's early obsession with slaughterhouses also suggests the rising concern with smell. Historians point toward an olfactory revolution occurring during the nineteenth century.[16] In response to miasma theories of illness, public health reformers worked assiduously to make cities less smelly.[17] This extended into a reorganization of domestic space as well, as toilets increasingly entered the home, but in ways that placed them at a distance, often separated by an anteroom, from the goings-on of the household.[18] Public health bylaws increasingly required attention to matters of hygiene and sew-

---

[15] See MacDonald 1973 and Valverde 2011.

[16] Ward 1999.

[17] See Johnson's (2006) *The Ghost Map* for a popular history of the overturning of miasma theory.

[18] Ward 1999; Wright 1981.

age disposal, forbidding waste from accumulating in ways that would cause public nuisance or health hazards. Sewer lines were easy to build in Vancouver, though they frequently ran just to the nearest shoreline.[19]

The rising concern with smell was balanced by the promotion of industry. The city was reliant on its canneries and lumber mills as producers of trade goods and jobs. Increasingly, these industries were joined by others, including breweries, smelters, and a large sugar refinery. Many of these were actively encouraged by the city with tax breaks and preferential treatment. Industrial interests frequently located facilities where they could make the best use of sea and rail transport, concentrating along the north side of False Creek and east of downtown, where the railway met the port. Others, like breweries, relied on the area's creeks for their water supplies. The arrival of a commercial electric streetcar network in 1890 (encouraged by the city) and its expansion through the 1890s helped spread industry more widely. Industries continued to compete for land with the residences spreading along the same lines, especially along the south shore of False Creek. Overall, the arrival of the streetcar drove up land prices, and landholders frequently paid streetcar companies to extend lines in their direction.[20] Interurban rail lines added to New Westminster in 1891 and to the canneries of Steveston in 1902 ("the Sockeye Express") further helped expand and integrate the region's industries and residences. Commercial uses for properties mingled with residential uses throughout the city, with many locals setting up shops on their ground floors.[21]

Vancouver's position as a transport hub on the edge of the larger British Empire quickly attracted a multicultural assemblage of immigrants. Sizable Chinese and Japanese communities grew in conjunction with distinctly European ones.[22] Men were far more likely than women to arrive as migrants in the early years, and they often found seasonal work in prospecting, lumberjacking, and fishing. Gradually others came to work on the railroad, took jobs with local industrial concerns, invested in real estate, or set up local businesses. In interconnected ways, the relatively large Chinese community became viewed as a source of cheap labor by industrialists, an impediment to labor organization, and ultimately a cause for concern by the

---

[19] Bartholomew's report to the Town Planning Commission notes that untreated sewage was still flowing directly into False Creek (1930, 32).

[20] MacDonald 1973.

[21] The Vancouver Heritage Foundation has published maps describing many of the old shops carved out of houses and townhouses in various neighborhoods around the older parts of Vancouver, with a map of Strathcona devoted entirely to identifying such historical icons.

[22] Other non-European communities also grew, including, for instance, the Hawaiians who took up in Stanley Park and other places around Vancouver for a time. However, intermarriage was more common, and this group never became as prominent as the Chinese and Japanese communities (Barman 1997).

colonial government. Most Chinese residents of the city, especially single men, took up rooms in the densely packed lodging houses of the Chinatown that developed in the swampy lowlands at the base of Vancouver's thumb, between False Creek and Burrard Inlet. Japanese residents tended to live a short distance farther east. Both communities also clustered around the extensive cannery operations in Steveston to the south. They were, in many cases, excluded from owning property elsewhere by the openly racist restrictive covenants and the real estate practices of the time.[23] It is likely that they also gathered together for protection, especially following the race riots of 1887 and 1907 that targeted both Chinese and Japanese residents of the city.

Despite private and contractual forms of discrimination, the city was prevented by higher governments from passing racially restrictive bylaws. Numerous attempts to use municipal powers to restrict and govern minority residents were shot down by the courts as unlawful, as in the United States.[24] Nevertheless, evidence suggests that the city disproportionately hassled minority property owners in Chinatown and elsewhere as failing to live up to city codes.[25] Local activists also lobbied the provincial government to pass more forthrightly racist legislation, and in 1895 British Columbia forbade Chinese, Japanese, South Asian, and First Nations residents from being listed on provincial voting rolls. As a consequence, these early residents were also kept from practicing in many of the higher-status professions.[26] The federal government, in turn, soon passed similarly racist legislation limiting non-European immigration.

If many of Vancouver's early residents took up rooms in lodging houses primarily because of race-based restrictions, discrimination, and self-protection, others simply took such rooms because of the seasonal nature of their work, or because they were new in a rapidly growing town, or because that was all they could afford in Vancouver's market.[27] Lodging rooms were often made available in larger houses and repurposed mansions after they were abandoned by the wealthy—frequently due to the industrialization

---

[23] Anderson (1991) provides an enlightening history of repeated efforts to regulate Chinatown and restrict the residential relocation of Chinese residents outside this area. See also Mawani 2009. Fogelson (2005) and Taylor (2009) provide discussion of the use of restrictive covenants for racial exclusion in the United States.

[24] Taylor 2009.

[25] Anderson 1991; Weaver 1979.

[26] Barman 1986; Anderson 1991.

[27] Galois (1980, 204) finds the Vancouver Board of Trade suggesting the quintupling of the population, from one thousand to five thousand, in the year following the City's founding, with relatively regular (if less dramatic) additions of people in subsequent years, all of whom would need places to stay upon arriving.

of sites nearby.[28] As in the United States, lodgers increasingly became a matter of public concern, especially under public health provisions. Public Health By-law 131 (passed in 1892) provided health inspectors the power to restrict the number of occupants that might be housed in dwelling places. In 1899, special legislation (By-law 341) was passed specifically to regulate lodging houses. It followed the licensing strategy earlier established for slaughterhouses, requiring that all buildings with rooms let out to lodgers register with the city and meet a set of minimum criteria with respect to living standards. A special concern was airflow, as associated with concerns about crowding:

> 2. The keeper of a registered house shall not permit to be let or occupied as a lodging, any room in such house, nor shall a lodger suffer any room under his control to be occupied by a greater number of persons, than will allow of the air space for each person according to the following rules:
>
> (a) The minimum space for each adult in any room in a registered house which may be occupied as a bedroom only, shall not be less than 384 cubic feet.
>
> (b) The minimum space for each adult in any room in a registered house which may be occupied as a sitting room and as a bedroom shall not be less than 400 feet.
>
> (c) For the purpose of the foregoing rules two children under the age of 12 years may be counted as one adult.
>
> (d) Every room shall have a window made to open at least two feet square with ventilation to the outer air.[29]

In addition, one water closet was required for every twelve persons living in a lodging house. By-law 765, passed in 1910 in replacement of the previous bylaw governing lodging houses, further defined such subdivided houses in a manner that grouped them together with hotels, but distinguished them from apartment buildings where cooking might be done in the apartments. This highlights how in Vancouver, as well as elsewhere, hotels and lodging houses became distinct from apartment buildings only in the early twentieth century.[30] Those living in single-unit detached dwellings but taking in boarders were technically defined the same way as hotel operators, though many may have avoided registering as such.

---

[28] Barman 1986, esp. 100–101.

[29] City of Vancouver By-law 341.

[30] Wright 1981 provides a history of the differentiation of apartments from tenements in the United States.

Along with the hotels and lodging houses, shacks thrown up around False Creek and along the mud flats also offered refuge for those unable or unwilling to compete with speculators and other landlords in the buying of property around the city, or to pay the rents they charged their tenants. Some 380 shacks were counted on the foreshores of Vancouver in 1894.[31] Across the early course of the city's history, these shacks were frequently torn down only to return soon after each campaign, along with large collections of tents that tended to be erected during the summer months.[32] Nevertheless, sturdier detached dwellings were going up at a rapid pace on the registered lots of land around the city, including both rudimentary cabins and fancier designs, built by owner-occupiers and builder-speculators alike.[33]

The designs for dwellings favored by more privileged residents were increasingly influenced by architects, at least seventeen of whom had set up shop in the city by 1891.[34] Housing for professionals, investors, industrialists, and assorted managers was thereby engaged with broader Victorian architectural trends. Living rooms, dining rooms, and spacious verandahs for the entertainment of guests were all required. Social historians suggest that among the elite classes, and extending to the growing urban middle classes, housing was becoming more and more about establishing a stage to support performances of privileged distinction.[35] Proper performances required room for both front stage and backstage. The sanctuaries built into the houses of the privileged took part in preserving various and newly important aspects of privacy. Separate rooms were established for separate functions, with parlors for receiving guests moved away from sleeping quarters, which in turn were increasingly partitioned between parents and children, and (at least by the late nineteenth century) between children by gender.[36]

Various progressive reformers kept a running conversation between the fashionable fads and social theories of the privileged and the living circumstances of the poor. The activism of progressives like Jane Addams, founder of Hull House in Chicago, exemplified the work taken on by prominent figures of the day. In Vancouver, groups like the Vancouver Council of Women

---

[31] Galois 1980, 428, 458.

[32] Wade 1994, esp. 18–19.

[33] R. Harris 2004 speaks to the early diversity of Canadian suburbs.

[34] McDonald 1996, 43.

[35] See Gillis 1996 and Wright 1981 for the United States and Ward 1999 for Canada. Frykman and Löfgren (1987) analyze similar trends in Oscarian Sweden (overlapping in time with Victorian Canada).

[36] See Ward's description of the Woolsley family (1999, 16, 82) for examples.

TABLE 3.1 COMPARISON OF INCORPORATION DATES AND EARLY TWENTIETH-CENTURY POPULATIONS OF MAJOR WEST COAST CITIES IN NORTH AMERICA

West Coast frontier cities	Population 1900/1901	Population 1910/1911
Los Angeles (1850)	102,497	319,198
San Francisco (1850)	342,782	416,912
Portland (1851)	90,426	207,214
Seattle (1869)	80,671	237,194
Vancouver (1886)	27,010	100,401

kept in touch with urban reformers elsewhere, in no small part by undertaking comparative investigations into household conditions.[37] Many progressives viewed good housing as an essential tool for promoting more inclusive citizenship. They worked to transform new ideas about decency and social inclusion into sets of standards for regulating the built environment, primarily via existing municipal licensing and permitting powers. For instance, by 1910, new restrictions on sleeping-quarter usage would make their way into Vancouver's updated lodging house regulations. Children were no longer to share sleeping apartments with those of different genders past the age of ten.[38]

Urban Succession: Escape and Reform

Through the first ten years of the twentieth century, Vancouver's free-market-driven growing pains would only grow increasingly intense. The city's population nearly quadrupled in size. Though it got a late start compared to its southern neighbors down the coast, Vancouver was hard at work trying to catch up (see Table 3.1).[39] But long-term growth was staggered with periods of sharp economic decline. The 1890s were marked by recurring financial crises and crashes in local property markets. The real estate boom of the early twentieth century, fed in part by speculation about what the Panama Canal might mean for Vancouver as a port city, once again turned bust in 1913.[40] As an indicator of the downturn in Vancouver, a lot fetching an astounding offer of C$125,000 at the height of the boom (1912) sold for less than a third of that price just five years later.[41]

---

[37] See, e.g., Wade 1994 on the VCW's actions in 1913 and Addams 1910 for examples of other contemporary reformist women's clubs.

[38] City of Vancouver By-law 765, article 14.

[39] Data are from MacDonald 1973, 28.

[40] Bartholomew 1930.

[41] MacDonald 1973.

Rapid fluctuations in trading value were joined by other crises associated with Vancouver's lax property controls. With the passing of the first decade of the twentieth century, it seemed increasingly clear to many that licensing powers and piecemeal regulations were inadequate for dealing with the threat to decency posed by Vancouver's metastasizing urban growth. The tasks of urban administration were simply overwhelming for city officials. Keeping up with the rapidly expanding licensing and inspection regimes in the context of a rapidly expanding city meant most officials moved from "crisis to crisis." Many resigned from overwork, stressing to the city council the need for more staff.[42]

The urban threat to decency, as tackled by progressives on behalf of the poor, remained a problem for the wealthy as well. For however they chose to design their own housing, those who could afford to purchase property and construct a dwelling in or around Vancouver still faced a particularly urban conundrum: their lots would be surrounded by other lots that they did not own and thereby did not control. After purchasing a home, they could no longer pick their neighbors—not even by race. The neighbors, in turn, could affect the quality of the owner-occupiers' residential life, not to mention the resale value of their property. True, after By-law 2, houses of ill repute on their neighbors' lots would be legally prohibited. After By-law 7, slaughterhouses would require licensing and would not be permitted within 150 feet of their own property. Some ways down the list, after By-law 341, lodging houses would be required to maintain a minimum of space and well-plumbed facilities for tenants (By-law 135, in an update to vagrancy prohibition, had already outlawed "answering the call of nature" in streets and public places). But the overtaxed licensing system was already breaking down, and who knew what new threat might arise from the chaos of the free-market city? For elites, at least, two solutions presented themselves, often in combination. The first was escape. The second was reform.

Elite enclaves held out the hope for the privileged of preserving the privacy and dignity that propriety demanded. Early on, many elites migrated to the West End of downtown, just south of Stanley Park and away from the industries concentrating to the east. But by the turn of the century, the West End was growing crowded and ever less exclusive. Moreover, it turned out that even the elite could become bad neighbors—mostly by leaving and subdividing their mansions into profitable rental apartments. As a result, the West End began to adopt tenant households that remained dignified, but further down the social ladder. Its classier apartments became a special draw for respectable single women.[43]

---

[42] Ibid., esp. 36–37, reviewing city council meeting minutes from 1899 to 1915; quote from p. 36.

[43] Barman 1986; McKay 2003–2004.

The process of neighborhood change and elite displacement within early twentieth-century cities was general enough that urban sociologists of the era began to study it. Those of the Chicago School termed this sort of neighborhood change "succession," and emphasized its relationship to ecological processes by which lower-intensity residential land uses were thought to be naturally replaced by more urban and higher-density residential, industrial, and commercial uses as cities expanded.[44] The general assumption was that a city's growth led to a kind of de-gentrification, pushing elites and the increasingly well-to-do middle classes farther and farther out into the suburbs by their disdain for the rough-and-tumble urban life.[45]

Urban succession processes tended to alter the landscape in both boom and bust periods. During the boom times, when the city successfully attracted capital and people, new developments were thrown up left and right, often rapidly changing the urban landscape. Licensing systems failed to keep up with the innovative ways people developed and redeveloped their properties, and new uses often seemed to portend bad neighbors. By contrast, during the bust times, capital dried up and development declined. Existing properties were frequently repurposed as resources for making a living, whether subdivided into rental properties, reconfigured as lodging houses, or provided with new storefronts and turned into commercial ventures. Real estate interests both decried and profited from the widespread perception of urban chaos. For instance, a local magazine article advertised a new bungalow design in 1911 by noting:

> The measure of a city's stability, financial soundness and attractiveness to the newcomer is not to be found in the palatial hotels, skyscraper office buildings and apartment houses. The dweller in flats is an uncertain and unsettled quantity. The man in the office may be a foot-loose adventurer. Homes alone indicate the extent and quality of citizenship. The home is the heart, the life and the index of a city. Vancouver may well be proud of her beautiful homes, and of her great industries that are directly concerned with the promotion of home-building.[46]

Detached bungalows—as opposed to conjoined flats, palatial hotels, and apartment houses—were equated by advertisers with home. Through such advertisements, a variety of land-holding developers outside Vancouver's downtown thumb looked to exploit fears and insecurities about urban life.

---

[44] Burgess 1925, 73. See also Burgess 1928.

[45] Fogelson 2005; Jackson 1985.

[46] Pemberly 1911, 1313–1315, as quoted in Holdsworth 1986, 23. Bourdieu 2006 and Fogelson 2005 note similar advertisements.

In a more systematic fashion, they worked to reassure potential buyers that they could live beyond the reach of urban succession by creating new, more exclusive elite enclaves on lands past the edges of the city. Perhaps unsurprisingly, the most successful developer in this regard was the Canadian Pacific Railway.

When the CPR opened up its land grant holdings on the hills south of False Creek to exclusive residential development in 1909, it offered both escape and reform. Lines formed to purchase the large new lots, laid out in natural contours by landscape architect Frederick Todd.[47] Shaughnessy, as the CPR's new enclave was named, quickly beat out contending neighborhoods for the attention of elites fleeing the West End and other locales. Like many of its competitors, Shaughnessy put in place restrictive property covenants, which were gaining prominence at the time as a deterrent to redevelopment.[48] Unlike its competitors, however, Shaughnessy also had friends in high places. To further ward off the threat of encroaching urban succession as it was absorbed into the newly created municipality of Point Grey, Shaughnessy's developers appealed to the higher power of the provincial government to place legal limits on land uses within its borders.[49] In response, the provincial legislature passed the Shaughnessy Settlement Act of 1914, allowing only single-family houses in the neighborhood. This appears to be the first legal recognition granted to the house as a specific regulatory technology for dwelling within the province.

Across the rest of the region, big development interests, like the Associated Property Owners of Vancouver, kept watch over the legal innovations taking place in Point Grey. Many seemed increasingly ready to contemplate restrictions on their property rights in exchange for greater stability.[50] Over the long term, urban succession tended to boost property values, bringing more intensive uses of land. But over the more chaotic ups and downs of the short term, gains remained uneven and properties often lost value. Given the era's rapid oscillation of boom and bust cycles, it was difficult for many property owners to hold on to their properties long enough to benefit from the Urban Core's outward expansion. Before further reform could occur, events overtook the city's reformers, and British Columbians were called to arms to defend the British Empire during World War I. The rapid construction of the metropolis of Vancouver, already rivaling Winnipeg as third largest in the nation, would more or less halt until war's end.

---

[47] Hayes provides a nice photo (2005, 81).

[48] Fogelson 2005, Taylor 2009, and Wright 1981 provide examples of covenant restrictions elsewhere.

[49] Shaughnessy was amalgamated into Point Grey in 1908.

[50] Weaver 1979.

A House to Guard the City's Gates

Landed elites were not the only people considering reform in urban land use. Nor were they the only ones placing protection of the single-family house at the center of reform efforts. As Vancouver was surpassing Winnipeg in size, Mr. Thomas Adams, progressive "Garden City" advocate and first president of the Town Planning Institute in the United Kingdom, was attempting to bring his ideas for guiding a new profession to North America. At a 1911 conference on city planning in Boston, he noted that town planning was a "world-wide movement," a chief object of which was to "maintain and extend the healthy detached home life of our people."[51] Adams would become an unabashed booster of the single-family house, transforming it from an idea into an active regulatory technology and placing it firmly at the heart of professional town planning. From this position, the house as a regulatory creature would soon go to work defending the ever-expanding Great House Reserve set up around city after city across the North American landscape. In 1917, Adams helped found the American City Planning Institute, and in 1919, just after the end of World War I, he took the position of the first president of the Town Planning Institute of Canada.[52] Just three years later, members Professor Frank E. Buck (horticulturalist) and J. Alexander Walker (engineer) began a Vancouver branch.[53]

The Vancouver branch of the Town Planning Institute of Canada quickly went to work encouraging planning at all levels of government. Following the example of its Shaughnessy neighborhood, the municipality of Point Grey adopted the first municipal zoning bylaw in Canada in 1922 in an effort to preserve its residential character against further urban encroachment.[54] Professor Buck would become appointed chair of Point Grey's Planning Commission, following the passage of provincial legislation legalizing more comprehensive town planning in 1925. A Town Planning Commission was also promptly formed in Vancouver with Walker as secretary. The commissions worked together, anticipating their future amalgamation. After considering Adams for their lead planning consultant, they instead hired pragmatically inclined U.S. planner Harland Bartholomew (based in St. Louis) to draw up a plan for the City of Vancouver in 1926.[55] This, of

---

[51] Adams 1911, n.p.

[52] Canadian Institute of Planners 2013.

[53] Haaf and Meredith 2011; Vancouver Town Planning Commission 1942.

[54] Point Grey's exclusive Shaughnessy neighborhood would obtain additional provincial protection the same year, with passage of the Shaughnessy Heights Act.

[55] Weaver (1979) suggests that Bartholomew—a consummate salesman/consultant of his era—was hired over Thomas Adams to placate developers wary of Adams's activism and disregard for property rights.

course, was the same year the U.S. Supreme Court reached its decision fully legitimizing use-based zoning south of the border. Bartholomew noted in his later write-up and history of Vancouver's plan the need for zoning, tying it to the recurrent problems faced by the city's beleaguered officials:

> In the case of the rapidly growing City of Vancouver, building dif-
> ficulties, which frequently tended to become a "storm centre of con-
> flicting opinion and personal animosities," beset the Council. The
> solution of these difficulties lay in the adoption of a modern zoning
> by-law, the preparation of which involves the study of those different
> phases of a city's growth, which, in combination, make up the city
> plan. . . . As a temporary solution of the problem, and largely to pre-
> vent the intrusion of apartment houses in single or two-family resi-
> dential areas, an interim zoning by-law was prepared and approved
> by the Town Planning Commission, recommended to the Council,
> and became law on 5th February, 1927.[56]

The interim zoning bylaw passed in 1927 and recorded by Bartholomew represented the city's first attempt at solving the problems associated with governing urban growth by directly defining and mapping what was allowed to be built on different lots rather than relying on a hodgepodge of licensing regulations conditionally prohibiting certain uses. In the process, the act both defined and wrote into law the single-family house as a protected and protective entity with its own reserve of "residential" land. And as demon-strated by Figure 3.3, the amount of land granted to the house took up most of the land base of the soon-to-be amalgamated city.

The fully completed zoning bylaw for Vancouver was passed in Decem-ber 1928. Ultimately it was similar to but much more detailed than 1927's interim measure, and the dominant position of the house as the guardian against urban encroachment remained. The plan brought together use-based zoning and transportation planning, envisioning in particular the arterials that would function as crucial links between the Urban Core and the newly frozen suburban neighborhoods. Commerce and higher-density housing (usually limited to two-family houses) were allowed along arterials, functionally extending tendrils of the Urban Core into the newly demar-cated Great House Reserve. Vancouver also absorbed the nearby municipal-ities of Point Grey and South Vancouver. As anticipated, Point Grey's plan was easily adjoined to Vancouver's, but the addition of South Vancouver's plan to the newly integrated city was not completed until September 19, 1929. Just a month later the events of Black Thursday kicked off the Great Depression.

---

[56] Bartholomew 1930; excerpt is from p. 211.

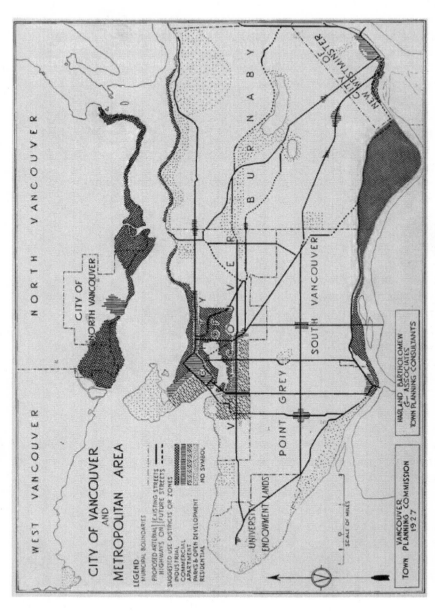

Figure 3.3 Diagram representing the interim zoning bylaw passed in 1927, as represented in Harland Bartholomew's 1930 plan, p. 222. (*Reproduced under Open Access Creative Commons license from https://archive.org/details/vancplaningen00vanc.*)

With the onset of the Great Depression, the extensive planning documents drawn up for the City of Vancouver were left with little new development to regulate. Instead, a Zoning By-law Board of Appeal was set up, and encouraged to provide relief to Depression victims by rezoning existing properties as needed. Altogether, historian John Weaver suggests, the impact of Vancouver's zoning bylaw on urban form was muted at first: "Given perpetual bargaining and concessions to economic circumstances, the impact of a zoning map on a city is bound to be less than dramatic." Despite his skepticism, however, Weaver notes a more lasting legacy: "On the other hand, zoning did reinforce the tendency toward single-family dwelling neighborhoods."[57]

Written into law, the regulatory form of the house went to work. Indeed, despite the lax enforcement of relevant bylaws in some areas during the Great Depression and World War II, Vancouver became an example for other municipalities as zoning continued to spread and expand in comprehensiveness.[58] In a 1946 letter congratulating the city on its progress since the original plan, Bartholomew noted:

Zoning is still the only logical method of protecting the character of residential districts and the value of the homes. This is clearly evidenced by the fact that nearly 2,500 communities in the United States have adopted zoning regulations since 1916—the year the first comprehensive ordinance was adopted [New York's]. More than seventy per cent of the urban population in the United States is protected by zoning.[59]

While he provided a glowing report overall, Bartholomew suggested that much work remained to be done in the city, enabled in part by "Technological Advancements" that had made zoning even more effective since the original plan. There was little to suggest that he had changed his mind about the role of the single-family house in cities. As he noted in his initial report, "That the one-family dwelling is the desirable unit for happy living is the general concensus [sic] of opinion of all authorities."[60] So it would remain.

---

[57] Weaver 1979, 220–221.

[58] The Vancouver Town Planning Commission's 1942 brochure noted: "Through the medium of its 'Plan' Vancouver has become well known for its progressive policies. Copies of the 'Plan' have been sent to many parts of the world and it has been on exhibition at several international town planning conventions in Europe and America." Weaver also notes that Vancouver's zoning plan set precedents within Canada, and brought "official enquiries" from "San Antonio, Spokane, and San Francisco" (1979, 212).

[59] Bartholomew 1946, 2.

[60] Bartholomew 1930, 234.

Throughout the Depression and World War II, the Town Planning Commission for Vancouver continued its work, justifying its efforts to plan for the future through promotional brochures attached to carefully produced zoning maps. These brochures help illustrate just how many parties were responsible for promoting and constructing the house as the guardian against urban succession. In addition to benefiting the city's beleaguered officials, the house also reflected the residential interests of many elites. Certainly, this group was best positioned to halt the outward progress of the city, and indeed, a 1931 commission brochure rooted the importance of zoning partially in how it combated the displacement of Vancouver's wealthier residents. Nevertheless, a variety of other justifications for zoning were also offered, reflecting, in many cases, the increasing professionalization of planners and their concerns for efficiency:

> In its short life the main business centre of the city has shifted at least twice and the high-priced residential districts possibly several times oftener, each shift involving loss of property values to the owners in the vacated districts and of utility values to the corporation. At the same time the city has spread itself over an unduly large area, leaving undeveloped sections behind with an enormous increase in the cost of all municipal services and public utilities owing to this undue and undirected expansion. The idea of planning is to prevent a repetition of this waste. The Zoning portrayed on the accompanying diagram is a scientific attempt to direct the growth of the various components, residential, industrial and business, that go to make up a city along sane, and as far as can be foreseen, permanent lines.

The attempt at halting the process of urban succession was underlined by the permanence intended for zoning boundaries. Echoing the nuisance-oriented logic of the Supreme Court, the brochure went on to note that the purpose of zoning was to "encourage the erection of the right buildings in the right place."[61] As in the United States, apartment buildings were categorized as decidedly distinct from residential land uses in these early schematics. At the same time, they were also set aside as separate from commercial and industrial districts.

Beyond officials, elites, and planners, zoning for the house was also promoted by publicly minded health reformers. "Ample side, front, and rear yards" were deemed important for air circulation and sun exposure—crucial tools in the fight against typhoid and tuberculosis.[62] The writing of the house into protective zoning bylaws, in Vancouver as elsewhere, seemed like

---

[61] Vancouver Town Planning Commission 1931, n.p.

[62] Ibid.

a solution to all sorts of people for all sorts of urban woes.[63] Correspondingly, there was no single author of the zoning bylaw in Vancouver. Instead, as historian John Weaver notes, the drafting of Vancouver's bylaw brought together a diverse set of idealists, consultants, real estate interests, and business interests, even if the process involved remained far from representative or democratic.[64] As for the planners, in the midst of professionalization, they were more than willing to sell zoning as a super-powered fix: faster than the speed of antiquated licensing regimes, more powerful than public health crises, and able to halt the process of urban succession within a single bound.

What of the rights of private property owners? What of the free market? Vancouver was founded and grew up within a profoundly revolutionary liberal market regime. Zoning seemed to strike at the heart of this system. By bonding land to narrow sets of uses—especially within single-family residential districts—it represented a dramatic communal intrusion into both property rights and market mechanisms. Through the early twentieth century, landed interests became increasingly willing to make pragmatic concessions in these matters. The Planning Commission promoted zoning as representing "common-sense and fairness in the use of private real estate," and encouraging "the golden rule" as a guide to relationships between neighbors. It made a patriotic virtue of thoughtful pragmatism in adopting zoning:

> Probably never before in history has it been more desirable that the student should have a proper conception of citizenship, the science of "how best to live to get the most out of life." Strange and unmeasurable social forces are being realized, causing perplexing problems to ferment in men's minds; the old and dignified warfare of "ideals" is giving way to a somewhat sordid complex of interests, individualism is being replaced by a demand for governments to meddle in every detail of our existence.[65]

If zoning represented a dramatic new restriction on property rights, the totemic appeal to the "science" of citizenship served somewhat paradoxically to both depoliticize zoning and to firmly disassociate it from any taint of socialist government meddling.[66] More progressive voices were sidelined by invoking fears of communism.[67] The Town Planning Commission defined its

---

[63] Valverde 2011.

[64] Weaver 1979.

[65] Vancouver Town Planning Commission 1931, n.p.

[66] Here as elsewhere, zoning might be considered a particularly powerful Polanyian "double movement."

[67] Valverde 2011; Wade 1994.

role as providing disinterested and technocratic expertise aimed at solving the problems of urban citizenship. The "maps, charts, and fine illustrations" produced in Vancouver's plan were meant to provide fetishized examples of the science of good planning.[68] As written into law, the house instantiated a new and high-tech form of patriotism.

The Invasive House

As a wall rose up between house habitat and Urban Core, cars became increasingly important means of getting people from one side to the other. So the advancement of the house as the default technology for dwelling quickly intertwined with the expansion of the car as the default technology for transportation. As elsewhere, the rise of the automotive was enabled in Vancouver by planners, who literally set about paving the way. A growing network of roads, expanded arterials, and bridges opened up lots further afield from the city center, allowing workers to commute to Vancouver from the surrounding suburbs of Richmond and Delta to the south; Burnaby, the Tri-Cities and further points to the east; and New Westminster and Surrey to the southeast. Both the Second Narrows Bridge and the Lion's Gate Bridge, funded by the Guinness family (of Irish beer fame), had been extended across the Burrard Inlet by 1938, allowing further suburban expansion into Vancouver's steeply sloped North Shore, where the Guinness clan owned substantial property interests they looked forward to developing.

Streets were widened as roads were increasingly built with the needs of cars and trucks in mind. Soon they were reserved nearly exclusively for automotive use through anti-jaywalking and related bylaw provisions. As pedestrians were kicked off of roads, cars were increasingly integrated into building bylaws through parking provisions. The Great House Reserve became intertwined with a similar Automotive Reserve, built to serve and interconnect the suburbs with the Urban Core they surrounded.

The land taken up by the expanding and increasingly auto-oriented road network represented a sizable portion of Vancouver's land base.[69] As the era's electric streetcars and interurban lines began to fail economically, they became viewed as obsolete by planners and other city officials. In 1944, the city began a process of replacing rail lines with bus services that could be run in a more integrated fashion along the same paved-over roads as cars. Petroleum asphalt would soon cover over a quarter of the urbanized land

---

[68] Vancouver Town Planning Commission 1942, n.p.

[69] In his planning report, Bartholomew (1930, 212–213) estimated that nearly 30 percent of the land of the densely settled pre-amalgamated City of Vancouver was already taken up by roads and lanes.

base of the City of Vancouver.[70] By 1946, Bartholomew pressed the city to begin integrating parking requirements into updated zoning bylaws, reserving off-street space for cars and further expanding the reach of the Automotive Reserve.

The end of World War II left other marks on Vancouver. The sizable Japanese communities of Vancouver and Steveston had been devastated by forced internment and redistribution to inland camps, and would never fully return.[71] Nevertheless, the city continued to grow, especially as workers arrived in response to the wartime demand for local labor. Despite a few wartime housing programs, including the building of Burkeville in Richmond (an unadorned residential neighborhood of single-family houses for wartime workers, located near the airport), the pace of construction failed to match the growth in population.

After the war, returning troops, often with war brides in tow, quickly found the low vacancy rates and lack of housing options intolerable. Servicemen occupied the Hotel Vancouver to highlight their plight, and to appease them, more detached houses were quickly built to the south of the city. Other veterans occupied the site of a former barracks in the city near Queen Elizabeth Park, which was set aside as the Little Mountain public housing project in 1954. Similar concerns over housing across the country were reflected in the adoption of a series of National Housing Acts, creating a modern, more standardized housing construction industry and an accompanying mortgage finance industry insured by the federal Central Mortgage and Housing Corporation (CMHC).[72]

The house, as written into municipal bylaws, quickly invaded the new habitat of federal mortgage finance regulations. The development of new financial technology relied on the "fee simple" ownership structure of the single-family house, and hence promoted its spread.[73] Through structuring, regulating, and insuring the mortgage market, the CMHC channeled an enormous amount of investment capital into supporting and profiting from

---

[70] Metro Vancouver Policy and Planning Department 2008 provides a figure of 25.3 percent of land base used for road and lane right-of-way, but this figure does not appear to include dedicated road right-of-way, and may be an underestimate.

[71] A Bartholomew report (1944) estimated that the proportion of Vancouver's population made up of "Orientals" had declined from 8.8 percent in 1931 to 2.2 percent in 1944 (predominantly Chinese), following internment of the Japanese.

[72] R. Harris 2000; R. Harris and Forrester 2003. The CMHC was later renamed the Canada Mortgage and Housing Corporation.

[73] "Fee simple" is a feudal term in common law referring to the highest-interest ownership of an estate. Other more complicated and more divisible forms of ownership could be found, but were relatively rare and untested. For instance, in many cities, row houses could also be purchased, with the simple legal obligation to maintain common walls. These were never widely adopted in Vancouver.

consumer purchases of single-family detached houses—and, for a long time, only such houses.

The development of a centralized and institutionalized mortgage industry also contributed to the spread of the house in other ways, directly promoting zoning. In the United States, mortgage-lending practices infamously promoted the redlining of neighborhoods. Building on the very same models of urban succession that zoning sought to halt, redlining occurred when the presence of minorities was taken as evidence that neighborhoods were in transition, and real estate appraisers were trained to code such neighborhoods as ineligible for mortgages and home improvement loans. Racist redlining practices kept many minority households—mostly black—from sharing in the widespread expansion of homeownership and wealth in the post–World War II era.[74]

Yet redlining took into account more than just race. In Canada, as careful research has demonstrated, it was primarily targeted at unregulated suburban neighborhoods, which lacked infrastructural servicing and the protection of zoning ordinances.[75] These were the neighborhoods deemed most at risk of urban intensification. Through their administration of the increasingly institutionalized financial technologies encouraging homeownership, real estate appraisers actively abetted succession processes in some neighborhoods—primarily those without existing zoning controls. But overall, their practices encouraged suburban developers and municipalities to adopt zoning ordinances as a means of maintaining access to the new lines of credit being opened up for home buyers. In effect, the heavily regulated mortgage finance industry at the federal level would adopt and, in some cases, refine the same regulatory devices first developed at the municipal level.[76] As a result, the house as a regulatory creature became a gatekeeper not just to land, but also to the newly structured mortgages under development through the postwar era.

The adoption of house-based standards in street planning and mortgage finance structuring helped fill up the Great House Reserve, as developers and builders marched outward from the Urban Core. By the 1961 census, the City of Vancouver held barely half of the overall number of dwellings in the rapidly expanding metropolitan area. Postwar growth was faster in the metro area's suburban municipalities, connected by the road network to the downtown. Dividing dwellings into detached houses and their increasingly distinct multiunit alternatives (e.g., apartment buildings,

---

[74] Jackson 1985; Taylor 2009.

[75] Harris and Forrester 2003.

[76] Jackson 1985 describes FHA involvement in setting minimum requirements for lot size, setback, and width of house and side yards, both endorsing and contributing to refinements in zoning in the United States.

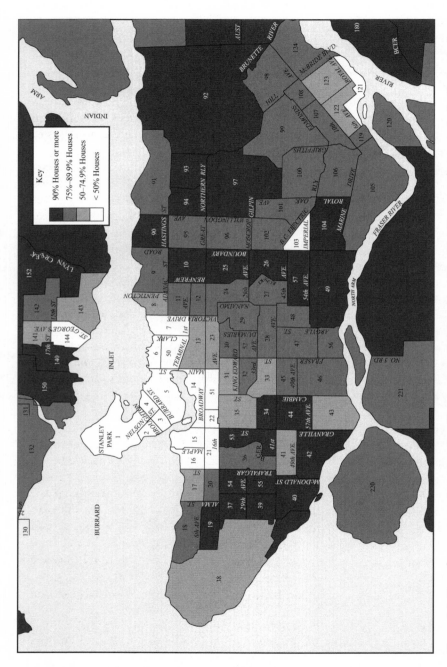

Figure 3.4 Map of census tracts in metropolitan Vancouver in 1961, by proportion of dwellings recorded as single-family detached houses. (*Graphic prepared by the author using 1961 census tract boundaries.*)

lodging hotels, row houses, and detached houses converted into apartments or duplexes), the City of Vancouver contained over three-quarters of the alternative stock of metropolitan housing. But these alternatives made up just over a third of the City of Vancouver's total housing stock, mostly contained within its pre-amalgamation (and pre–zoning regulation) borders. Detached houses accounted for more than three-quarters of the housing stock of the metropolitan area, and 70 percent of all housing was owner-occupied. Practically all multiunit dwellings were rentals, though owner-landlords still occasionally lived in apartments on the premises of their rental properties.

The map in Figure 3.4 identifies the metropolitan census tracts surrounding the downtown according to the degree of their domination by single-unit detached houses, as documented by the 1961 census. House-dominated tracts occupied most of the map, surrounding a core of multiunit housing around downtown and False Creek, all contained within the pre-amalgamated City of Vancouver. Within that core, the apartment districts of the venerable West End neighborhood (the bulk of tracts 1 through 4 apart from Stanley Park) and South Granville (tract 22) had especially few houses left by this point.[77] Outside the city's core, the old town sites at the center of North Vancouver (tract 144) and New Westminster (tract 121) retained mostly house-free residential stock. Nearly every other tract in the metro area was dominated by houses, including all tracts beyond the borders of the map.[78] Perhaps not surprisingly, the heart of the exclusive First Shaughnessy District (tract 53) remained especially dominated by houses for a tract so close to downtown.

A City of Two Tales

There are many stories that might be told about the spread of the house across the North American landscape, but two stand out. In the first story, Vancouver's history, like any other city's, may be written in the language of supply and demand, with the latter in the lead. Consumers demand houses. As soon as consumers' purchasing power and suppliers' costs reach an amicable meeting place, the market produces houses. To the minimal extent governments involve themselves in this process, they simply bumble

---

[77] The proportion of houses hovered around 10 percent or fewer of total dwelling units in each case.

[78] The triangular spot of land in Burnaby (tract 103) located along the old Electric Rail line to New Westminster contained primarily a park, but also a number of multiunit dwellings next to an industrial worksite, just barely edging out the small number of houses in the tract. On the whole, the higher density of urban alternatives, along with the practice of bounding census tracts with arterials lined with alternatives, means that the map likely understates domination by the house.

around, getting in the way. As in the old Chicago School of urban sociology, the spread of the house seems natural, based in the extension of choice to the consumer. In a more updated version, this is the basic tale provided by Robert Bruegmann to explain the spread of single-family houses in his aptly named *Sprawl: A Compact History*. Importantly, it remains counterfactual.[79]

As demonstrated in the second story, the story I tell above, in Vancouver and elsewhere municipal governments built the house into a powerful regulatory creature. No metropolis avoided its mark.[80] Across the continent, the house appeared as a sort of Frankenstein's monster, sewn together and brought to life through the work of multiple and divergent interests, including those of real estate magnates, municipal administrators, progressive reformers, middle-class homeowners, public health campaigners, and ambitious planners. Once it was written into law and legitimized by trial, the house became something more than the sum of its authors' diverse intents. Though built nearly a century ago, it remains at work today, and by now a large body of evidence supports the effectiveness of single-family residential zoning in freezing out alternatives. This is why we see so many houses boxing in the tiny Urban Cores of most of North America's cities. Though forged from culture during a particular moment in time, the house as regulatory creature is what structures the house as commodity and actively looks after and protects the house in concrete.[81]

Vancouver's experiences echo those across the United States, as revealed in works like Hirt's *Zoned in the USA*.[82] Importantly, the similarity in regulatory histories and urban landscape outcomes strengthens Hirt's larger argument about the importance of zoning but challenges her case

---

[79] Notably, Bruegmann mentions in an endnote (2005, 248n10) that he finds the rise of zoning one of the more convincing counternarratives.

[80] Houston is often offered as a counterexample by Bruegmann (2005) and others. It has no formal comprehensive zoning bylaw, and its general similarity in form (and house dominance) to other sprawling North American cities is at times presented as evidence that zoning does not matter. In carefully reviewing the evidence, Buitelaar (2009) notes and dismisses the "free market myth" for Houston, and summarizes the relevant land-use restrictions that effectively produce a zoning regime under a different name. These restrictions include the unusual municipal enforcement of deed restrictions and the exceptionally widespread use of master-planned communities in Houston.

[81] See, e.g., Baar 1992, Babcock 1966, Form 1954, Fleischmann and Pierannunzi 1990, Green and Schreuder 1991, Hirt 2014, Kimelberg 2011, Levine 2006, Shlay 1984, Shlay and Rossi 1981, Skaburskis 1989, Steele 1987, and Talen 2012. Doucet and Weaver (1990, 391) note that the decade of the 1920s produced an apartment unit boom across North America never equaled since. They blame the Depression, World War II, and the wariness of investors, but the rise and rapid spread of zoning during the same decade coupled with its choking effect on urban development seems at least as likely an explanatory candidate.

[82] Hirt 2014.

for American exceptionalism.[83] As an outsider, the Vancouver case also helps rule out some competing explanations for the rise of house dominance based in the particularities of the U.S. experience. For instance, the U.S. practice of enabling the deduction of mortgage payments from income taxes never crossed the 45th parallel into Canada. Though it might have furthered the rise of the house in the United States, it does not seem like a necessary part of the story.

More centrally, important works like Jackson's *Crabgrass Frontier* and Dorceta Taylor's *The Environment and the People in American Cities* speak to the key role of racial politics in the U.S. experience of suburbanization. Somewhat surprisingly, though he tackles many policy initiatives, Jackson largely ignores zoning, as when he suggests that unlike in Europe, U.S. "municipalities and states have traditionally imposed as few restrictions as possible on land developers." The house as a regulatory creature is made to disappear, but in actuality zoning made the suburban lands of North America less a free-wheeling "Crabgrass Frontier" than a carefully patrolled Great House Reserve.[84]

Improving on Jackson's magisterial work, Taylor, like Hirt, more directly and carefully links U.S. racism to zoning legislation. As demonstrated in this chapter, racism also played a role in the creation of zoning in Vancouver. But after that point, "white flight" proved unnecessary in promoting the rise of Vancouver's house-dominated suburbs. Racist legislation already prevented the large-scale immigration of most minorities, and Vancouver's Urban Core remained relatively white through the mid-twentieth century even as its suburbs sprawled outward.[85] On the whole, the construction of the house as a regulatory creature was capable of promoting the house in concrete across both Canada and the United States without features unique to the U.S. experience.

Interestingly, stronger forms of the "growth machine" story, though grounded in political economy, also overlook the importance of the house as regulatory creature.[86] Despite their political clout, developers and landowners faced real restrictions. Land was set aside for them to play with inside the Urban Core—often in conjunction with flexible regulatory environments.

---

[83] See also R. Harris 2000 and 2004 on this point.

[84] See Jackson 1985 (the quote is from p. 295) and Taylor 2009. Fogelson (2005) notes a similar overlooking of restrictive covenants.

[85] Bruegmann (2005) makes much the same argument against assigning racism too strong a role in determining urban form by comparing cities within the United States.

[86] See especially Warner and Molotch 2000; see also Logan and Molotch 2007, where the suggestion is made that zoning has been largely ineffective. In the former, Babcock's classic *The Zoning Game* is used as a reference to demonstrate this claim (e.g., pp. 10, 82), even though Babcock's overarching argument was that zoning practices in the middle of the twentieth century could not be blithely ignored.

But as multiple observers note, the zoning of the Great House Reserve was treated as far more sacrosanct.[87] As they crossed into the Reserve, developers seldom trod past the angel guarding the gates with anything but more houses in hand.[88]

All in all, the house as a regulatory creature was built to be tough. As noted by Jonathan Levine in his study of single-family residential zoning within Silicon Valley and around Boston, "A diamond is forever, a suburban R-1 zone nearly so."[89] The house quickly became invasive. Even the tiny rural township of Willingboro, New Jersey, which had experienced little in the way of growth, set up its own Planning Board in 1952 simply because, as a founding member put it, "We just went along with the crowd: everybody was doing it."[90] Perhaps even more impressive was the way the house jumped from covenants and zoning bylaws into new legal ecologies. Processes of standardization enabled the house to encode itself within mortgage financing and other regimes, making it more difficult to casually dislodge.

But the agency the house gathers unto itself as an urban actor also makes it vulnerable. Recognition that the house is out there—made of codes, bylaws, and regulatory practices—opens up possibilities for killing it off. Houses can be built around, built over, and renovated altogether. That is where our history of Vancouver continues. Having explored why the metropolis developed so many houses early on, let's investigate why it now has so few.

---

[87] Babcock 1966; Perin 1977; Steele 1987; Weaver 1979. Even Warner and Molotch (2000, 82) discuss Santa Monica's treatment of single-family zones as "sacred land."

[88] Here, too, Babcock (1966) emphasizes and provides firsthand accounts of the difficulties faced by developers in moving into single-family residential neighborhoods—as opposed to other zoned areas.

[89] Levine 2006, 76.

[90] Gans 1967, 15.

THE DEATH OF THE HOUSE IN VANCOUVER?

The retention of Vancouver as a city of single family homes
has always been close to the heart of those engaged
in the preparation of this plan.

—ARTHUR G. SMITH, CHAIRMAN,
VANCOUVER TOWN PLANNING COMMISSION, 1928,
QUOTED IN HARLAND BARTHOLOMEW,
*A PLAN FOR THE CITY OF VANCOUVER,
BRITISH COLUMBIA*

By 1961, Vancouver was one of the most house-dominated metropolises in North America. Less than fifty years later, it was very nearly the least. No other North American metropolis witnessed such a dramatic change in the character of its housing stock through the second half of the twentieth century. Vancouver in 1961 had proportionately more detached houses than any major metropolitan area of today, including even those, like Phoenix, infamous for their sprawl. By 2011 Vancouver had the smallest proportion of houses of any major North American metropolis, save for Montreal.[1] Figure 4.1 demonstrates the scale of the shift, comparing Vancouver's historical and present-day housing stock to the current stock of other North American cities.

In contrast to most of the old cities east of the Mississippi, all of the cities of the West have moved toward fewer houses in recent years, but Vancouver has moved the farthest and the fastest. This implies that a more targeted comparison might also be helpful. Looking southward, Vancouver has far fewer houses than its sister cities extending down the West Coast. This is striking for at least three reasons. First, the West Coast cities tend to share seemingly topographically limited geographies, caught between the mountains and the sea. Second, they all generally experienced rapid growth through the twentieth century. Third, the sizable historic cores of

---

[1] As the largest of the Francophone cities, located within the arguably separate "nation" of Quebec, Montreal remains within a region apart in many respects (Grabb and Curtis 2005).

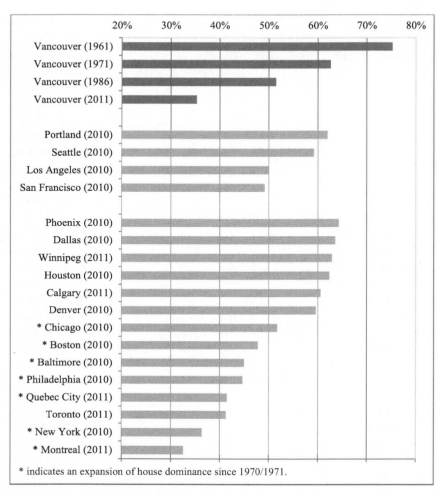

Figure 4.1 Percentage of metropolitan dwellings that are detached houses, comparing Vancouver's historical experience with selected contemporary metropolises. (*Based on census data from the United States and Canada. Graphic prepared by the author.*)

Vancouver's sister cities predate Vancouver's founding, as they predate the rise of zoning. The coastal metropolises to the south began the twentieth century with much larger stocks of historically dense housing. So what happened? How did Vancouver, a metropolis that exemplified the trend toward house-oriented expansion through the midcentury, become ground zero for the rise of urban alternatives some fifty years later?

The rise of the house in Vancouver, as elsewhere across North America, is really a story of unfolding and building the house into a regulatory form able to reserve house habitat and protect it from urban encroachment. Once installed to protect a Great House Reserve, the house had to be reckoned with in subsequent building, and could invasively move into other kinds of technical and legal habitats, like mortgage regulations. Just as the construction of the house and its Reserve altered metropolitan trajectories, new and well-placed acts of construction could alter the urban ecology all over again, involving the creation of new things with both regulatory and physical manifestations. In relation to the house, three types of subsequent building acts are worth noting in Vancouver: (1) those that built around the house (leaving the Great House Reserve largely intact, but limiting its growth or offering residential living elsewhere), (2) those that built over the house (intruding into and reclaiming the Great House Reserve), and (3) those that renovated and remade the house (correspondingly diversifying and remaking the Great House Reserve).

Each of these three building acts has contributed, in varying degrees, to Vancouver's dramatic shift away from house dominance. To understand where they came from and how they were enabled requires a return to Vancouver's history somewhere around where we left off. In the middle of the twentieth century, Vancouver was busy modernizing its planning processes and making the city and its suburban satellites look like every other major metropolis in North America, only more so. A funny thing would happen on the way to modernization.

A Modern Metropolis like Any Other

After the advent of zoning, midcentury metropolitan Vancouver contained a set of nucleic Urban Cores surrounded by a constraining Great House Reserve.[2] At the outer edges of the Great House Reserve, Vancouver's hinterland remained largely undeveloped. The solidifying boundary between Urban Core and Great House Reserve by midcentury had encouraged growth machines to operate something like the manufacturing corporations of their day—high-tech laboratories surrounded by house-building factories.[3] Within the Urban Core lands of Vancouver, developers worked out new building designs in conjunction and collaboration with technically sophisticated regulators and planners. With outward urban succession frozen, their

---

[2] Here I treat the Urban Core as consisting of those lots surrounded by the Great House Reserve. Most remained central, contained within the old boundaries of the pre-amalgamated City of Vancouver. But other pockets of Urban Core land were distributed more broadly. Some (e.g., along the Fraser River) were left behind by the distribution of industry prior to zoning. Others (e.g., in New Westminster and North Vancouver) remained when nearby municipalities with their own historic downtowns integrated into Vancouver's emerging metropolitan system.

[3] Nevertheless, as Walker and Lewis (2001) note, the hinterland was also sprinkled with industrial uses.

experiments remained controlled and contained by the walls of the house habitat. The Great House Reserve churned out a more uniform product. Here the factory machinery, both financial and land-based, enabled developers to input capital and output houses.

Farther out, at the border between house reserve and hinterland, a suburban form of succession continued, largely unhindered by municipal land-use controls. An infrastructural network tied core to reserve and expanded ever outward through the hinterland. This infrastructure paved the way for development of the hinterland and, in the process, came to constitute a major land use in its own right. As discussed in the previous chapter, roads frequently took up over a quarter of the land base as they were laid down across developed land. Bound together by bridges, the road network on the ground, the wire network above, and the pipe network below all increasingly tied the metropolitan area together, enabling new suburb dwellers to travel to work in the city even as they enjoyed urban comforts from home.

On the whole, the work of planning Vancouver through the post–World War II era was devoted to a project of modernization that further purified the boundaries between Urban Core and Great House Reserve first set up in the 1920s.[4] Municipal planners kept in touch with broader planning trends, aided by a loose form of metropolitan governance laid over the separate municipalities within the Lower Mainland.[5] Figures like Harland Bartholomew acted as conduits for the spread of new planning techniques at the same time as they pressed for cities to take a stronger stance against the intrusion of land uses that violated zoning. Despite advocating a certain flexibility regarding the distinction between the single-family house and very low-density alternatives, like duplexes, in his earliest planning, Bartholomew gradually took a more draconian position, arguing that the intrusion of two-family dwellings together with other multiple-unit dwellings contributed to urban blight. He went on to attack basement suites, in particular, as problematically unsanitary.[6]

---

[4] Latour 1993; Ley 1987.

[5] A great flood along the Fraser led to the creation of the Lower Mainland Regional Planning Board (LMRPB). British Columbia would rename and reorganize the LMPRB in 1969 after it criticized a new provincial railway and port plans for Roberts Bank, located to the south of Vancouver, as impinging on agricultural lands. Planning functions were henceforth consolidated within the Greater Vancouver Regional District (GVRD), which was later again rebranded as Metro Vancouver. See Garrish 2002 for a history.

[6] In 1930, Bartholomew noted of RS zones: "Whether or not these will remain one-family or become two-family districts can be safely left to the wishes of the owners themselves, and the by-law amended accordingly when occasion arises" (p. 225). Later, more negative quotes come from Bartholomew 1944, 27, and 1946, 20–21. Despite these concerns, Bartholomew made it clear in his 1946 suggestions for revision that he considered quarters for servants employed on the premises to be perfectly acceptable in single-family districts, since they were to be understood as family members (p. 21).

Within the city, new techniques for planning were codified within a brand-new and consolidated 1956 Zoning and Development By-law. This, in turn, was the product of Vancouver's newly integrated Planning Department, replacing the former Town Planning Commission. The new bylaw introduced more refined standards for determining what could be built, including for the first time the floor space ratio (FSR) limits linked to lot size. It similarly mandated how many parking spaces needed to be set aside for new construction based on floor space and use, fully integrating space for cars into legal building requirements. The bylaw allowed taller buildings to be built in the core neighborhoods of the West End and downtown, reflecting a new confidence in modern building and fire-prevention techniques some seventy years after Vancouver's Great Fire, and ushering in the development of high-rise apartment buildings.

The updated bylaw also added new zoning districts. The number of use districts had already expanded from five, in the 1927 preliminary bylaw, to ten by 1942. It jumped again to seventeen with the 1956 bylaw, and would reach twenty-two by 1965. The expanded set of districts included some adding new restrictions to existing single-family residential neighborhoods, while use-based districts laid out within the Urban Core were frequently expanded to add new flexibility. The bylaw gave new discretionary powers to planners and provided for both a design panel and a board of appeal. To the benefit of the developers and real estate interests who frequently moved in and out of city council positions, this provided the city justification for occasionally suspending restrictive height and FSR limits at the same time as it provided mechanisms for vetting new developments.[7] As a result of how these changes were implemented, the Urban Core became more flexible and more distinct from the increasingly rigid Great House Reserve.

Within the Great House Reserve, the modernization of planning coincided with a crackdown on the previous subdivision of houses. Despite zoning bylaws to the contrary, these had been permitted on the basis of hardship during the Depression, encouraged by national interest through World War II, and often ignored during the immediate postwar housing shortage. But neighborhood groups, like the Shaughnessy Property Owners Association (SHPOA), mobilized to protect the "sanctity of the single-family detached home."[8] By 1960, owners within the predominant RS-1 portion of the Great House Reserve more actively protested the doubling up (and more) of households within purportedly single-family districts. They worked with

---

[7] Punter (2003) argues that this "discretionary zoning" system combined North American and European influences.

[8] See Shaughnessy Property Owners Association 2013, n.p., for a brief history of the organization and an estimate, from a Vancouver survey, that some 30 percent of Shaughnessy estates were subdivided for rooming houses by 1957. Very little multifamily housing remains in the neighborhood today.

a sympathetic Council and modernizing staff to enforce the relevant by-laws and remove subdivided suites. By decade's end, over two thousand such suites were dismantled, further solidifying the boundary between Great House Reserve and Urban Core.[9]

A Fork in the Road

Despite its overall success, the boundary purification process was complicated by an antiquated and ambiguously situated road network. The lots along the arterials that were necessary to carry traffic across the boundary proved difficult to characterize as either reserve or core, and were often treated flexibly.[10] As Bartholomew noticed in a postwar assessment, they often failed to fill up with commercial uses when zoned for them, but were "not as desirable for residential purposes" as lots on minor streets. Bartholomew suggested special permitting procedures as one way to deal with these and other ambiguous sites. The zoning for such sites could be specially tailored to conform with their low-density suburban surroundings.[11] The City of Vancouver embraced the new technique, adding Comprehensive Development (CD-1) zoning to their planning repertoire in the same year they passed the new comprehensive planning bylaw. The designation's first use was for a large undeveloped lot at the intersection of major outlying streets, rezoned explicitly to enable the construction of an auto-oriented shopping mall.

The extension of commercial land uses along arterials had a dramatic side-effect: it slowed down traffic. Planners responded with new techniques for building integrated transportation systems. In the United States, passage of the Interstate Highway Act of 1956 ensured the expansion of limited-access freeways through and around the major cities of the country.[12] Freeways claimed vast swathes of Urban Core land for vehicular traffic, further connecting downtown work hubs to peripheral and house-dominated suburbs. The new Planning Department in Vancouver, though staffed by Englishmen, looked southward in envy. Under director Gerald Sutton-Brown, planners and city aldermen began working in earnest to bring a freeway through Strathcona, a densely populated and "racially suspect" neighborhood along the eastern side of the Urban Core.[13]

---

[9] Cheng 1980.

[10] Hess (2005) describes how these sites often languished across Seattle and other U.S. cities until developers found ways to fill them with poorly planned or integrated "garden apartment" buildings.

[11] Bartholomew 1946, 17–18.

[12] Jackson 1985.

[13] For geographic reference, see census tract 50 on Figure 3.4.

Adopting a common technique, planners used arguments about the improvement of living standards as a justification for the displacement of existing Urban Core residents.[14] In successive reports, affected blocks in Strathcona were characterized as hazardous slums—lacking in basic standards for crowding, cooking, and bathing—even though other areas (e.g., East Kitsilano) were considered at least as derelict and overcrowded.[15] As in previous eras, the standards evoked in such reports, often assembled by academics, enabled communication between activists, planners, and various related governing bodies. In Vancouver, they enabled the city to make a comparative case for attracting federal funds meant to support urban renewal.[16] A mix of cheap, run-down older housing would be replaced by new and centralized public housing, with room to spare for the freeway.

In 1958, the city froze property assessments and home improvement in the area to prepare for demolition. As with redlining, the report of substandard conditions was used to justify freezing out reinvestment in the area, contributing to keeping conditions poor. Then the city began the long process of buying and clearing the properties made ever cheaper by their policies. Echoing discriminatory patterns elsewhere, the demolition targets included Hogan's Alley, center of Vancouver's small but vibrant black community, and much of Chinatown.[17] While land had been forcibly claimed by the city for road expansion before in Vancouver, the attempted clearance of the Strathcona neighborhood for freeway construction added new scale to the endeavor.[18] An estimated three thousand residents were displaced.[19]

Unmaking the Modern Metropolis

The construction of Vancouver's freeway seemed inevitable, but in actuality it was never a sure thing. Every other major city on the continent had a downtown that could be reached by freeway by the late 1960s, but planners were still trying to make it work in Vancouver. Unlike the United States, Canada lacked a guaranteed source of federal funding for freeway development. While viaducts were constructed to be connected to the proposed

---

[14] Jacobs 1961; Taylor 2009.

[15] McKay 2003–2004; Murray 2011; Wade 1994.

[16] These funds were made available through the Federal Housing Act of 1949, amended in 1964.

[17] Hogan's Alley was home to the grandmother of guitar legend Jimi Hendrix.

[18] Previous road expansion carved away one lot in Chinatown to the point where only some six feet in width was left to the owner. Rather than give up his development rights, the owner constructed a two-story building on the lot, famously producing the Sam Kee Building, a regular contender for the title of skinniest building in the world.

[19] Harcourt, Cameron, and Rossiter 2007; Murray 2011.

freeway, the overall plan to hook them together through Strathcona required further funding applications. It also meant more people were going to have to be moved out of the way. But before they could get this work going, planners in Vancouver began to stumble over their past successes.

While various new techniques and bylaws increased the range of powers available to city planners and similarly produced new options for developers, these same powers also increased the public visibility of planning and development, especially within the Urban Core. The coveted patina of scientific objectivity attached to planning, harnessed to the public good through the goal of modernization, began to face a very public backlash.[20] In 1961, Jane Jacobs, then living in the Greenwich Village neighborhood of New York City, attacked the standardizing techniques and urban visions of the profession in her influential book *The Death and Life of Great American Cities.* In clear terms, she suggested that residential and commercial activities should be intermingled; that cities, no less than suburbs, were for dwelling; that redevelopment and renewal were destroying the urban fabric; that high-rises were blights on communities; and that freeways were an urban disaster. Jacobs's critiques, which rocked the planning profession, were taken up by activists across the continent. She would move to Toronto in 1969 and share her ideas and tactical expertise with Canadian activists.[21]

Within Vancouver as elsewhere, there is also evidence that developers, working in conjunction with planners and City Hall, may have overreached in their attempts to rapidly transform those parts of the city unprotected by the Great House Reserve. This tarnished the reputations of all parties involved. The 1956 Zoning and Development By-law left much of the Urban Core outside the downtown peninsula zoned for medium-density development. New buildings were bound to a maximum FSR of little more than 1.3, and were not to exceed 40 feet in height. In 1964, a little-noted amendment to the zoning bylaw tripled the height of buildings allowed in medium-density (RM-3) neighborhoods to 120 feet, simultaneously dropping FSR-based restrictions and replacing them with measures based on how buildings might obscure daylight.[22] This obscure technical change enabled the first real postwar attempts to extend the range of the profitable apartment towers, then going up in the downtown and the West End, into lower-density multiunit neighborhoods within the core. By the end of the decade, towers began to rise near the scenic and well-used beaches of Kitsilano.

In 1967, the already high-density neighborhoods of the West End and downtown were allowed to build even higher, to 300 feet. As the towers

---

[20] Punter 2003.

[21] One such activist, John Sewell, would later become mayor and chronicle Toronto's planning through the 1970s onward (Sewell 1993, 1994, 2009).

[22] Zoning Amendment By-law 4119, provisions 8 and 10.

began to go up and up, they provided concrete illustrations of obscure planning standards in action. Newly politicized activists started examining the standards themselves. Residents of the Urban Core began raising objections, some to the threat posed by potentially gentrifying redevelopment of their existing low-rent apartments, and others to the congestion and blocked views that came with new towers.[23] By 1972, in response to public outcry leading up to the civic elections, the city began to downzone, reversing some of the earlier height increases. Under the banner of preserving livability, activists began successfully installing more serious limits on development within the previously opened Urban Core.

Unbuilding the Freeway

Through the 1960s, residents of Strathcona also began to more effectively protest the destruction of their low-rent housing. As they made connections to broader networks of activists, they called attention to the destruction wrought by city policies and carried out in the name of both urban renewal and freeway construction. The Strathcona Property Owners and Tenants Association (SPOTA), often led by Chinese Canadian residents, worked with a new set of community activists and organizers to push back against the plans threatening their neighborhood.[24] Together with new, more sympathetic social planners (who waged an insurgent campaign against the established urban planners within the Planning Department), they turned arguments about living standards back against the city. It was far easier and cheaper to upgrade existing housing than tear it down for replacement. SPOTA and allies successfully appealed to an increasingly sympathetic and penny-pinching federal government to transform funding for urban renewal into less costly funding for residential rehabilitation, supporting renovations of existing buildings.[25]

While it occurred too late for many former residents, the shift in federal support toward renovation of Strathcona's existing housing was a devastating blow for Vancouver's freeway plans. By 1968, it became clear that Strathcona would have to be abandoned as a path to the downtown. By 1972, funding plans and public support for alternative routes had also crumbled, causing Tom Campbell, the colorful mayor of Vancouver at the time, to declare the freeway "sabotaged by Maoists, Communists, pinkos, left-wingers and hamburgers."[26]

---

[23] Gutstein 1975; Punter 2003; Price 2012.

[24] Harcourt, Cameron and Rossiter 2007; Hayes 2005.

[25] Murray 2011.

[26] Hayes 2005, 157.

It is difficult to fully envision the place of an unbuilding in a city's historical trajectory, but it is clear the collapse of Vancouver's freeway planning looms large. Unfinished roadwork towers over Vancouver's history, whether attributed primarily to the contingencies of bad timing and federal disinterest or the success of local activism. The empty spaces where the freeway might have run make Vancouver unique among major North American metropolises.

Three legacies are especially worth mentioning. The first, and most obvious, was related to traffic. Arterial streets remained the only means of getting into and back out of Vancouver's downtown, and compared to freeways, they moved slowly. It is still a chore traversing between Urban Core and Great House Reserve via car. The second and less often recognized legacy involved land use. The lack of a freeway left open an enormous amount of urban land that would otherwise have been covered in pavement and high-speed paraphernalia: on-ramps, off-ramps, and cloverleaf exits. Some of this land, as in Strathcona, would remain rehabilitated housing. Other parcels once slated for the freeway, especially disused industrial lands, opened up to new residential uses. The third legacy of this famous unbuilding was more political. The rolling back of the freeway, even more visibly than the downzoning of vulnerable neighborhoods within the Urban Core, provided a clear political victory for local activists to rally around. And rally they did. In fact, in the next city council elections, they took over.

A Growth Machine Turned against Itself

The defeat of the freeway and subsequent political oscillations in and around Vancouver resulted in decisive shifts in how the growth machine operated. New policies were constructed that came to redirect building activities on the ground. The construction of policies was fundamentally related to the building of political coalitions and to a broad set of guiding orientations. For this reason, it is worthwhile to examine the crafting of political coalitions through ideological differentiation and how these became translated into policy.

Through and after the Second Great War, Vancouver's growth machine remained relatively unified. The city council, the Planning Department, and local developers all played on the same team. Political leadership within the City of Vancouver adopted a stance similar to planners, emphasizing a pro-development and pro-business agenda as good for everyone and above more partisan bickering. This was reflected even in the name, the Non-Partisan Association (NPA) taken by the political party in power since World War II.[27] When engaged in collective building projects, the NPA fa-

---

[27] The NPA was formed in response to the Socialist-leaning Co-operative Commonwealth Federation (CCF), the party in the mayor's office from 1939 to 1940. The CCF would eventually merge with other pro-labor movements to form the New Democratic Party in 1961.

vored big infrastructural and redevelopment projects that promised to lead to growth and raise the value of big property holdings in the city. A similar bias toward growth, large projects, and big property holders ruled the provincial politics of the era, where the BC Liberal and similarly aligned Social Credit (SoCred) parties traded power, marginalizing labor-affiliated parties.[28] Indeed, comfort with shared political agendas may be evidenced in the City of Vancouver receiving a renewed provincial charter in 1953, leaving it with somewhat more legal room to determine its future vis-à-vis the province than was granted to other municipalities.

The right-wing coalitions of the growth machine, including the NPA in the City of Vancouver, along with the Social Credit and BC Liberal parties at the provincial level, generally wedded social conservatives with the interests of the propertied. The marriage was mostly happy, as long as everything remained in its proper place. The valorization of property rights supported the building of flexible and developer-friendly policies for governing the Urban Core. High-rise apartment towers could be accommodated, as long as they were not located near the social conservatives living within the Great House Reserve. After World War II, house dwellers increasingly tended to own their own properties and generally bought into the valorization of property rights, with the condition that the Urban Core would remain "over there." Big landlords and social conservatives readily forged alliances based, in no small part, on the reactionary marginalization of socialists, renters, and others viewed as urban degenerates (a.k.a. "Maoists, Communists, pinkos, left-wingers and hamburgers").

By 1972, the successful coalitions of the growth machine and the right began to fall apart. Provincially, unease with rapid and sprawling growth contributed to the election of a new government under the New Democratic Party (NDP). The NDP won on a platform combining socialist-leaning pro-labor policies with stricter controls on development.[29] Within the City of Vancouver, the NPA faced similar dissatisfaction with the pace and form of urban development. City councilors, including the mayor, were accused of conflicts of interest and attacked for lack of community consultation. Erstwhile conservative allies of the NPA began to take note of the addition of higher-density housing to major arterial developments nearby.[30] The inviolability of the Great

---

[28] Since the rise of the CCF at the provincial level during the Great Depression, the BC Liberals mostly merged with the BC Conservative Party to form a political counterweight, and should not to be confused with the Federal Liberal Party. The SoCred Party has a more unusual lineage, mostly tied to the figure of W.A.C. Bennett, though it effectively captured a similar constituency as the BC Liberals.

[29] Garrish 2002.

[30] An arterial development combining a shopping center with apartments and townhouses, known as "Arbutus Village," at the intersection of Arbutus and King Edward, was credited by Punter (2003, 23) as helping to ensure the loss of the NPA. Apartment towers were also on the rise near Oakridge Mall—the city's first Comprehensive Development district.

House Reserve's boundaries no longer seemed certain to the party's house-dwelling base. Heading into municipal elections toward the end of 1972, neither residents of the house habitat nor residents of the Urban Core fully trusted the NPA, and for the first time since its founding, the party was voted out of power in favor of the new and reform-minded TEAM party (an acronym for The Electors Action Movement). So it was that for a brief moment in the early 1970s, both the city government and the provincial government were controlled by reformist and/or left-leaning parties, both inherently suspicious of developers. The growth machine had turned decisively against itself.

On their way to power, the New Democrats, TEAM, and their allies drew populist distinctions between democratic rule and capitalist rule. They placed themselves more consistently on the side of the downtrodden, if often from the perspective of the urban professional. As reformers, they favored the interests of existing residents of various neighborhoods over the interests of developers and their property rights. They generally drew on coalitions of renters rather than owners. They valorized livability over growth, and a low-rise, back-to-the-earth environmentalism over high-rise modernism. In this, as eloquently described by geographer David Ley, the reformist left in Vancouver also made connections with the prevailing counterculture.[31] They celebrated diversity and individuation, and often derided the rationality and technocratic universalism they associated with modernism. They promoted social inclusion and justice, attacking the right as greedy, exclusionary, and square.

After the stars aligned for the reformist left in the early '70s, the political momentum would shift back and forth in subsequent years. Correspondingly, a Dr. Jekyll and Mr. Hyde act came to characterize Vancouver's growth machine. This act grew more pronounced with the increasingly mismatched power consolidations across city and provincial governments. Even at the federal level, power shifts through this era mattered and reverberated across the metro area. Table 4.1 lists ruling governments by city, provincial, and federal control, and sorts them roughly into reformist/left and growth machine/right affiliations. Drastically simplified in this fashion, the table demonstrates the rise of a split political personality within Vancouver's growth machine, frequently at war with itself from 1972 onward. The split extended into the politics of surrounding municipalities. To complicate matters further, major actors within city coalitions frequently moved on to provincial stages later within their careers. For instance, Vancouver mayors Mike Harcourt and Gordon Campbell, arriving to power from opposite sides, would both eventually take over as provincial premiers.[32]

---

[31] Ley 1987, 1996; Ley and Mercer 1980.

[32] Further illustrating such complexities, Bill Vander Zalm rose from mayor of Surrey, Metro Vancouver's second largest municipality, to the provincial premiership under the Social Credit Party.

TABLE 4.1 POLITICAL OSCILLATIONS IN CITY, PROVINCIAL, AND FEDERAL GOVERNMENTS

	Vancouver	British Columbia	Canada
1960s	Indep.—Thomas Alsbury 1959-1962	SoCred—WAC Bennett 1952-1972	Prog. Conserv.—Diefenbaker 1957-1963
1970s	NPA—Wm. Rathie, Tom Campbell 1963-1972		Liberal—Lester Pearson, Pierre Trudeau 1963-1979
	TEAM—Art Phillips, Jack Volrich (also Indep.) 1973-1980	NDP—Dave Barrett 1972-1975	
		SoCred—Bill Bennet, Bill Vander Zalm, Rita Johnston 1975-1991	
1980s	Indep.—Mike Harcourt 1980-1986		Prog. Conserv.—Joe Clark 1979-1980
			Liberal—Pierre Trudeau, John Turner 1980-1984
			Prog. Conserv.—Brian Mulroney, Kim Campbell 1984-1993
1990s	NPA—Gordon Campbell, Phillip Owen 1986-2002	NDP—Mike Harcourt, Glen Clark, Dan Miller, Ujjal Dosanjh 1992-2001	
			Liberal—Jean Chretien, Paul Martin 1993-2006
2000s	COPE/Vision—Larry Campbell 2002-2005	Liberal—Gordon Campbell, Christy Clark 2001-2015	
	NPA—Sam Sullivan 2005-2008		
			Conservative—Stephen Harper 2006-2015
2010s	Vision—Gregor Robertson 2008-2015		

Note: Unshaded = right-leaning. Shaded = left-leaning.

Ideas matter when they are put to work building things. The themes of both growth machine/right and reformist/left coalitions were translated into various competitively escalating policy-construction projects from the late 1960s onward, encouraging a baroque sort of regulatory diversification. These diverse construction projects worked to undermine the house in three ways: (1) they built *around* the house, enabling new and diverse entities to govern those lands outside the Great House Reserve; (2) they built *over* the house, reenabling forms of urban succession by encroaching into house habitat; and (3) they *renovated* the house, altering its legal character and correspondingly changing its very nature as a regulatory entity.

Building around the House

The acts of building *around* the Great House Reserve occurred across the relatively few parcels of metropolitan land left outside the reserve. We can divide such parcels into their Urban Core and their hinterland components. The Urban Core provided most of the residential alternatives to the house. But these needed to be enabled. The hinterland generally provided the room for the outward expansion of the land-hungry Great House Reserve. As new regulatory creatures were constructed to govern land use in each location, they began to shift the balance of development away from the house.

Opening Up the Urban Core

The growth-machine right generally kept the old Urban Core open for re-development. The reformist left tended to put in place stricter controls on this redevelopment. This back-and-forth ultimately produced a highly varied regulatory landscape, treated with more or less flexibility depending on who was in charge. The growth-machine right enabled Vancouver's many high-rises and championed new condominium forms of ownership. The reformist left may be credited for developing lower-rise livability, initiating cooperatives, and establishing rental protections. As the political winds shifted across the municipalities of the metropolitan area, Urban Core lands outside the City of Vancouver experienced similar regulatory diversification.

The rise of high-rise apartment towers began before the fall of the freeway, but mostly after the modernization of Vancouver's zoning bylaw. In this, if anything, Vancouver's growth machine came late to the game. Other North American cities had already taken to modernist high-rise development—especially for public housing projects. Vancouver's private developers remained uncertain at the outset whether high-rises should be oriented toward short-term hotel uses or longer-term rentals.[33] When tested, they seemed to rent well, and the new apartments were marketed to carefree single office workers, young childless couples, and genteel retirees.[34] With the city under NPA leadership, a decade-long building boom took off shortly after the 1961 census that would ultimately fill much of the West End with high-rise apartment towers.

---

[33] Price 2012.

[34] McKay 2003–2004.

If Vancouver's developers came late to their appreciation for high-rises, they adopted new condominium forms of tenure early. In 1966 the province of British Columbia, under the right-leaning Social Credit party (also known as the SoCreds), became the first in Canada to adopt legislation enabling strata (i.e., condominium) corporations, thereby allowing ownership of individually titled apartments within multiunit buildings.[35] British Columbia borrowed its legislation from Australia, hence adopting the term *strata* rather than *condo*, but the effect was the same as the condominium legislation spreading elsewhere through the 1960s, beginning in Florida and California.[36] As a result, multiunit buildings could finally be split into properties for individual sale, attached to common maintenance rights and obligations. Financial institutions had to adapt, as did the newly rebranded Canada Mortgage and Housing Corporation (CMHC) in enabling mortgage insurance for condominium properties. By 1980, more than 447 strata plans had been registered, covering over ten thousand units. By 2010, the City of Vancouver would contain over four thousand strata buildings and nearly one hundred thousand registered units.[37]

Reformist left governments took a decidedly suspicious stance regarding the development of high-rises and condominiums. In rezoning and long-range planning they sided, more often than not, with local neighborhood groups over the interests of developers, strengthening restrictions against the development of towers and conversions of existing rental buildings into condos.[38] They also installed new zoning districts, enforcing heritage designations preventing the tearing down of many old structures. But development continued on TEAM's watch, and there remained plenty of room for low-rise developments, including condominiums, within the Urban Core.

Overall, the obstructionist reputation of TEAM with regard to condo and tower development should not obscure its innovations in other regards. For instance, in their 1972 city council campaign, TEAM members championed opening up the formerly industrial waterfront for recreation and reclaiming the surrounding land for inner city residential use. After intensive consultation, the city partnered with the federal CMHC to redevelop the lands around and including Granville Island. Most of the former industrial tenants of Granville Island were replaced with the new Emily Carr Art School, a public market, and a variety of small, artisanal

---

[35] Douglas Harris (2011) details the innovations brought by British Columbia's condominium and related legislation. See also Lasner 2012, which details the rise of co-ops prior to condos. A few of these were built in Vancouver, but they never gained much traction, likely because of the uncertainty surrounding them, as discussed by Lasner.

[36] Van Weesep 1987.

[37] D. Harris 2011, 706–707.

[38] Ley and Mercer 1980.

Figure 4.2 Aerial photo of the City of Vancouver from 2013, overlooking much of the downtown Urban Core, False Creek, and (in the lower left corner) the beginning of the Great House Reserve. (*Photograph by the author.*)

industries. The city set up new zoning districts for the south side of False Creek (top center of Figure 4.2), and carefully worked to maintain a social mix within the surrounding residential developments. Generous leases were offered to residential developers, but the city kept title over the land in an experimental effort to keep prices cheaper. Planners encouraged the construction of multiunit, medium-density, lease-hold condominium buildings and purpose-built rentals.[39] Working closely with the federal government, the city also tried out another experiment—constructing housing cooperatives.

A new form of housing cooperative had been enabled by the National Housing Act of 1973, passed by Trudeau's Liberal federal government. Chartered as nonprofit corporations, cooperatives were run collectively, and all members were required to take part in democratic deliberations over their futures. Members purchased a share that never accrued equity, and paid rent corresponding to the size of their units.[40] But as nonprofits with access to low-interest government-backed mortgage loans, cooperatives tended to

---

[39] Ley 1987.

[40] This made new cooperatives different from previously established "equity" cooperatives, only a handful of which were ever established around Vancouver.

keep their rents quite low. Even so, federal subsidies provided help for those unable to pay full rent, geared to subsidize a fixed percentage of their income. Within Vancouver, one of the first federally supported housing cooperatives would appear in the new False Creek development. The False Creek Cooperative was founded in 1974 and would ultimately contain 170 units—a family-friendly mix of two-, three-, and four-bedroom units.[41]

Cooperatives fit poorly into preexisting categories of rent or ownership, and ultimately came to be governed under their own act. Altogether, some thirteen cooperatives would be built in British Columbia under the initial enabling legislation, containing 826 units. Today over one hundred cooperatives have been incorporated within the City of Vancouver alone, containing an estimated 5,605 units, with many more cooperatives spread across the broader metropolitan area.[42]

Various governments, both left-leaning and right-leaning, also developed and supported other forms of non-market housing as well over the years, often more directly targeted at the needy. Within the City of Vancouver, some twenty-five thousand non-market housing units have been preserved—about one unit for every two detached houses remaining in the city—most quite concentrated within the Urban Core.[43] Non-market housing also remains quite diverse, and though it is supported by the Province (BC Housing), it is managed by a variety of nonprofit organizations.[44]

Despite the diversity of non-market housing stock, the vast bulk of urban residents who do not own their property rent their units within the private sector. Here, the NDP government constructed residential leases as specific legal entities requiring protections, passing the Landlord and Tenant Act of 1974. Newly installed protections included limits on evictions, the ending of landlord rights to unencumbered entry, and officially backed rent control. A rentalsman's office was installed to administer the new Act. The defined tenant protections worked to preserve and protect existing affordable housing within the Urban Core.

The SoCreds were cautious about overturning the renter protections built in place by the NDP, and promised in the run-up to the 1975 election

---

[41] False Creek Co-op 2013.

[42] Co-operative Housing Federation of BC 2013.

[43] City of Vancouver 2013.

[44] This situation differs from that of other cities, like the City of New York and the City of Toronto, where large government organizations, including the New York City Housing Authority (NYCHA) and Toronto Community Housing Corporation (TCHC), manage most public housing. But in its diversity, Vancouver preserves more non-market housing units per person than either the NYCHA or TCHC (author calculations, based on City of Vancouver 2013 and figures provided by NYCHA and TCHC).

they would not do so.[45] After their victory, they remained wary of the perceived power of tenant groups, with a former official in 1980 likening adoption of rent control to jumping onto a tiger: "The riding is not particularly difficult. It's dismounting that's the trick."[46] Nevertheless, after another election win in 1983, the SoCreds made the leap. They passed a new Residential Tenancy Act that shed rent control and many of the other former renter protections, but kept in place the idea that residential tenancies deserved special consideration. When the NDP once again regained power in 1992, they tinkered with the Act once again, restoring rent control. Renter protections have officially remained in place ever since, even through subsequent shifts in political fortune. The lasting power of rent control provides further demonstration that regulatory creatures are difficult (but not impossible) to dislodge once they are built into the legal fabric.

Altogether, the regulatory environment produced by Vancouver's shifting coalitions became increasingly complicated over the years. The policies built by the reformist left were particularly important to ensuring that the residential stock within the Urban Core grew in a diverse fashion. They largely prevented the Urban Core from completely filling up with tall towers full of condos. Indeed, though Vancouverism is now most associated with the high-rise, the majority of Vancouverites actually live in various low-rise alternatives.

To provide a sense of the changes in Metro Vancouver's built environment, Figure 4.3 demonstrates the transformation of the housing stock by location within the region. The metro area is divided into the City of Vancouver, its near suburbs (Richmond, Burnaby, New Westminster, and the North Shore), and those farther out. The change over time speaks to the outward expansion of the metropolitan area as well as to the densification of the Urban Core. Between 1961 and 1986, the growth in houses was confined to suburban municipalities. The City of Vancouver experienced a net loss of over five thousand single, detached houses. Nevertheless, the city more than made up for the loss of houses with the growth of alternative dwellings. Of note, the high-rises favored by modernists (and only distinguished in census data in later years) accounted for a substantial portion of this growth, but definitely not the majority.

The growth of urban alternatives, including high-rise, low-rise, and other, was not confined to the city. By 1986, the near suburbs, and even the far suburbs (though to a lesser extent), were producing alternative housing. The near suburbs have also witnessed a real decline in the number of

---

[45] Lazzarin 1990; Tafler 1984.

[46] R. Williamson 1980, n.p.; quote attributed to Rafe Mair.

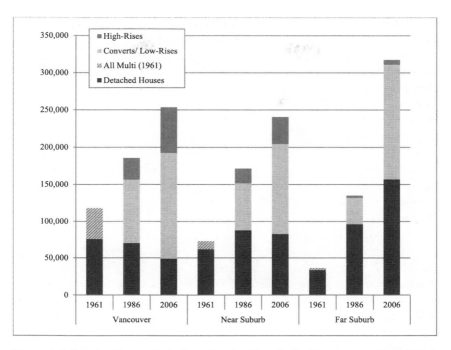

Figure 4.3 Detached houses and alternative dwellings in the Vancouver metropolitan area, subdivided by location relative to central city and year, 1961–2006. (*Based on census data. Graphic prepared by the author.*)

detached, single-family houses in recent years. The redevelopment of Urban Core lands across the metro area varied in implementation, but was facilitated by metropolitan planning. Through the process of documenting local priorities, the preservation of livability would become a guiding goal, one that extended clearly into the Urban Cores of each local municipality. The result of this effort was a broadly lauded Livable Region Plan, produced in 1975, that looked to the decade ahead and attempted to guide municipal land-use policies. The report recommended gradual increases in residential density, promoting more compact development meant to retain "the good qualities of single-family detached homes while using less land."[47] Though the report avoided promoting high-rises, or even low-rise apartment buildings, it clearly suggested that outlying municipalities should concentrate more on duplexes and townhouses, rather than further extending the Great House Reserve.[48] The plan also sought to develop a system of transit-linked

[47] Greater Vancouver Regional District 1975, 14.

[48] Ibid., 47.

Figure 4.4 "The Regional Picture in 1986," a map of Greater Vancouver drawn in 1975, projecting a decade into the region's future, including proposed "regional town centres." Excerpted from the original caption: "Our picture of Greater Vancouver in 1986 shows a regional community still in touch with nature: look out the window or down the street, go 15 minutes from home and there is the mountain slope or a stretch of water, a place to walk or play or game. Our picture of daily life deals with the basics: where a person lives, where he works, the Regional Town Centre where he finds community life and liveliness. These places are close together, for this should be a Region of complete communities—livable cities in a sea of green—each containing many of the opportunities a metropolis offers." (*From Greater Vancouver Regional District, The Livable Region 1976/1986: Proposals to Manage the Growth of Greater Vancouver [Vancouver: Greater Vancouver Regional District, 1975], 48. Reproduced with the permission of Metro Vancouver.*)

regional town centers in selected surrounding municipalities (Burnaby, New Westminster, Coquitlam, and Surrey), each containing shopping and office space alongside higher-density residential developments, and serving as a focus for local needs (see Figure 4.4).

The report would not be adopted in its entirety. But it led to various municipal growth coalitions competing over "town center" status as they sought to attract transit, attention, and prestige to local projects. Such competitions unfolding through the Livable Region planning process would promote densification of the Urban Cores within suburban municipalities, even if not entirely to plan. Through its focus on linking metropolitan hubs, the Livable Region Plan would also lay the groundwork for a more integrated regional transit system.

Shutting Down the Hinterland

Though all sorts of new alternatives were being built in the Urban Core, there was little in the early 1970s to prevent the Great House Reserve from further expanding into Vancouver's hinterland.[49] It seemed only a matter of time before the Great House Reserve would swallow up all remaining undeveloped tracts, replacing the farms and forests of the Lower Mainland with subdivided lots ready for houses—and only houses. Both urban and suburban residents of Vancouver appreciated the remaining farms and forests of the Fraser Valley. But what could be done to prevent suburban succession? The provincial NDP government, newly installed in September 1972, rode in to power in part by suggesting some ideas. After taking office, the NDP government wasted little time in freezing, by an executive order issued in December, the subdivision and development of all agricultural lands in the province.[50]

In the process of freezing development, the NDP quickly discovered it had to establish just what it meant by agricultural lands. The province initiated a technical process of definition similar to that defining the single-family house. A clarification in January 1973 defined agricultural lands as those in lots larger than two acres that were "assessed as farmland, zoned agricultural by a local government or rated CLI Class 1–4 agricultural capability."[51] Only once the NDP had defined agricultural lands in this fashion could it go about protecting them.

From the issuance of orders in council to freeze development of agricultural lands, the NDP government moved toward a more comprehensive and lasting solution. It passed the Land Commission Act of 1973, appointing a commission to establish and look after a new Agricultural Land Reserve (ALR). As multiple reviews note, in implementation the ALR was based on the government's zoning power.[52] Certain uses were defined as agricultural and bonded to the land. Other uses, including subdivision into lots for housing development, were disallowed. Fully mapped and official reserves were completed and set in place within each of the twenty-eight existing

---

[49] A patchwork system of parks had already been set up across the Lower Mainland by the early 1970s, extending especially up into the mountains. The park reserve seemed stable but small, or otherwise targeted toward parcels, as in the mountains of the North Shore, which were deemed largely unsuitable for development for reasons connected to the slope of the land and/or its inaccessibility. The Lower Mainland Regional Planning Board (LMRPB) had worked toward establishing a similar patchwork reserve for agricultural lands before being dissolved by the SoCred Party in the late 1960s.

[50] Garrish 2002; Hanna 1997; Harcourt, Cameron, and Rossiter 2007; Runka 2006.

[51] The latter designation was based on the Canada Land Inventory, which rated all lands on a scale of one to seven, with one being the most suitable for agriculture, and seven "having no agricultural capability." See Runka 2006, 1–2.

[52] Garrish 2002; Hanna 1997; Runka 2006.

administrative regions of British Columbia by 1975, ultimately preserving 4.7 million hectares of land for the ALR. Then the commission turned its work toward administering the land and handling the applications for sub-division and land-use change that began to pour in.[53] Though controversial at the outset, enraging many farmers and developers, the ALR quickly be-came popular across most of British Columbia, especially for those living in and around Vancouver.[54]

Though the Great House Reserve and the Agricultural Land Reserve were based on the same principle, only the latter has provincial standing and formally bears the name of a reserve. The ALR would ultimately remove parcels of land from potential development within nearly every municipal-ity in the Vancouver metropolitan area. For some suburban municipalities (e.g., Richmond, Delta, Surrey, and points farther east), the parcels reserved for agriculture comprised a strikingly large portion of their total land base. Figure 4.5 displays the size of the Vancouver metropolitan area placed off-limits by the ALR. By protecting lands for agriculture, the ALR effectively prevented the Great House Reserve in the metropolitan area of Vancouver from expanding much farther outward, halting the loss of an estimated six thousand hectares of farmland per year.[55]

There remain few other examples of such encompassing efforts at con-taining suburban development across North America. Initiatives from the 1960s in Hawaii and California provided some inspiration to British Co-lumbian policymakers.[56] Quebec also froze the urbanization of much of its agricultural land.[57] Oregon's urban growth boundaries were put in place at roughly the same time, but their effectiveness in constraining sprawl around metropolitan Portland (thereby preventing the spread of detached housing) has been limited, both by the nearby border with the state of Washington and by the fact that a gradual adjustment of the boundaries was built into the system. In British Columbia, preservation via zoning power was placed at the heart of the Land Commission's work, providing a different and less readily adjustable foundation for the ALR.[58]

---

[53] Runka (2006) notes that some thirty-five thousand applications had been submitted by 2006.

[54] Garrish (2002) notes that some 80 percent of British Columbia residents approved of the ALR in informal ministry polling in 1994–1995. See his footnotes, p. 26, for additional evi-dence of widespread public support. As noted by Rome (2001), high levels of support from suburbanites would not be surprising.

[55] Runka 2006; Hanna 1997. Garrish (2002) includes the 6,000 ha/year figure as on the high end of an estimated range of 4,000–6,000 ha/year.

[56] Garrish 2002.

[57] Hanna 1997.

[58] Garrish (2002) remains critical of this characteristic of the ALR, especially as applied across the province outside the Lower Mainland.

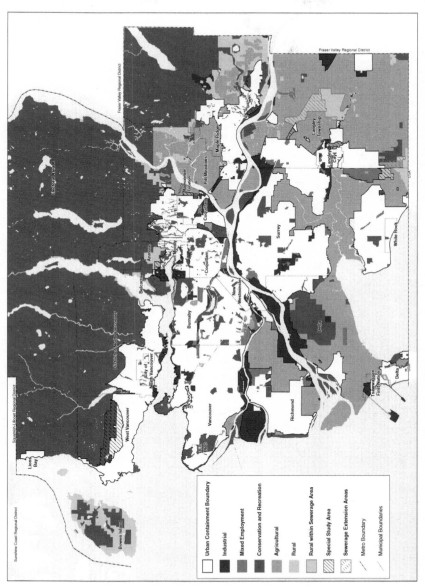

Figure 4.5 Urban containment boundary of metropolitan municipalities, confined by the Agricultural Land Reserve and conservation and recreation areas, with special study areas under consideration. (*Regional Growth Strategy from 2010 [map 12], Greater Vancouver Regional District By-law 1136. Reproduced with the permission of Metro Vancouver.*)

Even though subsequent provincial governments would prove much less supportive of the commission's work than the NDP, they would never roll back the ALR in its entirety. Opposing party leaders found the popularity of the Agricultural Land Reserve intimidating, and it remained, as one observer called it, an "NDP ghost" that would continue haunting the province even after its authors had fallen out of electoral favor.[59] The persistence of "ghosts" reinforces a theme: the regulatory creatures built by various authors—governing the house, agricultural land, and even rental contracts—tend to stick around and keep on doing things. Right-leaning governments mostly settled for whittling away at the Agricultural Land Reserve's edges rather than dispensing with it entirely, and even their whittling activities (e.g., redefining golf courses as agricultural land uses) produced scandals.[60]

The forests of the Lower Mainland, especially as they spread down the mountainsides of the North Shore, were protected by a different set of regulatory creatures. Laws and policies kept older parks and watersheds surrounding reservoirs mostly development-free, with the new Cypress Provincial Park added to the roster in 1975. But setting aside parks and watersheds still left a fairly large portion of the North Shore open to development interests, the largest of which remained the Guinness syndicate's British Pacific Properties. Though developers began advancing houses up the slopes shortly after the Lion's Gate Bridge opened in the 1930s, they faced increasing zoning and servicing restrictions from local municipalities. In the district of West Vancouver, policy from 1958 onward forbade development above twelve hundred feet in elevation, initially for servicing reasons (water and snow clearing). The policy was reconfirmed through subsequent planning, with added protections meant to preserve "the forested character of the community." Since 2001 the policy has come under advisement, resulting in a "special study area" recognized by both the district and Metro Vancouver and designed, in no small part, to explore whether development rights below might be traded for development rights above to "provide for a more natural appearance of the mountain side as opposed to the straight-line demarcation between forest and development that the twelve-hundred-foot restriction would continue to produce." In 2015, a working group convened to study the issue brought back to council the recommendation that the twelve-hundred-foot development restriction should remain in place, and the area protected should be

---

[59] Maitland 1981, 8.

[60] Hanna (1997) estimated a net loss of about 0.2 percent of land in the ALR between 1974 and 1993, with losses driven mostly by government agency requests rather than private applications for land removal. Currently the BC Liberals are once again reviewing the policy, but have vowed to leave the ALR alone within the Lower Mainland.

extended even further by municipal purchasing of remaining undeveloped lands.[61]

A map produced by Metro Vancouver to note sewage-servicing expansion and special study areas (Figure 4.5) draws on ALR and various "conservation and recreation" reservation boundaries to demarcate an Urban Containment Boundary around development for metropolitan municipalities. The sizable special study area in West Vancouver is cross-hatched at the upper-left corner of the map. Nevertheless, as a whole the map reveals just how little rural land remains open for additional development, most of it concentrated farther east up the Fraser Valley.

Building over the House

Historically, the city under all parties has remained cautious about tinkering with the Great House Reserve itself. Single-family residential zoning laid down clear boundaries that largely reflected the alliances of the growth-machine right. Developers were enabled to do whatever they wanted within the Urban Core, as long as they avoided offending their socially conservative allies in the reserve. Indeed, perceived violations of this bargain seemingly led to the downfall of the growth-machine right. The reformist left's distrust of developers and valorization of neighborhood consultation suggested similar respect for the status quo. Once the Great House Reserve had been installed, remarkably few intrusions were allowed.

Figure 4.6 enables a comparison of zoning maps across time, from the 1930 zoning bylaw to the updated one of 2013. The maps here simplify categories dramatically, distinguishing between Urban Core (Core) zones, single-family residential (RS) zones, and the more ambiguous two-family dwelling (RT) zones. The comparison reveals that overall the boundaries of the Great House Reserve have remained remarkably stable through the years, especially outside old (pre-amalgamation) Vancouver. The patches of Urban Core lands intruding into former RS zones by 2013 were almost exclusively Comprehensive Development (CD-1) zones. Most often these enabled low-density developments to be put in place along major arterials, as in the old Oakridge Mall, Women's and Children's Hospital, and Van Dusen

---

[61] District of West Vancouver 2001. Quotes are from pp. 14 and 3–4, respectively. See District of West Vancouver 2015 for the final decision, in which density transfers and zoning variances directly encouraging the development of denser alternatives to single-family houses were the suggested mechanism for protecting valuable undeveloped lands below the twelve-hundred-foot line. Of relevance to claims that topography rather than regulation serves as the primary limit to further development up the slopes, the Upper Lands Working Group confirmed that the vast majority of the land in the Upper Lands Special Study Area is located on an appropriate slope (<35 percent) for development (District of West Vancouver 2014).

Legend

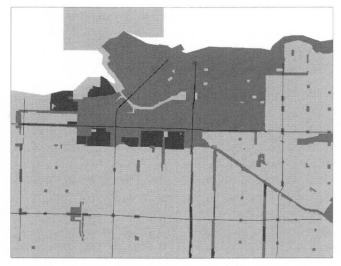

Map 1. Current Vancouver Zoning Map

- Core
- RS
- RT

Map 2. 1930s Vancouver Zoning Map

Kilometers

0 0.5 1   2   3   4

N

Figure 4.6 The spread of inclusive Urban Core zoning and two-family residential (RT) zoning into single-family residential (RS) zones between 1930 (Map 2) and 2013 (Map 1), surrounding downtown Vancouver. (*Graphic prepared by Joseph Tohill.*)

Gardens. Overall, there have been strikingly few expansions of density beyond transfers from RS to RT zoning across Kitsilano, to the west of the core, and around its eastern borders. As discussed more below, these transitions betray some of the ambivalence planners felt initially about the relationship between duplexes and houses.

Despite the overall strength of the Great House Reserve in fending off intrusion, close inspection reveals that the areas supporting multiunit alternatives to the detached house have occasionally, and in very limited form, been allowed to grow into more exclusive neighboring residential areas, either in block-by-block increments or through bleeding along arterials. Recently such encroachments have intensified, reflecting a paucity of alternative sites for development.

By the turn of the twenty-first century, fewer transformable old industrial lands remained to support the rise of new higher-density housing forms in and around Vancouver. The few industrial areas still working were often gathered around the ports, and threatened to take the metropolitan economy down with them if they were rezoned. This began to turn the interest of developers toward other properties, including those, like the Oakridge Mall, supporting lower-density commercial outlets. The city began rezoning its major commercial arterials to support taller structures, with retail continuing to operate on the lower levels and residential space, in the form of either apartments or townhouses, located above.[62] But even with mixed commercial and arterial redevelopment, fewer and fewer options remained for residential densification without intruding into the Great House Reserve.

The densification of Vancouver's Urban Core occurred alongside new moves toward the reunification of Vancouver's growth machine. Toward the end of the twentieth century, local politicians, city planners, and developers all began to converge on a central branding strategy for Vancouver, bringing the achievement of livability through planning (e.g., "Vancouverism") together with the surrounding wild and scenic natural environment. These issues were merged into the cultivation of "EcoDensity" during the colorful NPA mayorship of Sam Sullivan. He attempted to copyright the term while promoting "big, shiny towers" as the antidote to the greenhouse effect.[63] Vision Vancouver, the left-leaning reformist party that ultimately ousted Sullivan, stuck with many of the themes of EcoDensity, but rebranded earlier initiatives within newer "Greenest City" packaging.

Under the banner of EcoDensity and in its race to become the Greenest City, all of Vancouver's major governing parties have come to look favorably

---

[62] Mixed Commercial Multiple Dwelling (CRM) districts were introduced in the 1976 Zoning and Development By-law.

[63] See D. Wood 2012, an article in the *Georgia Strait* wherein Sullivan also lionized former mayor Tom Campbell, credited his vision of EcoDensity to David Owen's (2004) "Green Metropolis" article in the *New Yorker* magazine, and remarked that after his epiphany, "I realized I wanted to bury Jane Jacobs under concrete."

on rezoning applications resulting in denser housing, especially when constructed to green (e.g., LEED-certified) standards and located near transit hubs and regionally planned town centers. Speculation concerning the new push toward densification runs rampant in local real estate ads—even within the Great House Reserve. For instance, a 2013 real estate ad for a house, listed at a sales price of C$1,498,000 in a single-family residential (RS-5) zoned neighborhood, described the following:

> Fabulous Renovated Home in Dunbar with Gorgeous 2 Car Garage. Packaged with other homes on block for potential DEVELOPMENT/ ASSEMBLY for Potential Future Townhomes Site. Currently a Beautiful 5 Bedroom Renovated Home with 3 Beds Up & Fully Renovated Two Bedroom (suite potential) Down. Great Investment/Holding Property. Garage has "Laneway House" Potential. Best School Catchment for Lord Bing and Other Top BC Schools. Package with 3617 West 21st, and Possibly Other Lots. Buy "End of Block" lots! Fantastic Holding Package and Listing Agent Working on Assembling Other Lots on Block if Possible. RS-5 Zoning. Wonderful Rare Opportunity in Hot Dunbar. 2 blocks from Multi Fam zoning. Hurry on this one![64]

The breathless description reads as if the lot owner will soon be enabled to rezone at a higher density, particularly for townhomes. The concern with assembly speaks to a normal difficulty developers tend to encounter in the Great House Reserve: it is not always easy to pull small residential lots together into larger parcels enabling big redevelopments. Nevertheless, realtors and developers have a great deal of experience working around this problem.[65] Two further items are of note: the ad mentions potential for a suite and laneway house. This reflects renovations in the very meaning of the house as a regulatory creature within Vancouver—another sort of building exercise entirely.

Renovating the House

While TEAM and its allies would mostly leave the Great House Reserve alone within the city's boundaries, it is notable that reformist-left parties expressed interest in relaxing restrictions against secondary suites after taking power. Public meetings concerning secondary suites found representatives of wealthier neighborhoods generally opposed to relaxation, reinforcing the distinction between Reserve and Core. As one Point Grey resident noted:

---

[64] MLS Listing V989962, accessed April 26, 2013.

[65] Ley (1996) provides vivid descriptions of block-busting practices in the Fairview neighborhood above False Creek during the 1970s, involving developer enlistment of Hare Krishnas to drive away neighbors.

"When the numbers of these suites rented out by absentee landlords is [*sic*] allowed to increase without restriction, the neighborhood rapidly deteriorates into a commercial area."[66] Nevertheless, other neighborhood organizations were more open to such options, and an internal city council report recommended rezoning to allow secondary suites in some locations as early as 1974.[67] More conservative TEAM alderman Jack Volrich would push back, suggesting that rezoning should be accomplished only after ensuring widespread support within neighborhoods, further noting, "At all times we should strive to preserve the single family home atmosphere."[68] Volrich also suggested the licensing of all secondary suites enabled within the city. Back-and-forth ambivalence within TEAM spoke both to concerns about obtaining neighborhood consent for planning shifts, and to the perceived importance of preserving the single-family neighborhood.

After plebiscites, the city rezoned two areas within the Great House Reserve in 1977, creating new RS-1A districts that allowed secondary suites. The new zoning category, along with the relaxation of enforcement (based only on complaints) and liberal interpretation of hardship claims, helped turn the house on paper into something of a paper tiger within the city. As a result, the practice of carving out suites to rent, especially in renovated basements, expanded. This was most common through the more working-class eastern half of the city, where many detached houses were effectively converted into two-unit apartment buildings. Most other municipalities in the metropolitan area would similarly relax their regulatory regimes over time, resulting in the transformation of many houses into duplexes, usually separated into a main home and a basement suite.

The vernacular "Vancouver Special" style of architecture, shown in Figure 4.7, made conversions of houses especially easy. Vancouver Specials were designed to cheaply maximize their allowed roominess, as set by the rigid floor-space-to-lot-size ratio (FSR) regulations of Vancouver's post-1956 zoning bylaw.[69] Architects and builders began early on to exploit loopholes in the bylaw, allowing them to ignore unfinished basements in the calculation of floor space. They made basements as shallow as possible, for all practical purposes making them first floors of large two-story houses. The technically unfinished first floor did not count as floor space, but could quickly

---

[66] Quoted in *Vancouver Sun* 1974.

[67] Vancouver Archives, Memo of the Department of Permits and Licenses to the Chairman and Members of the Standing Committee on Community Development, May 10, 1974.

[68] Vancouver Archives, Memo from Alderman J. Volrich to Community Development Committee, May 16, 1974. Volrich would become mayor in 1976 and then turn rightward to win again in 1978 as an independent with NPA backing. In 1980, he would lose to Mike Harcourt, also a former TEAM member, who moved left to ally with COPE.

[69] Terriss 2008.

Figure 4.7 "Vancouver Special"–style houses, built to maximize allowable floor space and enable easy conversion to duplexes. (*Photograph by the author.*)

and surreptitiously be finished by owners. The ability to easily separate the upstairs living space from the resulting downstairs living space, carving out two separate apartments, made this an attractive option for those eager to rent out a basement suite.

In effect, tolerance for such suites opened up a new front in Vancouver's transformation of its housing stock. The city again expanded the range of legalized secondary suites in 1986, and later formally altered the bylaw regulations so that nearly all buildings in areas zoned for single-family house use (RS designation) could be modified to include a secondary rental suite, a practice expanded on further by the Vision-controlled city council in 2009. Using 2006 census data, the City of Vancouver estimated that some 19,440 secondary suites had been added to its rental market.[70] All told, this probably reflected the conversion of around a third of the former single-family houses within the city.

Very recently, Vancouver also began to permit the construction of small, single-unit "laneway houses" along the alleys of single-family residential neighborhoods. Assuming that the lots met a relatively lax set of conditions, owners could apply to build laneway houses above or within existing garages. As a result of these shifts in bylaws, most city lots that formerly supported only a single-family house can now legally support three separate dwelling units, including one large duplex in front and one small house on the laneway in the back, all adjoined to the same lot. With respect to the revised zoning bylaw, these would all now be classified as legal RS, "One-Family Dwelling" district uses.

It is worth noting that lots remained legally indivisible regardless of the addition of secondary suites or laneway houses. Apartments could not

[70] City of Vancouver 2010.

be turned into condominiums. Additional units added within the Great House Reserve could only be rented out, not sold. Vision Vancouver justified this policy as a purposeful boost to the rental market, where investment interest had diminished ever since the rise of the condominium. Nevertheless, the policy retained the added advantage, with respect to encouraging density, of more readily allowing rezoning and densification at a later date. From a developer's perspective, it more readily enabled the assembly of larger lots.[71]

Elsewhere the city has tried to promote other forms of "green" densification, including, for instance, a "Skinny Streets" proposal aimed at reclaiming some of the width from wider residential streets for housing. Infill townhouses might be built on property formerly ceded to the city's grander avenues. Together with the bike lanes also viewed as cutting into city streets, this has prompted much hand-wringing over Vision Vancouver's "war on the car." Diversification away from the automobile has accompanied diversification away from the house.[72]

Building the Great Green Growth Machine

Building around, building over, and renovating the house all helped Vancouver to overcome the stranglehold of single-family residential zoning. Building around the house (limiting its reach and encouraging urban alternatives) had by far the largest impact on the transformation of metropolitan housing stock. But the city and its near suburbs also lost detached houses in absolute numbers, speaking to the work of building over and renovating the house, transforming it into something else. Growth was nearly a constant for the metro area, despite its move away from the house. Indeed, within the City of Vancouver, densification of the housing stock was a prerequisite for growth; it was the only way to fit more people into the city's fixed boundaries.[73]

How did the growth machine manage to keep directing people (and their money) to Vancouver, while directing development away from houses? There is much to be said for Vancouver's prime location as Canada's gateway to the Pacific Rim. The region was well disposed to benefit from the liberalization of trade and immigration regimes. But it seems plausible that the reformist

---

[71] Co-ownership remains an option, and financing options are available from VanCity Credit Union, but lack of knowledge and legal uncertainties surrounding this option continue to keep it from being widely adopted (on the history of these options, see also Lasner 2012).

[72] Mason 2014; Quinn 2012.

[73] Population declined in the City between 1971 and 1976, when the new reformist left actively worked to downzone and slow development. Even then, population continued to grow across the metro area.

left's focus on promoting urban livability also helped. Moreover, the growth-machine right threw some great parties, attracting global attention.

In 1986, the World Exposition on Transportation and Communication (Expo '86) arrived in Vancouver after eight years of planning by the province. Shortly after planning commenced in the late 1970s, the promise of the mega-event contributed to a dramatic and speculative run-up in local real estate prices. This was catnip for the growth machine, though the subsequent property market crash in the early 1980s gave Vancouver an especially nasty withdrawal. During the build-up, the industrial lands along the northern rim of Vancouver's False Creek were exempted from the regulations installed by more progressive city regimes. Then they were sold off by the province to Hong Kong billionaire developer Li Ka-shing, who began filling them up with the towers full of condos that were increasingly beloved by Vancouver's developer set, often attached to townhouses at the base.[74]

Together with Canada's increasingly liberal and stratified immigration regime, the high-profile international deal would prove a boon to the local growth machine. Wary and wealthy residents of Hong Kong, anticipating the planned handover of their city to China in 1997, came to view Vancouver as a safe harbor. Many arrived as privileged "investor-class" immigrants and purchased properties across the Vancouver metropolitan region.[75] More recently, the 2010 Winter Olympics provided another giant advertisement for Vancouver on the world stage.

It is important to remember that foreign investment and global capital flows were always a big part of Vancouver's development, but the scale of the Lower Mainland's transformation into a destination for wealthy immigrants nevertheless astounds. The patterns on display in Figure 4.8, tracking relative house prices and the arrival of investor-class immigrants, speak at least somewhat to the success of the growth machine in attracting international attention and money to the area. For property owners, the wages of growth were high. Evidence suggests that the simultaneous arrival of new residents and new money contributed to driving up the prices of detached houses around Vancouver and neighboring suburbs.[76] By 2010, the province had received over seventy-five thousand investor-class immigrants since the immigration program's start in 1985, the vast majority settling in the Vancouver

---

[74] Despite the controversial nature of the provincial deal, it is notable that Li Ka-shing would eventually work closely with the City (under returned NPA leadership) on the development of North False Creek, and the negotiations came to form much of the basis for Vancouver's Amenity Contribution strategy of extracting concessions from developers in exchange for providing density. See Berelowitz 2005 for a glowing review of these developments and Ley 1987 for a more negative contemporary take.

[75] Investor-class immigrants were required to have a net wealth of C$1.6 million as of 2012, and to provide C$800,000 as a loan of sorts to provincial governments upon arrival.

[76] Ley 2010; Mitchell 2004.

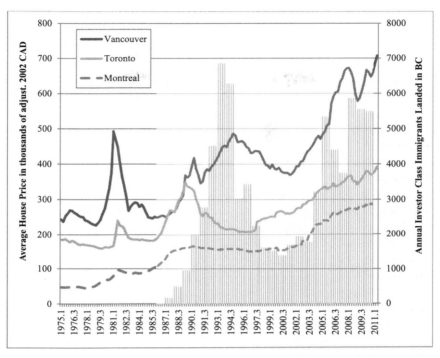

Figure 4.8 Average sale price of detached houses in inflation-adjusted 2002 Canadian dollars, by major metropolitan area and quarter, from 1975 to 2011 (University of British Columbia–Centre for Urban Economics and Real Estate data), with annual investor-class immigration to British Columbia highlighted in the background (*BC Stats data. Graphic prepared by the author.*)

metropolitan area. In sum, the number of extraordinarily wealthy immigrants arriving in the area well exceeded the number of detached houses remaining in the City of Vancouver (under fifty thousand), providing an idea of the pressure such wealth might have added to the local real estate market. From the late 1980s onward, the metropolis of Vancouver has remained by far the most expensive place to buy a house in all of Canada.

Given the dramatic wealth accruing to local property owners, one might expect they would welcome densification. But many emerged as champions of the house instead, joining with residential neighborhood associations devoted to defending local ways of life. Within Vancouver, the Dunbar Resident's Association (DRA) became one of the most prominent champions of the house, representing a West Side neighborhood of the former Point Grey municipality. In spring 2011, the Dunbar Residents Association newsletter ran with the headline "The Death of Single-Family Neighbourhoods?"[77]

---

[77] Dunbar Resident's Association 2011.

The newsletter contained articles attempting to muster outrage at the recent changes to city bylaws allowing secondary suites and laneway housing, and provided information to help residents get involved in resistance to such policy changes.

The success of such activism may have been reflected in the tendency for local residents to vote against the incumbent party (Vision) in 2011 civic elections. That the incumbents easily won anyway suggests that the political might of those remaining within the Great House Reserve in Vancouver has diminished following the long-term rebalancing of the population into the denser Urban Core. The electoral vote maps relatively nicely onto suburban resistance to Vision's densification policies.[78] Votes for the NPA harken back to the historical growth-machine party's implicit agreement to avoid threatening the tranquility of house dwellers with new development.

Given the population shift to the Urban Core, suburban electoral resistance within the City of Vancouver likely remains futile. Furthermore, whether under the NPA's "EcoDensity" initiative, or Vision Vancouver's "Greenest City" race, the city's growth machine seems relatively unified on the issue of enabling more development across the Great House Reserve. Does this portend "The Death of Single-Family Neighbourhoods?" Maybe it does in the long run, especially when coupled with similar development patterns in other municipalities across the metropolitan region and an Agricultural Land Reserve largely preventing further outward sprawl. But there are still plenty of houses around. To be sure, many of them have mutated into forms no longer recognizable under older, more restrictive single-family zoning, but so far this seems more adaptation than extinction. On the whole, the old house habitat, protected by RS zoning, remains. But overall both the regulatory ecology of Vancouver and the habitat that has been constructed for its residents have grown more diverse, more inclusive, and more robust.

In covering the spring meetings of the Urban Land Institute (a developer think tank) in 2014, a local reporter repeated a common refrain about Vancouver, describing its "unique situation" as a site of global investment. The metropolitan area's "restricted space for growth" arose from its "being surrounded by mountains, sea and the American border."[79] The refrain raises questions about any regulatory lessons that might be learned from Vancouver's experience. Can they be transported elsewhere?

Three responses seem pertinent. First, all cities are uniquely located in space and place. They all face differing environments for growth.

---

[78] See "2011 Mayor Race Results by Voting Division," posted by the City of Vancouver at http://vancouver.ca/images/cov/content/2011VancouverMayorRaceByVotingDivision.png.

[79] Bula 2014.

Nevertheless, policymakers and developers frequently draw on examples from other metropolitan areas as they craft local solutions to their dilemmas. Vancouver's downtown planning traditions are already part of a transnational policy discourse. Its lessons are already being adapted to places as similar as San Francisco and different as Dubai. But what Vancouver has to say about single-family detached houses is currently missing from its regulatory lessons, despite how important the metropolitan history of building around and over them is to explaining the city's downtown success.[80]

Second, all of the metropolitan areas extending down the West Coast of North America remain nestled between mountains and sea. Though none run up against international borders, Portland, at least, has to deal with a state border limiting its planning capabilities. Despite their broadly similar topographies and geographic barriers, Vancouver looks very different from its southern sister cities. The difference is telling, underscoring just how large a role Vancouver's regulatory creatures have played in determining its urban form.

Finally, and perhaps most powerfully, we might question the naturalness of the barriers to growth preventing Vancouver from sprawling outward. As it turns out, what surrounds and constrains Vancouver's outward development are mostly creatures of policy rather than features of geophysical location. The sea seems implacable, but in fact Vancouver's reclamation of a large portion of False Creek demonstrates otherwise. Only a host of environmental protections keeps the city from expanding further into the sea, together with regular patrols along the shores evicting informal settlements. Looking toward the mountains, most Vancouverites can see the houses ending their climb up the slopes at the twelve-hundred-foot mark. But they are met at twelve hundred feet by a regulatory limit rather than by the sudden onset of natural mountain hazards, and beyond that boundary they face the legal preservation of park lands and reservoirs. Even looking southward, as the map in Figure 4.5 makes clear, development is mostly restricted by the Agricultural Land Reserve far before it hits the guards at the U.S. border.

In short, the creation of diverse regulatory creatures permeates Vancouver's history. Though locally grounded, these remain much more transportable that might be suggested by focusing on unique features of metropolitan geography. The only things that really limit the spread of regulatory creatures are policy environments. This is important insofar as the ecology of policy changes with each new creature added. If Vancouver can change, other cities can too.

---

[80] See Boddy 2003, 2005 and Peck and Theodore 2010 on Vancouverism and transnational policy mobility.

Vancouver's dramatic transformation from one of the most to one of the least house-dominated metropolitan areas in North America provides an important example of what is possible elsewhere. To be certain, the construction of Vancouver's policy environment remains unique—full of intriguing contingencies, including a monumental unbuilding, political machinations across multiple scales, and extraordinary good luck. But it points the way toward a few common strategies for overcoming the stranglehold of the house: build around it, build over it, and renovate it from the inside out.

Vancouver's story is also far from over. Though modified, old single-family residential zoning remains in place across large swathes of the metropolitan landscape. Within the Dunbar neighborhood, a new watchdog group called Dunbar Re-vision continues to mobilize against densification. Recently they targeted a six- to seven-story retirement housing complex proposed along an arterial within the neighborhood, with one protester noting the desired outcome: "I hope that maybe it's a four storey or somewhere else where they're not going to disturb the neighbourhood, somewhere where there's actually an area for this kind of development, not in the middle of where people are living."[81] As this quote suggests, the prospect of people "living" outside single-family neighborhoods still remains hard for an especially privileged set of Vancouver residents to imagine.

Dunbar Re-vision's conceptual blind spot echoes the ignorance etched into stone with the 1926 Supreme Court decision justifying zoning. The best justification for the Great House Reserve has always been the protection of urban space for living. But this justification has been carefully constructed to perpetually overlook all of the myriad people living in places other than single-family houses. Maybe it is worth giving those people a voice? That is where the next chapters take us.

---

[81] Cowan 2012.

INHABITING THE GREENEST CITY

> We are, all of us, creatures of habit, and when the seeming
> necessity for schooling ourselves in new ways ceases to exist,
> we fall naturally and easily into the manner and customs which
> long usage has implanted ineradicably within us.
>
> —EDGAR RICE BURROUGHS, *THE BEASTS OF TARZAN*

The latest branding effort has sought to turn the City of Vancouver into the world's "Greenest City." Painting the town green has relied on a variety of initiatives, from community gardens to bicycle paths to green building standards and densification, all plausibly intended to reduce environmental impacts. The single-family house mostly gets in the way here, as described in previous chapters. But for all of the city's efforts at building over and around its houses, some 80 percent of its residential land base remains zoned for their protection.[1] The vast majority of Vancouver's residents can see all these protected houses, but they cannot touch them. The benchmark (expected) price for a detached house ranges from nearly C$1.3 million on the city's East Side to over C$3 million on the West Side.[2] This suggests a green painted in the shades of money and envy rather than ecological consciousness. It also raises a very important question: is Vancouver becoming uninhabitable for everyone but the ultra-rich?

In this chapter, I plumb the depths of this question by listening to what Vancouver's residents have to say about it. In the process, I explore the kind of habitats that houses create for people. What makes them different from other urban habitats? I take up claims of universality and particularity—the

---

[1] Rough figure drawn from Metro Vancouver Policy and Planning Department 2008 land-use estimates for 2006 for the City of Vancouver.

[2] Benchmark obtained from Real Estate Board of Greater Vancouver's (2016) "Home Price Index" for March 2016: www.rebgv.org/home-price-index. The figure for the metro area as a whole roughly matches that for East Side Vancouver at just over C$1.3 million.

house as living standard versus just one of many lifestyles. I also attempt to fit habitats to a working model of habits, investigating how they relate to our concepts and feelings of being at home. In so doing, I move from the history of buildings toward giving voice to their residents. How do people come to think of themselves as at home in Vancouver? Do they ever get to feel that way at all?[3]

Not surprisingly, feelings of envy, and even outrage, are not very hard to find in Vancouver. They often come tethered to claims that the Lower Mainland is becoming uninhabitable. When I spoke with her, Amanda Garrison was a married mother of two with a history working in relatively low-paid service work. Like many others, she took the metropolis to task for failing to provide for the living needs of families:

> I can't believe it's difficult to ask for space, you know—for, like, affordable space for a family. I mean, it is what you need. Kids are kids. They run around! They need space!

Amanda laid out a strong claim for a universal set of housing needs. In this, she echoed the thirty-year-old preaching of Edward Broadbent, former leader of the socialist-leaning New Democratic Party in Canada: "Only the rich can afford houses and this is wrong. . . . [B]uying a house is not a luxury like buying a cabin cruiser or a trip to Jamaica."[4] Elements within the progressive movement since shortly after its creation have attempted to rally the troops around raising the single-family detached house to a universal living standard. But really, I can include Amanda within this group only by interrupting the entirety of her quote. I return to where she left off:

> They need space! They can't live in a . . . well, I mean, people *do* live in a small apartment. But, I guess, North American–style living . . . is, uh, what we're accustomed to.

Amanda began by drawing on a universal sense of need, especially related to children, but then she quickly corrected herself. The force of her argument seemed to weaken as she turned to the "North American–style living" she had grown "accustomed to" as justification for her outrage. Why should she not have access to the lifestyle she grew up in? The question still resonates,

---

[3] The questions here lead me away from more dominant (Mulder 1996) and flawed (Callon and Law 2005; Joas 1996; Kemeny 1992; Shiller 2000; Storper and Manville 2006; Swidler 1986; Tversky and Kahneman 1986) rational choice theories, which tend to have little to say about habits (excepting Becker 1992), inhabitability, conceptualizations (though see approaches like Coolen and Hoekstra 2001; Lindberg, Gärling, and Montgomery 1989), feelings, and home.

[4] Canadian Press 1981. Extending even further back, there is a reason Jill Wade's (1994) finely researched history of social housing in Vancouver through 1950 was titled *Houses for All*.

but not in quite the same way as when she started, transformed from righteous anger to more run-of-the-mill envy. Maybe only the rich get houses in Vancouver, but if that is just one of many possible lifestyles, what does it matter?

Lifestyles do not pack quite the punch of living standards, but maybe they should. At the very least, they raise an interesting line of questions about where our habits come from. How seriously should we take the process of becoming "accustomed" to a style of living? When does this process transform a lifestyle into something ingrained, preventing adaptation? How do such habits contribute to defining the uninhabitable? Very quickly we return to our starting question: is Vancouver becoming uninhabitable for everyone but the ultra-rich?

In a different sense, lifestyles offer an implicit critique of the notion of living standards, packing a punch all their own. Why standardize ways of living at all? Meeting fundamental needs seems important for promoting justice, but enforcing sameness in styles of living erodes freedom and diversity. Furthermore, it seems inevitable when standards are enacted that the lifestyles and idiosyncratic concerns of more dominating cultures move to the fore as the basis for establishing what should be considered universal, undermining justice itself as a multicultural concern.[5] In the process of eroding her own argument about universality, Amanda thoughtfully reasserted the centrality of cultural difference.

Ultimately, both lifestyles and living standards can provide room for defining what should be considered uninhabitable, but with different implications. Integrating each with the language of habits and habitats helps to make their similarities and differences plain. The word *uninhabitable* seems foremost a good marker for poor matches between particular sets of habits and habitats. But as suggested by the cultivation of diverse lifestyles, people remain adaptive. So what is to prevent people from adapting? The truly uninhabitable match is one where *new* habits that might make the match work are prevented from forming. Embracing a universalizing living-standard approach defines the uninhabitable by specifying what environments prevent new habits (or "decent" habits, as defined with all the cultural imperialism that entails) from forming for everyone. By contrast, a lifestyle approach grounds the definition of inhabitability within the flexibility of particular sets of people.

So habits are an important part of defining what might be uninhabitable, meaning that it is worthwhile to draw an additional distinction between two different ways in which people's habits work. Habits can be considered

---

[5] This is a central concern of Young's (1990) work. Lauster and Tester (2010) provide an example in working through the implications of using the Canadian National Occupancy Standards to measure crowding for Inuit households in Nunavut.

aspects of cognition insofar as people learn to associate different symbols with one another until their fitting together seems natural and automatic. These are the sort of habits learned as part of culture, the habits that structure our reflective thoughts. But there are also more directly embodied habits, structuring the thoughtlessness of our actions. These are the habits that enable us to flow through the materials of everyday life, cued from one moment to the next by familiarity and routine.[6]

Roughly speaking, these two sorts of habit carve out notionally separate dimensions concerning how people consciously and subconsciously interact with the diverse materials of their everyday lived environments. The distinction makes it possible to separate what *looks* like home from what *feels* like home.[7] It enables us to subdivide our starting question into two parts: How might people find Vancouver uninhabitable given that the house remains an important cultural symbol? And how might they find it uninhabitable given the way housing physically structures their everyday routines? This returns us to the various forms of the house regularly encountered by people, as introduced in the first chapter. The inaccessibility of the house as a commodity in Vancouver has raised real questions about its necessity in culture and concrete. The rest of this chapter mostly concerns the cultural importance of the house, but I return to its concrete manifestations near the end.

The Green of Envy

Samantha Lyeung was born in Vancouver. Her husband came from small-town Ontario. Despite their different origins, Samantha noted, they shared the same general expectations:

> In terms of how we grew up, we both lived in a house. Almost everyone that we know did, right? Everyone grew up in a house with a backyard, and I guess that just . . . has become a part of what was

---

[6] The two kinds of habit described here fit within and inform dual-process models of cognition and action, as described across a variety of disciplines. For examples, see Gross 2009 and Vaisey 2009 within the sociological literature; Evans 2008 and W. Wood and Neal 2007 for research in psychology; and Redish, Jensen, and Johnson 2008 and Yin and Knowlton 2006 for neuroscience. Associative habits of perception and classification inform reflection, at the same time as they form part of the cuing for impulsive actions (Strack and Deutsch 2004). Within sociology, cultural theorists like Bourdieu (1990, 2005) and Swidler (1986) are often viewed as adopting and mixing together these two sorts of habit in their concepts of "habitus" and "cultural toolkit," but habits may be usefully separated into their classificatory and practical components (Lizardo 2004; Lizardo and Strand 2010), and derived from broader pragmatist conceptions of the flow of action (Gross 2009; Joas 1996) that have until recently remained relatively neglected within sociology (Camic 1986).

[7] Blunt and Dowling (2006), Mallett (2004), Manzo (2003), and Rybczynski (1987) provide critical and useful reviews of the literature on home.

taken for granted would be part of our future? And it hasn't come to fruition in Vancouver, here . . . so . . . I mean, there's just this . . . um . . . I'm not sure how to explain it. It was just taken for granted that that was just how we would grow up, when we had kids, when we got married, that we'd own a house with a backyard, and so there's kind of a disconnect between what we expected and what we're actually living.

Samantha did everything "right" to get to a home that looked like a house. She stayed in school, received an excellent education, got a good job, and married well. She knew where this story was supposed to go, and it should have taken her into a house. But it did not. As Samantha's great expectations and subsequent disappointments reveal, people's careful work to insert themselves into particular storylines does not always work out the way they expect. Sometimes the setting to the story changes in ways beyond their control. For Samantha, now with children of her own, it appears that Vancouver has become an unsettling place to live. She is far from alone.[8]

Marlene Darcy also grew up in a house, but in a more working-class step-family in a small northern town.[9] She was the first in her family to attend university. There she wrote research papers on single mothers living in housing cooperatives and emphasized the benefits of dispensing with patriarchal social conventions. But despite her militant resistance to other norms, Marlene described how her inability to afford a house in Vancouver really bothered her. Through the course of her interview with my research assistant, she tried to rationalize away the demoralizing affect her housing situation had on her, and found she could not honestly bring herself to do it:

> MARLENE: I personally couldn't give a dang about having a piece of land. Like, I really don't care about that. For me it's about . . . um, having a financial avenue . . . like, you know, it's a good investment, to have a piece of property, but also . . . [pause] You know what? I think it's not true that I don't give a dang about it, 'cause now that I think about it, it's also a bit of a status thing. Like, you know, if I say to people, "Oh, I'm renting," or "Oh, I live in a co-op," it just doesn't seem right. Like, I sort of feel like when you're a grown-up you should own a house and, you know, it should be a nice house in a nice neighborhood.

---

[8] Storytelling typically provides people with a context for working out identities (Ezzy 1998; Robertson 2007), and with coherent-seeming lines of action formulated as cultural scripts (Townsend 2002). That it failed to work in either sense in Vancouver provides substance to Swidler's (1986) distinction between settled and unsettled contexts.

[9] Marlene's hometown had fewer than twenty thousand residents in 2006. Over 75 percent of residences were detached houses—similar to Vancouver's housing figures in 1961.

MIA: And, sort of, at what point does that shift over? 'Cause that's also another thing that's come up. At what point?

MARLENE: I think once you have kids. Once you have kids then you're considered like a grown-up, then you should be able to afford a house, in a good neighborhood, and, uh, kind of build your sense of community and your network and your community by the fact that you live there.

Marlene's interpretation of why she felt bound to the house dramatically changed course mid-description. She *did* give a dang! It was not really about the investment values associated with houses, a finding that seemed broadly applicable to most interviewees.[10] Instead, it was about how Marlene connected owning a house to being a grown-up, even as she clearly tried to maintain a critical perspective on those feelings. This influenced Marlene's notion of her quality of life in general, fitting into an overarching story about how things were not quite coming together for her, at least not in Vancouver:

Oh, I spend lots of time thinking about my quality of life, because sometimes I go back to [my home town], where my family lives, and their quality of life seems so much better. Because they're not racing from one activity to another activity, you know, they don't have to work as hard . . . like, as you have to work around here. They can afford more kids than I could. You know, I mean, they each get to have more than one child, because they can afford it.

Returning to her home town and interacting with her family there heightened Marlene's awareness that she was not where she wanted to be. For both Marlene and Samantha, the house had become part of an associative habit, a habit of mind. Both wrestled with breaking free of this habit. Samantha could not quite articulate its hold on her. It manifested as a mental disconnect, an unmet expectation. For Marlene, the house was associated with a sense of what a "grown-up" should have. Her discussion cast most of Vancouver into a weird sort of Never Never Land where adults were prevented from growing up but children were provided only limited entry.

Sadie Carter took a slightly different tack in describing how the house became a cognitive shortcut for her. A highly educated mother of two, Sadie found herself looking backward to a telling episode in her childhood, growing up in a Toronto suburb, which she thought amusing as she found herself renting the top floor of a character house in Vancouver:

---

[10] Indeed, most interviewees had an understandably poor grasp of investment and financing fundamentals.

Where I grew up, it was largely people like me. Just . . . you know, comfortable, well-off, like, white families. And everybody had a pretty big house and a yard, and went to school . . . private school. And I do remember as a kid, when I'd meet someone who maybe rented a house or lived in an apartment, or lived in a house that was maybe quite narrow or smaller than mine, and I would think, like, "Oh, poor them." [Which] I'm kind of shocked at now, 'cause I'm living in that house, you know? . . . I do remember, like, this one boy, they were Russian immigrants, and his family moved to Toronto, and he became a friend of my brother's. And one day, I walked with my brother and dropped him off, and he lived in an apartment. And I just remember thinking, "Oh, how terrible, I hope he has enough to eat!" [*Laughter.*] But that's not how I feel now. But it definitely is still under here somewhere.[11]

For Sadie, her childhood home, as reinforced by her interactions in the community, provided the house with a special sort of symbolic importance. Those who owned and lived in a big house with a yard (the full house package) were normal and successful. Those who lived somewhere else, like an apartment, were to be pitied. She resisted this association in her interview, mirthfully laughing it away, but she also acknowledged its remaining hold on her. Here we see evidence of historical differentiation between the haves and the have-nots informing Sadie's habits of cognitive association. To lack a house is to be a failure. In Vancouver, this interpretive habit leaves little room for success stories.

Children growing up in dwellings other than houses might be expected to develop some resistance to these kinds of interpretive habits. Their family environments could predispose them to better appreciate housing alternatives, passing along distinct familial subcultures. However, they may also pick up on the pity of others ("Oh, poor them"), and learn of their abnormality in this fashion. Stephanie Bryson, who as a girl had lived with her mother in a rented, one-bedroom apartment in Vancouver's West End, noted, "Nobody was growing up in a one-bedroom apartment on TV." Stephanie also came to learn in even starker terms how she did not quite fit in as a child living in an apartment building:

Growing up in Vancouver, in the '80s, a lot of apartments were actually "adults only." They had a policy of adults only, and we had some management . . . when we first moved into the building I was four, and the management didn't have a problem with that. Then the

---

[11] As Zavisca (2012) notes, Russians often view mortgages as debt bondage, providing a possible alternative understanding of the friend's situation.

subsequent management came in who truly wanted to enforce this policy of no children, but they couldn't. They couldn't evict us, but they tried everything possible. . . . [T]hey brought in these new special magnetic keys so that we could get into the building, and then they said that I wasn't a tenant, so they wouldn't give me one. So for a time period I had no key to get in to the front door of the building, and I would have to ask strangers to get into the building. And, uh, it was only after we had a community meeting for the building where they were talking about security issues and they had a policeman there. And so my mom went to the community meeting and said to the policeman in front of a bunch of tenants, "Don't you think it's bad that, you know . . . an eight-year-old girl comes home from school and she can't get in the front door because the management won't give her a key?" So the next day we had a key.

In these ways, Stephanie found herself heavily (and punitively) influenced by the way apartment building managers discriminated against children. Evidence suggests such discriminatory practices continue in a variety of forms.[12] A number of parents renting apartments described fears that their newborns would cause problems with their managers. They often described their difficulties in finding and keeping apartments as related to landlords' normative ideas about what constitutes a good home for children. Discriminatory practices work to reinforce the understanding that children belong in houses. Children often know when and where they are not wanted. It is perhaps no surprise that even though Stephanie's childhood provided her with an alternative example by which she might come to understand a different configuration of home, the house still asserted itself in her imaginings:

> Not that it was the worst place to grow up, but it's kinda funny that I've always kind of yearned to have, you know, like, space—a house and a yard sort of thing.

Stephanie considered herself "a nontraditional person and a nonconformist" and actively worked to avoid the notion that she was someone to be pitied. Nevertheless, as a child she clearly longed for something different, more in line with the norm. As a married university graduate and a newly expecting parent, she also noted that she wanted to provide something different for her own child, and always expected that she would be able to do so by following a more normative storyline than her mother's:

---

[12] See, e.g., Lauster and Easterbrook 2011.

I never grew up wanting to be rich, but I always thought by the time I got married and ha[d] kids, I would have kind of . . . you know, I wouldn't be living in a rented one-bedroom apartment, you know? Like, I think that's the big thing. I thought I would be more . . . not settled, but . . . I'd be more comfortable with where I was living, that I would feel I had space, that sort of thing. Whereas now I feel like, just to have a two-bedroom sort of place is this extravagant sort of thing only for the wealthy, you know? It's kind of crazy.

Stephanie, too, felt unsettled by Vancouver, even though she grew up in an apartment in the city. The house gets in people's heads through their social-ization as children. They may come to learn that the house is part of home through their own experiences of home growing up. They may also learn this through their interactions with restrictive policies and discriminatory practices, coming to understand the association between house and home as a reinforced norm. The norm is learned by most North American children from an early age, and the process of reinforcement never fully ends.[13] For Vicky Chenowith, married mother of one, it happened all over again every time her parents dropped by:

My parents were just here on the weekend, and every time I see them, literally, there's questions about whether, when are we going to get a house: "You've got a kid now; you gotta get a house now!"

The men we talked to tended to perceive the house in similar ways as the women, though at least one contextualized his ideals in a more markedly patriarchal vision of the past. Scott Engeman came to us as a middle-aged, down-on-his-luck artist temporarily sharing a three-bedroom basement apartment with friends after moving out of his former girlfriend's small apartment. Scott described his working-class belief about what a single in-come household should entail:

Basically, bottom line, I believe that a family, with one working member making a decent income . . . should be able to afford a mod-est house. I'm not talking about a very fancy one. Very modest, you know, maybe, you know, maybe [a] nine-hundred-square-foot dwell-ing. . . . But it has to be [a] safe and, you know, healthy place to live. I really do believe in those values, and I don't believe that can happen here, or, or really anywhere now. . . . So that dream's kind of gone. Seems it's disappeared out of the '60s and the '50s. But I still believe it's important.

---

[13] See Morris, Crull, and Winter 1976.

Through cognitive habits of association the house has acquired symbolic value.[14] Many people still believe it is important.[15] It has become a means of negotiating distinction and belonging—a stage on which to display one's worth as a grown-up, a success in life, a good mother, a decent man. But hardly anyone can afford a house in Vancouver these days. Living in the area can seem unsettling whenever friends, family, or even past expectations get in the way of people's ability to perform an adequately successful self without access to a house for staging material. But does the symbolic power of the house really leave Vancouver uninhabitable for all but the ultra-rich? Or does the metropolis also support the formation of new cognitive habits and cultural associations?

A Vancouver State of Mind

Many Vancouver residents we talked to did not seem especially oppressed. Instead, they shrugged off or even actively resisted the symbolic importance of the house, forming new and different associations that drew on their material environments to stage successful performances of self. Kathy Martin and Ted Demarest lived with their daughter in a small one-bedroom apartment in Kitsilano at the time of our interview. They discussed how they received gentle reminders of their unusualness in this regard, but despite Ted's occasional anxiety about securing their future, the present did not seem to bother them much. As Kathy noted:

> I'm sure plenty of people, my parents included, think we're living with not quite enough space. Um . . . but that's ok. People can judge us. We made this decision for our family at the time, and then if they don't like it, they can make a different decision. For their own lifestyle.

Kathy and Ted cultivated a live-and-let-live attitude. Shrugging off the perceived judgments of others, they adopted the rhetoric of lifestyle. Their laid-back stance challenges the primacy of cultural norms and social sanctions in people's lives. Perhaps it is no coincidence that this fits in well with Vancouver's reputation as an alternative-lifestyle Mecca.

---

[14] See Paulsen 2013 on the ways this symbolic value is used as a sales device.

[15] When asked directly in surveys, people tend to say they would prefer to live in detached houses over other common sorts of housing (townhouse, apartment, mobile home)—80 percent in a recent U.S. survey (Belden, Russonello, and Stewart 2011). The preference may be interpretable simply as evidence that people want to be successful in life, with a house representing success as discussed here, rather than evidence that houses provide the most livable environments (e.g., Michelson 1967), though this is discussed more ahead.

Many other Vancouverites also found it relatively easy to reshape life without a house into an individualized story of success. Like Samantha Lyeung, Janice Akers-Kearney grew up in a house in Vancouver, married, and had a child. Similarly, she found herself unable to afford a house of her own as a schoolteacher, even with a second income in the household. She and her husband bought their eight-hundred-square-foot condo in trendy Kitsilano while she was pregnant, as she described it, "because we wanted to buy a place of our own, and, uh, we wanted a little bit more space for the baby." But unlike Samantha, as Janice described her career trajectory, she worked backward from her present circumstances to create a coherently successful life story.

> Well, the reason—one of the big reasons, not *the* reason, but a *big* reason—I became a teacher is because I knew I wanted to have a family, and I knew that being a teacher is conducive to that, with the hours, and also, just stable income. So it was easier to get a mortgage. It was much, much easier, in that respect, 'cause it just . . . made it . . . uh . . . made it much easier to get the mortgage for this place. Yep!

Here Janice reversed the ordering of events in time so that they seemed to vindicate her long-held expectations. Her pregnancy motivated her earlier condo purchase, which motivated her much earlier career choice and educational trajectory. But in other moments she revealed that her thoughts on what good housing looked like had actually changed quite a bit along the way:

> So I used to . . . have to have . . . I really wanted to have space, and I thought that was ideal. And now, you know, I feel really lucky to be where we are . . . to have a nice space [*cooing to baby*]. Yeah! I feel lucky. And he doesn't really care. As long as he gets a good night's sleep.

Janice was able to bend her story as needed to shape it into a success story. Either she knew what she wanted from the start, and she went out and got it, or she once wanted something different, but ended up getting lucky with how she lived now. The alpha and omega of her success story, her son, was decidedly nonjudgmental about her housing. It seemed ironic, then, that when asked directly whether she had planned ahead for her baby, Janice replied:

> JANICE: Uh, yes, I'd say so. Well, sort of half and half, but I'd say so. We, we had that in mind, yeah. And, um . . . I knew I could get maternity leave, so, yeah.

MIA: Um, and so, in that sense, if you didn't have the opportunity to take mat leave, would you not have considered having a child?

JANICE: Yeah. I would have been, yeah, a lot more careful, so we wouldn't have considered it.

Janice's son was planned for far, far in advance, yet he was also the result of a certain "half and half" carelessness with contraception that would not have occurred were Janice's maternity leave prospects less secure. All in all, Janice demonstrated a kind of individualistic, life goals–oriented flexibility in crafting a narrative of self and success that seemed quite at home amid Vancouver's yoga-centric and enlightenment-through-self-awareness culture. With that kind of room to maneuver, who needs a house?

Where Janice was able to squeeze into a successful individualized identity, and Kathy and Ted shrugged off cultural norms and social sanctions as the stuff of divergent lifestyles, Katrina Gower developed a more strikingly oppositional orientation from the vantage point of an apartment in Vancouver's West End. Katrina, a married and highly educated researcher, grew up in a house in a small town, but she did not see that arrangement as ideal for her daughter. Likewise, she responded in contrary fashion to broader suggestions that she might need a house for her family:

> I think for me, I don't . . . I don't like being . . . told what to do, you know? I like to kind of find it out for myself. And we were told a lot that we wouldn't have space, especially by family and friends who live in suburbs, or smaller cities. Um, you know, that we would need a house. That we could never do it, you know, that we could never do it without in-suite laundry, all those things. And I think that really bothered me, because, you know, I don't do suburban living! I don't think there are any benefits. You gain in space, you lose in access to people, to culture, things like that. So I was really resistant to that idea . . . telling us we needed a house. I really didn't like that. . . . You know, maybe, maybe before all [that] started, I had thought we needed a house. But the more, like, when we were actually pregnant and preparing for her, um . . . I was pretty determined to just not need more space.

Katrina had many of the same experiences as others interviewed above. Like Sadie Carter, Katrina came to understand that a house was associated with wealth and success. Of those she knew who had grown up in other types of dwellings, Katrina noted, "maybe they grew up in a small trailer, and their parents had them when they were teenagers and they went on to have kids when they were teenagers, that kind of thing." Despite, or perhaps because of learning these associations, Katrina rebelliously wanted something different for herself.

She did not seem entirely clear on where it would take her, but Katrina knew she did not want to work with the normative blueprint for a home she had been given. Vancouver's cosmopolitan air offered Katrina ready justifications ("access to people, to culture") for her rejection of the norm. Similarly, when I asked Linda Jones, a married mother of one living in a Yaletown high-rise condo, whether she felt influenced by the suburban house she grew up in, the strength of her reply took us both by surprise:

> No. No!!! . . . It really . . . [*startled laughter*] I, I, I, it didn't faze me. I don't know, I've always been drawn to urban centers . . . even though I didn't grow up in them. So, I can't say that any of the way I grew up . . . I mean, it's nostalgic, and it's nice to romanticize about it, but you know, every time I go back for a visit, after a visit I go, "Damn, I'm going home!"

Linda reacted strongly against the notion that the house of her youth should feel like home. Time spent in the suburbs left her longing for the city. Like Katrina, Linda seemed to reactively feel her way through her objections to the house. But she was also able to draw on some of the environmental discourse that made its way into Vancouver's "EcoDensity" and "Greenest City" initiatives to justify her positions. When Linda noted she would feel bad about living in a house, I asked her why, and she responded:

> I just, I don't know, I guess when you, when you're, when you live in an urban center . . . my brother lives in Edmonton. There's four of them. They have a five-thousand-square-foot house. And, you know, it's lovely, but I just, I just can't fathom that—the amount of space that they have, the amount of heat cost that they have. And it just . . . I don't know, it doesn't seem environmentally friendly, you know? I just think, you know, our society is moving away from everybody having their three-thousand-square-foot house, and now that we feel that we were being a little bit more environmentally sustainable by living in a smaller space, and especially because of the fact that we don't have to drive, and 'cause we walk to our amenities, and we like to support local amenities.

Linda remained vague on the abstract details of her environmentalism, adding frequent "I don't know" statements as she described her system of beliefs, and later clarifying, "I'm not, I'm not holding the drum for being environmentally conscious." But when she seized on the details of how her brother lived, she sharpened her critique. She was not following the more normative path that he had, and drawing on the local environmentalist ethic provided a way to explain why she felt good about it.

Both Katrina and Linda grew up exposed to the notion they should want a house, but somehow it did not take. In Linda's case, she seemed to develop a specific allergy to suburban housing. In Katrina's case, the allergy seemed more generally directed at being told what to do. Though they began as reactive rebels without causes to guide them, Vancouver provided a green and cosmopolitan explanation for why they should not want what others had.

As both a lifestyle destination associated with a vibrant historical counterculture and an urbanized gateway to a West Coast wilderness, Vancouver provides its residents ample cultural scaffolding for rebuilding the meaning of success.[16] But Vancouver serves as a gateway city in another sense as well. After all, some 40 percent of the metropolitan area's residents were born outside Canada. They and their children provide Vancouver with much of its multicultural diversity. This diversity could offer an important well of resistance to the idea that a house necessarily signifies success. But does it?

Of the immigrants and minorities we spoke to, many adopted a house as a goal. Strikingly, they often did so not as a demonstration of belonging in Canada, but as an affirmation of their distinct cultural heritage. Married suburban house dwellers Cathy Kwan and Matt Ng provided an intriguing case in point. Cathy grew up in Hong Kong, and believed her "Asian" cultural heritage came with a particular disposition "because we always thought, oh, if you have money, buy a house. Don't rent!" Cathy further rooted these cultural norms in marriage practices:

> They think that before you get married you have to buy a house. They're like, "Oh, you don't have money? Buy a house for my daughter [or] I'm not going to let her marry you!"

Matt, born in Vancouver to parents who emigrated from Hong Kong, seemed more circumspect about cultural influences as he considered various people he knew who had become house owners. He ultimately turned to a more universal logic that he thought of as particularly Asian, which he then undercut with reference to its counterpoint:

> I guess Asians probably tend to rent less, because they think the money's going into someone else's pocket, kind of thing. So . . . but then there's benefits of renting, too.

Cathy and Matt's back-and-forth illustrated something of the complexity that multiculturalism offers in disrupting or reinforcing cultural habits. Indeed, with backgrounds rooted at least in part in the high-rise metropolis of Hong Kong, where public housing accommodates at least 30 percent of

---

[16] See Lizardo and Strand 2010 on cultural scaffolding.

households, Matt and Cathy might seem well prepared to resist considering buying a house a necessary component of success.[17] But they found plenty of material within their interpretation of "Asian" culture that instead overdetermined the necessity of a house.

Cultural heritage may be interpreted in different ways, depending on context, and other migrants, including some from Hong Kong, had different stories to tell about how their culture influenced their understanding of housing.[18] The processes by which some people choose to become immigrants while others do not, or are not successful in their applications, may also play an important role in how culture comes to matter. The wealthy, educated, and highly motivated are most likely to leave their countries of origin to navigate Canada's immigration regime. They may arrive with very different orientations than most of those left behind.[19]

If some immigrants enthusiastically embraced the house as an affirming symbol of success and belonging, finding it curiously applicable to their lives across multiple cultural contexts, others remained open to trying out new ways of living. For many, that is why they came. Arriving from Russia, Lada Kurochkin moved into a two-bedroom apartment with her husband and daughter "just to see what it's like here—maybe Canada would be better for us." Lada quickly formed an impression of Vancouver corresponding to its cultural reputation: "Vancouver is just relaxed and, you know, all nature-oriented and all this stuff, so the whole feel is different." She was not sure she would stay, but she was happy trying things out—including differing housing arrangements—to see how they might fit. Regardless of culture of origin, this sort of adaptable curiosity is also a hallmark of who is likely to become an immigrant.[20]

Regardless of whether or not immigrants themselves adopt critical stances with respect to the importance of a house, their addition to the

---

[17] City of Hong Kong 2007.

[18] See, e.g., Enid Ngai's discussion of housing in Chapter 6.

[19] Cathy, for instance, grew up mostly in a house in Hong Kong that was built by a Canadian developer, and lived in a high-rise condo for only a couple of years. Of note, the CMHC (Canada Mortgage and Housing Corporation 2007) has prepared an official brochure for immigrants, titled *The Newcomer's Guide to Canadian Housing*. Ownership of a house frequently acts as a default category within the document, for instance in the note, "Apartments can be ideal for people who cannot afford a house" (p. 3). Immigrants thinking of buying are assumed to be buying a house and are given this advice: "You don't want to buy a house in a neighbourhood where house prices have been steadily falling. Nor do you want to buy in a neighbourhood where future plans will affect house prices and property taxes. Your dream home won't be much of a dream if there are plans to put a highrise next door. Contact the municipal office and ask about planning regulations and zoning bylaws in the area" (p. 27).

[20] Relatively little has been written about how immigrants relate to detached housing in modern regimes, though there is a sizable literature on immigration and home ownership. See, e.g., Haan 2005, Hiebert 2009, and Hiebert and Mendez 2008.

multicultural mix of Vancouver reinforces a local awareness of difference and interpretive possibility. Like Amanda, correcting her train of thought midstream, most Vancouverites come to recognize that there are multiple ways of living, challenging the privileging of North American lifestyles as universal living standards. Such an awareness, often achieved through travel, also brings many people to the city.

After growing up in Ontario's suburbs and exurbs, Greg and Charity Rattner took professional degrees as engineers, then traveled and lived out of their VW Bus for a while. They settled down to raise a child in an urban neighborhood of Vancouver as an extension of their search for novelty, for a broadening of their horizons. Reference to difference and multicultural awareness informed their contentment with the idea of raising their daughter in a small, one-bedroom apartment:

> CHARITY: I think, we keep reminding ourselves, there are people all
>   over the world who . . .
> GREG: Live in tight spaces.
> CHARITY: Whole families, multigenerational, in smaller spaces, and
>   they manage to do it, so we don't need more space. That's kind of
>   our mantra right now.

The Force of Habit

The house is widely recognized as an important symbol of success and belonging in North America.[21] Vancouver is unsettling because houses have moved so far out of most people's reach. But the region also provides a number of cultural scenes in which people find ample room for reinterpreting the importance of the house.[22] Its laid-back celebration of alternative lifestyles and individual enlightenment, its widespread environmental ethos and cosmopolitanism, its multicultural mish-mash and easy access to otherness—none of these are unique to Vancouver, but all enable and encourage adaptation among the locals. At the same time, they signal to malcontents and lifestyle adventurers elsewhere that they might find a home in the city.

When it comes to culture, which force wins? The force of habit by which people come to interpret the house as an important component of successful adulthood? Or the force of adaptation and curiosity, supported by Vancouver's cultural scaffolding encouraging lifestyle diversification? Building on and contributing to the suburban dread of change, media depictions suggest

---

[21] Pugh (2009) suggests that belonging is a primary motivation in the consumption process for children as well as adults.

[22] See Silver and Clark 2015 for exploratory work on scenes.

a widespread concern with residents fleeing the Vancouver metropolitan area—especially the young and families with children. Headlines declare, "High priced Vancouver losing residents" and ask, "Will young homebuyers say goodbye to Vancouver for good?"[23] But beyond the anecdotal, there is very little systematic evidence of the young, of families with children, or of anyone else taking their leave in a disproportionate fashion. All in all, many more people continue to come to Vancouver than appear to be leaving.

Even when net migration figures are broken down by age, as in Figure 5.1, there seem to be no alarming trends.[24] People of nearly all ages, including parents and their children, are still flocking to Vancouver, much as in the comparably growing metro areas of Edmonton and Toronto. On the whole, Vancouver's net migration profile between 2006 and 2011 looks very similar to that of other growing metropolitan areas, except that the elderly do not flee mild Vancouver like they do the far colder metropolis of Edmonton.

If families with children are not leaving Vancouver, then where are they living? In Figure 5.2, I draw on census data regarding the distribution by housing type of children living in family households.[25] The data come from Vancouver in 1976, Vancouver in 2006, and Canada as a whole in 2006. They demonstrate a dramatic reshuffling of children between different sorts of housing within metropolitan Vancouver, both compared to recent history and compared to the rest of Canada today. Over a period of thirty years, children in Vancouver went from being especially likely to live in houses to especially likely to live elsewhere, within a more urban alternative—mostly, but not entirely, of a low-rise variety.

Many North Americans associate the house with success. And indeed, some people, like Samantha, Marlene, Stephanie, and Scott, had not gotten over its symbolic importance when we spoke with them. As suggested by Marlene's comments about being able to afford more children elsewhere, it may be the case that Vancouver's housing situation contributes to its somewhat lower total fertility rate relative to other Canadian metropolises.[26] But

---

[23] For examples, see Mann 2012 and Lazaruk 2012; see also Bridge 2011 and Kirby 2011.

[24] Author calculations based on census data for 2006 and 2011, broken down by age. Canadian age-specific death rates for 2008 were applied to adjust for expected deaths between census periods.

[25] Statistics Canada regards family households as those containing a couple (married or cohabiting) and/or a parent and child. Here I follow children under the age of sixteen (in 1976) or fifteen (in 2006). In the 1976 census results, no distinction was made between high-rise and low-rise apartment living, and in the figure, all apartments in 1976 are grouped together as low-rise.

[26] As estimated by Milan (2011) based on 2008 data, Vancouver's Total Fertility Rate (TFR) was 1.36 relative to Canada's overall TFR of 1.68. (TFR is the expected number of children likely to be born to women across their lives based on current age-specific birth rates). See also Lauster 2010a, 2010b, and 2012.

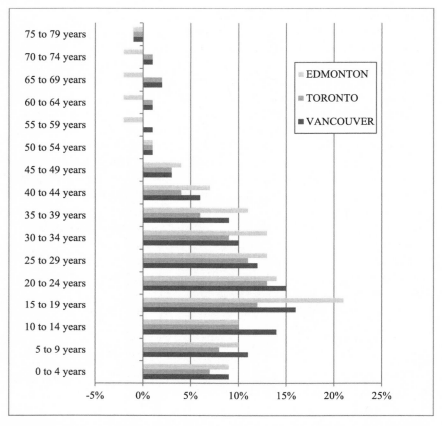

Figure 5.1 Net migration estimates for 2006–2011, by age (in 2006), for the metropolitan areas of Edmonton, Toronto, and Vancouver. (*Statistics from Canada Census data. Graphic prepared by the author.*)

on the whole families are adjusting, and Vancouver's demographics look quite similar to the rest of the country. The force of cognitive habits can make Vancouver seem uninhabitable, but only for some people, and even then maybe for only a little while. Indeed, many residents we spoke with described histories of personal transformation that mirrored the dramatic change in Vancouver's built environment.

Emma Miller, a retired public servant, was the oldest person we spoke to in our study. She had experienced a variety of different living situations as a single woman navigating her way through the latter half of the twentieth century, but grew up mostly in houses as a child. When we spoke to her, she had lived in her historic Vancouver apartment building, converted into condominiums, since the early 1990s. Asked whether her thoughts on what

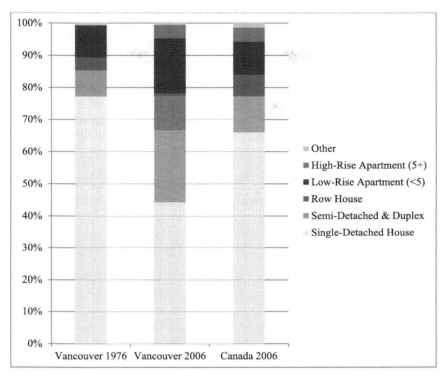

Figure 5.2 Proportion of children living in different housing types in Metro Vancouver (1976 and 2006) and across Canada as a whole (2006). (*Statistics from Canada Census data. Graphic prepared by the author.*)

constituted good housing had changed over her life's course, she noted: "I would never have bought an apartment, never in a million years, until I moved to Vancouver, and it took me about three years to go, 'Huh, I guess a house is beyond my ability.'" Now Emma found her old dream countered by her lasting contentment with her living situation:

> I sometimes think, well, maybe I will move out of Vancouver, and then I could have a house . . . but whenever I do that I think about this neighborhood and all the things I like about it, and how, how much I like the building and my apartment. And it passes for a while. [*Laughter.*]

For Emma, as for many others, satisfaction with everyday life in urban Vancouver came to trump broader cultural ideology valorizing the house. Indeed, even a few of those who managed to eke out the North American dream of buying a house in Vancouver's suburbs spoke with seeming wistfulness about more urban paths not taken. Toward the end of our interview, suburban house dweller Matt Ng expressed curiosity about how the other two-thirds of the metropolis lived:

> I'd like to know if other people, making the same money we are, think the same way we do. . . . Yeah. I want to know if they are actually happy and how they think about [living] down there. 'Cause I was wondering how it would have been if I had lived down there. Like, I can only imagine, but it's different.

Matt's wife Cathy deflected his reverie, suggesting, "You probably can't sleep 'cause it's noisy," to which Matt responded, "Well, then I'd have to find a unit that is quiet, or else [has] double windows or something!" Vancouver's many urban alternatives to the house provided shape to Matt's curiosity, enabling him to work through all sorts of ways to make them livable.

Vancouver actively draws people toward alternative lifestyles, suggesting that cognitive habits remain malleable for people. In many cases, as for Katrina and Linda, residents' habits never seem to map onto cultural norms in the first place. In other cases, living in Vancouver encourages residents to modify their cultural associations. Habits can take a long time to die, but symbols can be renegotiated. People can adapt. Metropolitan Vancouver keeps on growing as it encourages this process, leaving the house more lifestyle than living standard.

What Really Makes a Place Uninhabitable?

When I met Joanie Folsom, a gregarious single mother of a daughter with special needs, she described her desperation over finding a new place to live. She was unemployed, as she explained, due to the demands of caring for her daughter. She noted that her current apartment had mold in the walls, a relatively common problem amid Vancouver's damp climate. The mold presented a further threat to her daughter's health, but Joanie was unable to find anything else she could afford:

> Like, my daughter says to me, like, "Mom, I'm coughing all the time!" And I'm like, "I know, like . . . I have spent every day for the past two, three weeks looking at places"—in between, you know, other appointments. But I'm on Craigslist, like, all the time and [looking] at classifieds.

The mold in Joanie's walls produced an embodied response in both Joanie and her daughter. Its material presence constituted something different from a thought they could dismiss or a symbol they could negotiate away. The coughing and queasiness interrupted daily rhythms and, in so doing, made establishing a routine impossible. No old habits could be maintained, nor could any new habits be formed enabling Joanie to feel at home in such a place. She could not adapt; it is not clear that anyone could. Joanie's place seemed truly uninhabitable.

Joanie would have liked to have non-market social housing options, with rent geared to her income. However, there was not much in the way of so-cial housing located in the near suburb of Vancouver where she lived, and Joanie felt she had worked too hard to get services for her daughter within the school district there to consider leaving. These services, in turn, were what made Joanie's daughter's school life bearable, given her special needs. As Joanie frantically searched through alternatives, she described a variety of dwelling situations from her past that she had come to place off-limits as possible homes. On living with her sister:

> I wouldn't mind it, if I had the space, you know, and you know, their lifestyles were to be healthy role models for my daughter, right? You know? [But] they have been known to be alcoholics and drug addicts.

Joanie had, in fact, brought her daughter to live with her sister before, but left after she perceived the drug use to be a problem. She needed less drama. But when she left, she was forced into other circumstances that she again found unacceptable in her present search:

> [My daughter] and I had to live in a shelter. You know, because had it been me I could've lived in my van, but I wasn't prepared to do that to my daughter. She needed some sense of stability.

Absent a sense of stability, a living situation can become uninhabitable quite fast. Without some stability, it is difficult to support an everyday routine or form new habits.[27] It should come as no surprise that routines and habit formation loom especially large for parents. In Joanie's case, she needed a dwelling that served as an ally in bringing up her daughter, in stabilizing the world and making it predictably cozy.

Stabilizing the world is important for everyone. We all organize large portions of our daily lives by habit, and correspondingly we need allies able to keep things predictably in place for us. Within this context, housing acts as an agent on our behalf when it provides a material environment that

---

[27] See Logan 1988 and W. Wood and Neal 2007 on the environmental requirements for habit formation, emphasizing stability and interactive repeatability.

enables habits to form: an anchor to our interactions, carved into space over time—in other words, a home.

Home as an interactive anchor for our bodily routines is felt more than seen.[28] People interact with its material components directly, rather than at a distance. We may not even be aware of the interactions as they take place, tuning out as we engage in everyday life. Home gathers together its many interactive components and assembles them into a stable and traversable network, enabling people to move from one interaction to the next on autopilot, guided by habit. As suggested by anthropologist Mary Douglas, this sort of home must start "by bringing some space under control."[29] Good housing exerts a measure of control over some space, stabilizing it for human inhabitation.[30]

In theorizing about what home does for us, it is important to acknowledge that people do not always want to feel at home. Spending too much time amid the familiar can get boring and come to feel oppressive, especially as our everyday routines come to involve accommodating others. As Douglas notes, "The more we reflect on the tyranny of home, the less surprising it is that the young wish to be free of its scrutiny and control."[31] It is no surprise that all of us sometimes crave excitement and new experiences, and this often motivates people to move. Callista Allen, a teacher now living in a converted house in a dense urban neighborhood, described this kind of a trajectory as spurring her departure from the suburbs of her youth: "I loved it until probably I was mid-teens, and then I was thinking, you know, ok, this is a little redundant, little too small, little, you know—I wanted to experience different things."

A stabilized home motivates and enables outward exploration, constituting a haven "to which one withdraws and from which one ventures forth."[32] Each new adventure provides the possibility of outwardly expanding one's sense of home, wherever new interactions can become routinized and made comfortably familiar.[33] The excitement wears off as the interactions become

---

[28] Or, as Gillis (1996) might suggest, it is lived with rather than lived by.

[29] Douglas 1991, 289. Overall, Douglas paints a marvelous picture of home, blending the lived-in version with the ideal version, where home is really about "the realization of ideas" (p. 290). I think it worthwhile to separate these analytically, but keep in mind they tend to work together—if not in perfect communication—in practice.

[30] Bratt (2002) offers a similar emphasis on security and stability, based on a review of research literature.

[31] Douglas 1991, 287.

[32] Tuan 1971, 189.

[33] In this sense, one might also build on Interaction Ritual Theory, as propounded in particular by Randall Collins (2004). Recognizable social interactions become rituals, which produce emotional energy and solidarity. A key distinction of Collins, which I reject throughout this

domesticated, but familiarity comes to extend our home networks in new directions. We begin to feel at home doing new things.

If a sense of home can expand, it can also retract. When stressed, or overwhelmed by situations where we do not know how things work, we look to retreat to where everything comes naturally to us. In this way, emotional dynamics both lead us from and return us to home as a network of interactions, traced and retraced through time by the act of dwelling. Correspondingly, the network itself can expand, reflecting an imminently inhabitable environment. But a sense of home can also retract as conditions become less stable and predictable, as control over space erodes, reflecting an environment turned uninhabitable.

The kind of stressful events that erode people's senses of home pack a double wallop, forcing them to retreat to a safe haven made smaller by every blow. For Jackie Eberhardt, living with her boyfriend and daughter in a low-rise apartment building, this kind of event seemed to be a persistent problem.[34] The conditions within her building would not even let her make a secure routine out of doing the laundry:

> There's drug users that come in and go downstairs by the laundry room, and you know, somehow they get in, and they sit down there, and they do their drugs and stuff. And, you know, I go down to do my laundry with my daughter and . . . they're sitting down there and it's really scary. Like, I've been . . . some lady [was] sitting down there, and this is before [my daughter] was born, and she said she was going to spray me with bear mace! So, you know, luckily my landlord was in the apartment and I went and told him, and he just took water and dumped it on her, and she left! But you know, to be threatened with bear mace in my own apartment! Well, not my own apartment—my own building.

These kinds of threat to taken-for-granted routines produce existentially uninhabitable living situations. How do people respond? Some, like Joanie, start frantically looking outward for someplace new to live. But others, like Jackie, simply retreat further into what is left of the familiar. The more we spoke, the more Jackie's odd self-correction, troubling the distinction of

---

book, is that such interactions must first be social in the sense of involving other people, rather than simply involving things. An expanded definition of the social, as in actor-network theory, provides much to be gained in expanding Collins's framework to more fully incorporate interactions with nonhumans.

[34] "Boyfriend" was Jackie's term, though they had a child together and had lived with one another long enough to qualify as married under common law.

what she considered her own between building and apartment, came to seem strangely telling of this process of retraction.[35]

Despite the many problems she recounted (e.g., noisy halls, thieving neighbors), Jackie and her boyfriend had successively rented many different apartments within the same building over the years since they moved to Vancouver from small-town Ontario. Describing her current one-room apartment as too small, Jackie was looking to move again when we spoke. Her boyfriend was working a blue-collar job in a nearby municipality, and she claimed they were searching for places closer to his work, but in our conversation Jackie seemed more interested in yet another apartment opening up in her building. As she noted, somewhat unconvincingly:

> With the dog it's really tricky, and we know right now there is one next door that's open, so we're kind of going for that right now until we can find another one. . . . 'Cause we don't, we don't want to be picky, you know, we kinda just want to get in there.

The persistent paradox was that when asked about whether she could think of a worse housing situation than her current arrangement, Jackie replied, "No, I don't think so; I don't—you know, it's pretty bad." So why not move someplace else in the area? Why not move to a different building entirely? As Jackie explained, "This is just what we know; since we've been here, this is where we've been, and it's kinda, just a home, I guess, this building."

In many respects, clinging to the building seemed more like a response to feeling away from home than an indication she was already there. Jackie missed her old, familiar life in Ontario: "I want to go back home. . . . I miss my family. But [my boyfriend] wants to stay." Jackie's commitment to her boyfriend prevented her from returning to Ontario and also added a different sort of disruption to her sense of stability in British Columbia. As she described it, not so long ago, "he was drinking, and he had hit me." As a result, Jackie's boyfriend was temporarily banished from their apartment. Unfortunately, so was Jackie: in order to keep her daughter, protective services said she could not bring her "back to the danger zone" of the building.[36] So Jackie and her daughter stayed in a shelter or transitional housing for nearly three months, while her boyfriend slept in a tent in the park with their dog.[37] All the while they continued to pay rent on their apartment, and Jackie

---

[35] Many experiences related here speak to Rossi's (1980) guiding research paradigm positing that residential dissatisfaction produces mobility, but Jackie's experiences throw a wrench in the works of Rossi's and subsequent mobility models.

[36] Without revealing specifics, I ran the scenario by an official at the Ministry of Children and Family, who confirmed that this was an entirely likely outcome.

[37] Jackie noted that shelters would not take the dog.

noted that some of their former neighbors robbed the place in their absence. Ultimately they took counseling and returned to living together, and after an unexpected pregnancy, they were expecting another child in a few months.

Many of the components of Jackie's world seemed to conspire against stability. Left in her apartment, she seemed to have little control over her everyday life, and little space for home. For a time Jackie supported the family by working full-time in low-paid jobs in the service sector while her boyfriend "got lazy and stopped working." This arrangement made her happy, ironically providing the closest thing to a haven she had found in Vancouver: "I was away from everything, and I was happy to come home, and happy to come to whatever they're ready to give me." Once she was left without that kind of sanctuary—a place to which she could securely withdraw and from which she could venture forth to take on "whatever they're ready to give me"—Jackie seemed to find the thought of trying anything new more unsettling than retreating to what remained of the familiar. These remnants she both complained about and tenaciously held on to, like "her" building. Her shrinking sense of home closed down avenues of exploration, even when it came to the possibility of adapting beloved old habits into new connections to place:

> Back in Ontario we have little streams and rivers all over the place and you just go sit beside any river you want and fish for carp. I like carp and bass and stuff like that, and I'm not into salmon or trout or anything, you know? I think being in BC is a lot . . . [it] changes a lot of things, the things I can do, you know? I could just walk down any stream I wanted and fish, and now I, I don't know how to do this kind of fishing.

Home starts by bringing some space under some control. It grows by progressive outward exploration. New habits form on top of old habits, rooted to interactions made stable and grown familiar over time. We become more and more at home in the world. But as control over space is challenged, whether by mold or threat of violence, home can also retract. Interactions rooted to specific places can become less and less inhabitable.

Both Joanie and Jackie found their cheap housing uninhabitable. They responded differently to their situations—Joanie looked for an exit, while Jackie clung on all the harder. But their experiences had other characteristics, like their low income, in common. And in each case, what made their housing uninhabitable extended beyond the cognitive habits of culture and interpretation.[38] What made their housing uninhabitable had to do with

---

[38] Nevertheless, it is notable that both Jackie and Joanie articulated the cultural importance of houses too.

their embodied experiences of place and their fundamental inability to put together a safe, stable routine with them.

So is the decline of the house turning Vancouver uninhabitable for every-one but the ultra-rich? No. Most residents do not seem to need houses. Vancouver provides ample cultural scaffolding for locals to dismiss or re-interpret norms about the importance of having a house. Moreover, people keep coming to live in Vancouver. Despite widespread concern, there is no sign that young families are leaving. Instead most seem to be adapting to the options on offer.

Does this mean that *all* housing should be considered inhabitable? No. Joanie and Jackie's experiences suggest that housing can work to disrupt rather than enable and stabilize the formation of the everyday routines of home. But their experiences probably do not have much to do with Vancou-ver's relative lack of houses. Single-family houses can become infested with toxic mold, just like apartments. Living in a house might have overcome some of Jackie's barriers to feeling at home, but others seem like they would have remained firmly in place, and she could have ended up feeling even more isolated than in her apartment building.[39] More to the point, even if there were more houses in Vancouver, they would still be too expensive for Joanie or Jackie to afford.

Still, laying out examples of uninhabitable situations sets the terms for continuing the debate in two important ways. First, houses might do more for us than simply acting as stages on which to demonstrate our social worth. The material sanctuary they provide might also be important, providing more control over more space than other types of dwellings and enabling residents to feel more at home. Second, people might be flocking to Van-couver, but still never find themselves feeling at home. Rather than leaving, Vancouverites could end up clinging to their diverse buildings in an increas-ingly isolated fashion, retracting their sense of home rather than expanding it into engagement with the surrounding community.[40]

---

[39] For all the problems, Jackie expressed great fondness for and gratitude toward the landlords, and despite her mistrust, her neighbors seemed quite friendly while I visited. Indeed, a neighboring mother was just dropping by to check in on Jackie and see how she was doing as I left.

[40] Though the findings remain disputable, a survey by the Vancouver Foundation (2012) famously suggested that this pattern was a real problem for the city, and linked a lack of community connectedness to high-rise living.

WHAT DO HOUSES DO BEST?

A man's house is his castle.

—James Otis,
ARGUING BEFORE THE SUPERIOR COURT
OF MASSACHUSETTS IN 1761

Once upon a time, the British colonies of North America all relied on common law, and just a decade and a half before the American Revolution divided the United States from the fragments of Canada in the making, an advocate in a Boston lawsuit drew attention to the continuing equivalence of house and castle.[1] Evoking something vast and well protected, the castle still speaks to what the house does best. "Home starts by bringing some space under control," and relative to their denser urban alternatives, detached houses generally work to *maximize* the elements of space and control.[2] Physical form and configuration as part of a house package (providing roominess, a moat-like yard, and ownership) all work together in this regard. Does this mean houses do home best? Are they, in fact, the most inhabitable of dwellings?

Thinking specifically in terms of habit formation, the more spacious the house, the more room people have to bring home new activities and play with them, transforming them into routines. Similarly, having more space enables residents to share more easily. The more control offered by the house, the fewer interruptions people will be forced to endure in their routines, making their dwelling spaces all the more inhabitable. The more control, the greater the security that everything important will remain in place. All in

---

[1] James Otis was arguing in court against the anti-smuggling *Writs of Assistance* enabling customs officials' entry into homes. See "James Otis: Against Writs of Assistance," archived by the National Humanities Institute at http://www.nhinet.org/ccs/docs/writs.htm.

[2] Douglas 1991, 289.

all, the house package offers a firm yet expansive anchor for feeling at home. It solves important problems of everyday urban living.

So what kind of habitats are houses? In what ways do they offer something more inhabitable than alternatives? This chapter builds on Vancouverites' descriptions of everyday problems associated with city life, showing how they often look to houses as offering ready-made solutions. In so doing, the passages ahead provide a basis for understanding both why people still love the kind of space and control houses provide and how we might deal with the troublesome results.

Space for Assembling Routines

Many Vancouver residents felt crushed for space for all sorts of different reasons. A house seemed like a ready solution for this multifaceted problem. Jill Sampson spoke to us of the difficulties associated with space in her previous apartment, where she lived before moving to the roomier townhouse she came to occupy with her husband and two children, Michael and Stephen.

> We got to the point where we were having to . . . to just have enough space to live and have the space to play, well . . . obviously Michael was too little, but for Stephen to have a place to play. . . . [W]e were having to get rid of things that started to feel like necessary things, not just extraneous things. [They] were going to storage or were just getting put aside, sent to the "Sally Ann" or whatever.[3] So . . . that was sort of stressful. And I think there's this sort of stress that I feel about not having a space of my own to do hobbies or things that I enjoy doing, because just physically there's no little niche.

In this, Jill spoke to many different reasons she felt they did not have enough space in their old apartment. She began by discussing how more room was needed to assemble a "space to live" as well as a "space to play." In this, Jill explicitly connected living to space, though the manner in which her living required space went unspoken, at least temporarily. Room was required in order to assemble the actors, both human and nonhuman, needed to perform the rituals of everyday life in proper and ultimately habitual fashion. Jill also recognized that her children required space for playing, as distinct from living. In effect, as the children played, they put together all sorts of different interactions, only some of which they eventually repeated and learned from until they became habitual. Playing is part of learning how to live. It is how people come to expansively inhabit some portion of their interactions with the world around them—especially as they grow.

---

[3] "Sally Ann" is a colloquialism for the Salvation Army.

As she quickly moved past what seemed to her obvious needs for space to live and play, Jill took up the need for storage. She needed room to hold on to the "necessary things," even if she did not use them every day. Many things serve as important components of living and playing, of expanding one's interactions with the broader world over time periods extending beyond the everyday. Similarly, there were many things Jill enjoyed doing. Where to put them when they were not in use? When she had to do something else, but did not want her things disturbed? Jill expanded on this theme when asked whether she felt like she had enough room at the time of the interview, living in the new townhouse:

> No, actually, strangely, I don't! [*Laughter.*] You'd think I would. You'd think that [since] we moved, I would've gotten it! Um, we have . . . we have more space, so I'm not feeling cramped, like, I'm not feeling as though the children are on top of me all the time the way I did in the old place. But, um, I still . . . we have a very large, off of our bedroom, we have a very large walk-in closet, which, sometime—very soon!—is going to turn into sort of a closet. Without stuff in it. Except I'm going to have a sewing machine. Well, the sewing machine is in there, but I can't even get at it because it's piled up with tons of other stuff. But: sewing machine, and shelves for my wool, knitting, and that . . . that kind of stuff. So, although I don't sew or knit terribly frequently, at least I will have a sense of a place that I could go where . . . my projects can sit, uninterrupted, in the weeks that intervene between the start and the finish of the projects.

Most of us have projects of some sort or another, and it often takes space to keep them going, especially to be able to pick them up where we last left them. Projects and play offer means of exploration and outward expansion. Home is the place from which we venture forth. Having space enables people to keep many of their adventures easily accessible, making the world both more inhabitable and more readily contained.

How does work relate to home? Whether or not it is treated as an adventure, work often defines the biggest of our projects. Correspondingly, bringing work home has become part of how people assemble their lives into inhabitable routines. No surprise, then, that having an office was frequently mentioned as a reason people wanted more room. Tina Tremaine, an athletic expecting mother living with her husband in an apartment on Vancouver's West Side, wished for office space, noting:

> I find that I have stuff everywhere right now. And you know, trying to go through my paper work, and I always have papers. We don't really have a proper office, so . . . there's always stuff on our dining

table, so we always end up in the living area, eating off our laps, watching TV or something, right? When we never sit down and eat . . . uh, together.

Having space for an office, where she could maintain an assembly of papers unmolested, was important for keeping Tina's projects separate from where she and her husband did their living. Without that space, the dining table became colonized by paperwork, making it impossible to put together a dinner ritual in the way Tina wanted. She continued discussing how she and her husband used to use their den as an office, but were transforming it into a nursery. Tina, who traveled via wheelchair, commented that these transformations were taking a toll on her mobility.

> Um . . . also, I find that for me, uh, you know, we have a den in there, which is where we had the office, which worked well, but I also have some workout equipment that I can't set up in the house now, because you know, there's absolutely no way I would be able, even able to get into a room . . . with that in there. Even in the spare room. So . . . yeah. It's . . . just, uh . . . [it] would be nice to be able to move around a little bit better. Less furniture, less stuff.

More room provides for fewer conflicts: between the assemblies we put together for everyday inhabitance and those we maintain for longer term use and play, between mobility and office space, between our own projects and those of the others we share our lives with. As Tina continued talking about how a house might solve problems for her, the prospect of needing space to accommodate others while still preserving space for herself came to the fore:

> I think if you were to talk to [my husband], you know, one of the reasons why he would like to be in a house is because he would love to be able to work from home and have, like, a, you know, a garage or a studio wherever that he could work. I would also, you know, I like to design clothes, so I would like to, you know, be able to have sort of my own craft area that I could design and [use to] work with people. So you take that outside of your family area. And yeah, so I—we—definitely don't have that here, for sure. So I think it would definitely be great for both of us. I mean, it would be great if we could both stay at home, and, you know, have equal amounts of time with our kids, right? But still, you know, have your own thing going on, that, so you don't lose yourself. Which I think is important when you become a family.

Space to Share

How to construct an integrated family without losing yourself? Tina's ideal tiny household democracy would preserve space for each. Similarly, most of the discussions about why people felt they needed more room in and around Vancouver concerned, in some way, the preservation of space for living with—and apart from—others.

Other people's things were often a major issue. When my research assistant spoke to Scott Engeman, he was a single and unemployed musician living on the south side of the city. He began sharing a basement apartment there with friends, a single mother and her daughter, after breaking up with his ex-partner. He discussed how space constraints in his ex's apartment contributed to the breakup:

> My ex-partner and I dealt with living in, it was a 462-square-foot apartment. It was very small. It was one bedroom. My musical equipment was strewn out in the living room so it made it very . . . um . . . it led to a certain amount of tension between us. It, I definitely wouldn't say that it caused the breakup, but it was definitely a factor, absolutely.

Scott's description of the otherwise amicable breakup was corroborated by his former partner, who also agreed to be part of our study (Scott learned about it from her). As she noted of her space: "It was definitely not comfortable for two people. For me it's adequate." Lack of space makes it difficult to share by constraining residents' ability to assemble and maintain both solo activities and couple activities. Speaking to the latter, Shivani Ryan, a married mother of one living on the East Side of Vancouver, praised the space she had obtained in her new house relative to her former apartment, especially in the kitchen:

> If you have a bit more space you can cook in the kitchen together, which is kind of nice. [In] our old apartment the kitchen was kind of small, so really only one person could be in there at a time, and, um, yeah. My husband and I both like to cook, so being able to cook together in the kitchen is probably important. The kitchen was the first room we renovated in the house!

A house made living together seem easier.[4] Roomier dwellings accommodate not just more stuff but also more people, providing them space they can

---

[4] Spurred by Calhoun's (1962) early research on rats, there is an extensive and surprisingly inconclusive literature on the effects of residential crowding on stress and social pathology (Lauster and Tester 2010; Myers, Baer, and Choi 1996). If there are any overall effects, they seem small (Baldassare 1978; Booth and Edwards 1976; Booth, Johnson, and Edwards 1980).

inhabit jointly as well as separately. Division into private and public spaces within a dwelling mirrors broader divisions into private and public spaces across larger polities. More space enables less fraught negotiation over the shared governance of daily life. Put differently, people need space to assemble both their things and their loved ones into their networks of inhabitance, making of them a home.

Accommodation of loved ones often extends beyond household members. People felt they needed room to bring over and assemble larger networks of people, including both family and friends. In this sense, people need room to play with their networks of people, just as they need room to play with their networks of things. As Kathy Martin and Ted Demarest noted, their lack of space created a real constraint on their social life:

> We have some friends who have some very large homes that they live in and entertain in, so we spend more time at their houses than they . . . We rarely invite people over to ours because we only, we have the four seats, so we could invite two people over for dinner at a time. But, um . . . we can't have twenty people over for a party like other people can.

Similarly, Karen and Gary Shen, a highly educated couple with a child living in a two-bedroom condo, noted how their family lived relatively far away, commenting that it would be nice to have room for them to stay when they visited. Gary expanded on this theme, referring to a culturally informed philosophy of hospitality—that they would like to have room for anyone to stay with them if need be:

> It's kind of important for us to have, like—we've always been kind of working with the philosophy that we'd always like to have an extra room for someone. So whenever anyone comes into town, they can stay with us. No problem.

As people described their needs and desires for more room, they often spoke to how space structured their activities, including the social nature of those activities. For most people, home meant sharing at least some portion of their space at least some of the time. Household members made everyday claims, but friends and family could also lay some claim to space, though often at lengthier and more irregular intervals. Overlapping claims to space speak to the complicated social ties people navigate in opening and closing their homes to inhabitance by others. But despite the various negotiations over how much space partners and other intimates, family members, and visiting friends might need, the most common concerns over space inevitably arose from the accommodation of children.

Space for Children

If adults can negotiate over how much room they need to maintain a role within each other's lives, children occupy space in a different way. There are no clear guidelines for how much space either adults or children need. But unlike adults, children are not always considered capable of advocating on their own behalf (though in fact, past a certain age, they often advocate quite loudly). They have a special status as household citizens. Though they do not get a full vote in many matters, they are often placed at the very center of how households organize everyday life. The parents we spoke with usually ordered their household space around their children, extending to regularly negotiating with themselves on a child's behalf. As Vicky Chenowith noted of her newborn daughter:

> She comes with a lot of stuff. You need to get rid of furniture and things for her, and I sold a lot of stuff on Craigslist.

To Vicky, it just seemed natural that her daughter came with stuff—as if it magically appeared alongside her. She portrayed her daughter's needs as self-evident and indisputable. But it is clear that Vicky herself was the one sorting through what these needs were. She later continued this theme. Even though her daughter was not yet crawling, Vicky felt the baby had already transformed how she and her husband could use their space:

> If you have a kid, you're not going to have the house the way that it used to be. You know, we didn't used to have all these toys around. We used to have, you know, more furniture, and we used to have an office in there. So you have to be really flexible with your space, and [when you have] something that totally transforms [it, like kids, you have to be] patient with them, as they ruin your house too, probably, right?

In part because infants cannot really negotiate on their own behalf, prospective parents are tasked with preparing room for a new occupant without fully understanding what their child will want or need. The task is filled with uncertainty. In many ways, giving birth to the child only embodies that uncertainty, rather than ending it, since parental interactions with children continue to change and develop over time. In many cases, drawing on cultural prescriptions—"You've got a kid now; you gotta get a house now!"—can help assuage parental fears.[5] But when parents find these prescriptions unattainable or otherwise reject being told what to do, they find themselves in

---

[5] See Vicky quoting her parents in Chapter 5.

uncharted territory, trying to work things out and negotiate directly with their housing, their partners, and their ever-changing children.

Negotiations do not always arrive at satisfactory solutions. At three years old, Jackie Eberhardt's daughter was older than Vicky's. This meant a new set of concerns associated with her daughter's mobility and emotional demands as well as her need for sleep. Jackie was sharing the bedroom with her daughter, while her boyfriend slept on the couch due to his early work schedule. As she noted:

> JACKIE: He wants to come back to the bedroom, but . . . he won't. You know, I don't mind getting up first thing in the morning, doesn't bother me. But he doesn't want to wake [our daughter] up first thing in the morning. [With a two-bedroom apartment] she'll have her own bedroom, so we can do that, and . . . so hopefully we can become more of a family again. Because it's kind of being, you know, being in such a short, small area, we kind of separated as a family, doing what families do, and kind of just going our own ways . . .
>
> NATHAN: So that's really interesting. So . . . having a smaller space has made you actually separate as a family?
>
> JACKIE: Yeah. It has. And you know, we're kinda at each other's necks sometimes, and . . . I, I don't like it, having to go to the bathroom, obviously she knows how to open the door so I have to lock it, so she can't come in and bother me if I need a time-out myself. I put myself in quite a few time-outs, instead of her. I feel I'm the one that needs a time-out, not her! [*Laughter.*] So yeah, definitely, it's pulled us apart instead of bringing us together more.

More room—specifically another bedroom—would have reduced the need for Jackie's partner to sleep on the couch.[6] It might also have reduced the degree to which Jackie felt everyone was "at each other's necks." As I discuss ahead, some people actually described smaller spaces as drawing them closer together with their family members. In Jackie's case, she clearly felt that the small size of her space drew her apart from her daughter, as well as from her daughter's father. There was not enough space to distinguish together activities from apart activities. Another relevant aspect of Jackie's account was that her daughter's needs were given priority, once again, by both Jackie and her boyfriend. Indeed, Jackie imposed time-outs on herself

---

[6] However, a different interpretation from Jackie's account here might emphasize her acknowledgment of the boyfriend's history of violence as a possible factor in his couch-sleeping arrangement.

on her daughter's behalf, reinforcing her daughter's role as at least an equal claimant on household space.

As children age and enter school, they are exposed to new environments. Housing heavily conditions these environments. Parents often make moves based on school districts, though likely less so in Vancouver than in many U.S. cities.[7] Nevertheless, school districts still made a difference to people across Metro Vancouver, as in Joanie's case, when she had worked too hard to get her daughter's needs met in a particular school district to consider leaving for another one where decent housing might be easier to come by. Schools also introduce children to peer socialization. In addition to worries about settling children in good schools, Marlene, a divorced mother missing her small-town upbringing, expressed concerns about ensuring adequate space for her primary-school-age son to maintain a social life.

> I had a townhouse and it was probably about seven hundred square feet, and it wasn't large enough for [my son] to bring his friends over. It wasn't, uh, large enough for him to, uh, stretch out really, so yeah. It needs to be big enough to have friends over, it needs to be big enough for them to play activities, um, yeah. It needs to be, uh . . . I think that's about the main—those two things. That would be good.

It is worth noting, especially given Marlene's previously discussed sensitivity to cultural ideas about what constitutes good housing, that her demand for space may have been as rooted in her concern that her son not be exposed to mockery or pity, as in the more vague idea he might need room to stretch out. She certainly would not want any of his friends to worry that he was not getting enough to eat—as Sadie, for instance, might have assumed during her childhood. Indeed, Marlene seemed quick to follow up with precisely this sort of judgment, noting that it "seems inhumane to raise a child in nine hundred square feet."

Figuring out how to make a home for children is especially fraught with cultural baggage. Habits of mind associate children with houses, reinforcing ideas about their needs. Yet parents may come to the same conclusions just by watching their children play. They need more space for that game, more space to run around! Ultimately, culturally negotiated meanings and everyday interactions with place influence one another. The spaciousness of houses seems like an obvious solution to the need for room to accommodate children. A house could provide space for children's things, for play, for a

---

[7] The Vancouver School Board maintains catchment areas for schools, but also enables parents to move their children freely between schools as long as spaces remain available.

friend-filled social life, and for an escape when needed. Crucially, it could also help assure parents that they are doing everything right.

Control over Sensory Disruptions

Sharing space with others means disruptions are a constant threat. Keeping things in their proper places does not mean we can enjoy them whenever we want. Sensory disruptions can scatter one's ability to inhabit place, to flow seamlessly from one interaction to the next. Noise can prevent people from feeling at home. Bigger spaces, especially those with the possibility of closing off one space from another, can prevent co-residents from getting noisily on each other's nerves. For Mark Patterson this was an important issue as he described his negotiations with his girlfriend over how much space they would need in order to move in together:

> MARK: We, in discussing this, we, uh, determined that having the ability to close doors and isolate ourselves from each other within the same, within our living premises was a really important feature. We can't do that in my place. That's the single biggest problem.
>
> NATHAN: That is really interesting. So, um, why, if I can ask, is that so important?
>
> MARK: Um, on a practical level, we both work in types of work that require us to work from home. So in a very practical sense, having a quiet space that's free from the other person just allows us to do work. Um, further, or sorry, beyond that, um, personality-wise, the two of us very much like our own space, and . . . [pause] part of our compatibility or why we work as a couple has to do with how at peace we can be with each other when we're not actually interacting in the same room, but we're present in the same room. Uh, so it's related to that. It kind of goes hand in hand with that, just that, you know, if I want to watch TV or . . . listen to music or something like that, she's not subjected to that, and vice versa.

As with space, children have a special relationship to noise. Indeed, they were often described as both especially sensitive to noise and especially likely to produce noise. Their sleep is easily disturbed, and they can also disturb the sleep of others, including both parents and one another. As the mother of one, contemplating having an additional child, Shivani Ryan reflected on noise as a reason why she felt each child would need their own room:

> I think there's so much disruption with having a newborn that you don't want to totally throw off your eldest child. Already, their life has been turned upside down by this new arrival. Then if they can't sleep

through the night, they get cranky, and [*laughter*], so yeah. Having, I think, children with their own bedrooms is easier. I mean, you can have a baby in your room probably, for the first four or five months, or whatever. But my husband's a light sleeper, so having a baby in the room just didn't go over so well. . . . I didn't know that little bodies could snore! It's like, "How come you're snoring?!" [*Laughter.*]

Like many people we spoke with, Shivani noted that noise was also "the biggest reason" they moved from their previous apartment to their current house. As it turns out, noise travels—not just within a housing unit but also between housing units. The design and materials of a building can contribute to a lack of control over noise between units. Walls both conduct sound and often prevent people from exercising control over the noisiness of their neighbors. As Shivani noted of her former apartment:

It was just one of those live/work spaces, so it was really loud and echoey, 'cause a lot of, you know, hard surfaces . . . and the, the people who lived beside us did coke all night long. Had parties. So it was a little hard listening to that, night after night after night after night.

Houses, unlike apartments, typically install multiple walls and a buffer of air—usually attached to a yard—between housing units. As a result, house dwellers should generally be exposed to less noise from neighbors. This potentially makes houses seem like better homes, both for those especially sensitive to noise and those especially likely to produce it. Annabel Marks, a teacher married to a musician, felt displaced by noise on both fronts. As she noted, "Because of my husband's job, we could be considered noisy people." She and her husband attempted to audition for landlords and neighbors, in order to ensure amicable relationships. In a previous basement apartment, this worked out well for a while. Given the noisy proclivities of their landlords above, they thought "it would balance out." Unfortunately, when their landlords told them they were going to have another child, Annabel felt the noise from upstairs would be too great. As she noted:

ANNABEL: The second baby was going to be sleeping in the master bedroom with the parents, which was directly over our bedroom, and I was not getting up at four-o'-clock feedings for a baby that wasn't mine . . . [*Laughter.*]

NATHAN: [*Laughter.*] . . . You moved preemptively, or that was after the . . . ?

ANNABEL: We moved preemptively. . . . I just sort of felt like, you know, I mean, infants are infants. There's no reasoning with

them. There's nothing else you can do. . . . I just didn't . . . you
know, we're not kid people; we don't plan on having kids.

Arriving at her current basement apartment, Annabel and her husband once
again offered to audition for the landlord above, but were turned down. Her
landlord suggested there was no need:

> He said he didn't really have a problem with it. Single guy, working
> in the film industry—wasn't a big deal. It's a big deal now, though,
> 'cause now he's engaged and the new fiancée, she can't stand it! So
> this is the whole reason we're moving. It's because now, three years
> in, he wants to change the spirit of the agreement. And it's frustrat-
> ing for us, because we were clear, and open, and honest about it, and I
> recognize his situation has changed, but you know, ours is the same,
> and, uh, with him now wanting to change.

With the change in her neighbor's situation, Annabel felt increasingly unwel-
come in her own apartment. As she described it, "I don't feel comfortable in
the house, I try to get out of the house as much as possible right now, even
though there's, you know, nothing going on." Annabel was looking for a new
place, where the noise issues would not be a problem. While a detached house
seemed like an obvious solution, she, like many Vancouver residents, was
frustrated by how financially out of reach it seemed for her:

> If we could get a detached property, um, I'd absolutely do it. And I've
> talked to people who own their own homes, and oh my god! Own-
> ing's such a pain, because you have to repair everything yourself.
> And there's all these things that go wrong with houses, stuff like
> that. And I think, if you had, like, a standard family with standard
> jobs, that's probably really true, you know, not having to worry about
> needing to call somebody, or whatever. . . . But for us, because of the
> special needs that we have, kind of regarding autonomy . . . we'd be
> better off having our own space. And I think it's kind of ironic, in
> the way, you know, society's set up: the people who don't really need
> the gigantic houses get them, and the people who need them, you
> know, we're deprived, we're unacceptable! You know, because we're
> going to "make all that noise, blah blah blah." So it makes more sense
> to shove us into our own place, and be like, "Stay over there and leave
> the rest of us alone." You know . . . we have no chance of pulling that
> off. And, you know, I don't see that changing.

Annabel notably rejected the normative idea that a house was for everyone—
strikingly, she saw owning a house for a "standard family with standard

jobs" as more of a chore than an aspiration. Nevertheless, Annabel was willing to take on all the things that could "go wrong with houses" in exchange for the solution they seemed to offer to her immediate noise problems. Even though she did not see a house as part of an important cultural norm she needed to fulfill, Annabel still found herself drawn to the house as a solution to the everyday problems of not feeling at home. Not surprisingly, many parents described feeling the same way about their noise issues, and correspondingly also felt drawn to living in houses. For instance, Kathy Martin, living in a low-rise, noted:

> Nobody's bedroom borders on our apartment, which was fortunate, and that was part of our decision to stay here, knowing that we wouldn't be hopefully too much of a "wake people up constantly" [kind of neighbor]. . . . And he actually sleeps really well, and he doesn't cry for very much when he's awake at night. So we were a bit nervous that we would cause people grief by there being a screaming baby and we'd be like *those* people in an apartment, whereas—in a townhouse, the same thing could happen—but in a detached house you would be less likely to hear a baby crying next door.

Like Annabel, Kathy wanted to be a good neighbor. But given her son's potential noisiness, she needed good housing to make it work. It is worth noting that noise is not the only sort of sensory disruption urbanites experience. Exposure to other sorts of activities also disrupted people's daily ability to feel at home. Smell, in particular, travels both within and between housing units. It also wafts up from intersections, bearing air pollution into homes. Janine Harmon, a single mother trained as a lawyer and living in a one-bedroom apartment in Vancouver, made the case for air pollution as a housing concern. She put this in the broader context of her growing awareness of environmental health issues and her concern over her newborn baby's health. If she were to move, she noted,

> I'd also be thinking about how close I am to any major intersections, in terms of particulates in the air. Near any industry [too]. Especially with the baby now, and, you know, his developing respiratory system, I'd be worried about asthma.

Due to their location in the denser parts of cities, often near "major intersections," and industries, multiunit buildings are regularly more exposed to noxious pollutants that might seep in from outside. Zoning intentionally spared single-family residential areas from such threats, in many cases by using apartment zoning as a buffer.[8] But Janine did not stop here; she moved immediately from air pollution to smoking:

> And smokers. I mean, I just can't stand it. . . . Oh, the guy downstairs was a smoker too![9] And so I was really concerned about my baby breathing in. Because you know now, like, [smoke] comes through cracks, and electrical outlets, it seeps through into other units, right? I think they've pretty much proven that. Umm, so, uh, I would not live anywhere near a smoker.

It is no surprise that many people felt smoking was a major problem. A variety simply found themselves disgusted by the smell of neighboring smokers. Others, like Janine, couched their concerns in the language of health risks. Broadly, we may speak of all sorts of things that "seep through" as sensory disruptions. Those living in multiunit buildings, located closer to historically noxious areas, and sharing walls, floors, or ceilings with neighbors seem especially susceptible to this kind of seepage.

Control over Intrusions

Sensory disruptions represent a challenge to dwelling, a threat to one's control over space made tenuous by urban proximity. A more immediate threat in many cases is that one's control over space will not be recognized or respected by others at all. Jackie's discovery of an intruder in her building's laundry room provided a poignant example of this. But a variety of other people also described break-ins as a problem for them.

My research assistant spoke to Christina Chu, a married mother of one living in a small condo building and working for a technology company. Christina noted her concerns about break-ins in her neighborhood: "We've had break-ins at the neighbors', [but] we've been lucky so far, being on the ground floor is always . . . [it provides] opportunities for break-ins." Asked to describe a neighborhood that would feel safer from such problems, Christina described one containing neighbors who were "quiet people with, uh, with people that are sort of in the same economic background as we are, and . . . where space generally is not a major issue, so there's no crowding." Asked to expand on what made living among people of the same economic background feel safer, Christina worked through an explanation:

---

[8] To compound matters, Valverde (2012) observes that city officials and judges tend to use less stringent metrics in determining how much noise constitutes a nuisance in apartment-dominated neighborhoods.

[9] "The guy downstairs" was a neighbor she had earlier described as especially loud and rude about displaying his bad taste in music to the building.

> People are not, then, if they're sitting in the same . . . or better, I guess. Same or better . . . um . . . they're able, more capable of affording, they don't have to resort to other means of getting resources to meet their needs, in a sense. So if they have the same—we're pretty comfortable—and if others around us are the same or better, it's, uh . . . I don't have to worry about my cars getting broken into, or my house getting broken into. Although, yes, other people can travel into the area to do break-ins, but they don't live there.

For Christina, the proximity of poverty seemed like a clear and present threat to control over her space. By contrast, living around those of "same or better" economic background provided a sense of safety. Despite their ground-floor accessibility, houses usually provide for neighborhood homogeneity, making them seem like ready solutions to the problem of intrusions. Similarly, the normative feel of houses provides some assurance that one's neighbors, in keeping with social norms, are likely to remain predictable in their behavior. In marked contrast to Jackie's experiences, Christina spoke to how the *fear* of intrusions may be felt even without the experience. Christina's comments lend some support to those critics of zoning who suggest it operates primarily as a tool to promote social exclusion.[10] It is particularly easy to imagine her speaking out against the densification of her neighborhood out of a concern over break-ins. Leila Ferreira, a married mother of two, tied a similar concern with social exclusion to her thirteen-year-old son's well-being. In this, her sense of control over space was tied to her control over her son's interactions with others. She described wanting to stay on the West Side of Vancouver because of who he was likely to encounter during and after school.

> Wherever you are, there's always different people, but I feel like for me, if he's around . . . um . . . you know, people that are a little bit on the wealthier side, he might be a bit easier growing up, just for, you know, the friends he hangs around with, and there's a lot of parents that I guess are on the East Side that aren't home as much, and, you know, their kids do their own thing. Whereas the kids here, they have a nanny, you know, on the West Side, if their parents aren't home, there's a nanny.

Though Leila lived in a townhouse complex along an arterial, she was surrounded by a single-family-zoned neighborhood on the West Side. She thought the relative wealth of the West Side brought more parental

---

[10] See, e.g., Babcock 1966, Perin 1977, G. Power 1989, Sewell 1994, Shlay 1984, and Shlay and Rossi 1981.

supervision of children, even if only via paid surrogates. When I asked her whether her impressions about the East Side came from personal experience, she demurred: "When I'm watching the news, I just see more trouble on the East Side—I don't usually hear about any of it being over this way." Living on the East Side, house dweller Shivani Ryan offered a more localized view. She described her neighborhood as "gentrifying" (a plus in her book) and divided into pockets: "You can have a bad pocket right beside a good pocket, and then go back to bad." Asked what distinguished good pockets from bad, she offered an uncertain but intriguing answer:

> I don't know. I don't know if it's the, you know, amount of apartments relative to houses, you know? So if the area is more transient . . . ?

Shivani had a notion, even if only partially developed, that houses came with stable neighbors, and stability created good places to live. Asked to define what made bad pockets bad, Shivani referred back to the potential for intrusions: "A lot more break-and-enters—there's, you know, visible drug trade, prostitution." Notably, concerns about intrusions into private space bled into concerns about public morality. As respect for law was reimposed on a neighborhood, it became a better place to live. Shivani relayed a friend's pet theory of how this might guide smart real estate investment:

> You just follow the hookers. [*Laughter.*] . . . 'Cause wherever they used to be, then you know, if you can buy just as they're getting kicked out, then things will improve in the real estate quite quickly. [*Laughter.*]

Getting the law on your side can help establish stability within neighborhoods, imposing rules over the respectable use of both public and private space. Shivani knew she would end up on the right side of these rules, while local street prostitutes would not. In practice, this sort of mobilization has led to quick profits for some and tragic results for others. Evidence suggests that Vancouver's various crackdowns on "hookers" have driven sex workers toward riskier and riskier situations, linked to a string of subsequent murders and disappearances.[11]

Officially, control over public space is maintained primarily by city bylaws. Control over private space is recorded through legal categories of property ownership and governed, as well, by rental contracts. Street prostitution and break-ins represent obvious violations of these forms of control. But as noted in the work of social scientists like geographer Nick Blomley, control over space in Vancouver and elsewhere remains fundamentally unsettled

---

[11] Ross 2010.

and contested.[12] This goes all the way back to the competing claims at the heart of Simon Fraser's early tussles with the First Nations communities located in and around Vancouver. The varying cultural claims people make to control over territory do not always match their colonially imposed legal claims, and even the legal claims leave considerable room for ambiguity. Detached houses, especially when owner-occupied, may be appealing in part because they *seem* to offer more solidity with regard to competing claims over control than are available via other housing situations. Indeed, the way houses crowd out more public and contested spaces and exclude the poor may still be viewed as a plus by many residents.

Control over Boundaries

Once people establish shared residence, their overlapping claims to space do not tend to be recognized in much of a legal fashion. Household governance remains messy. This can create friction between household members, including both family members and housemates with less clearly institutionalized relationships to one another. Marta Perez, a Latina immigrant to Vancouver, was a single mother of one at the time of our interview. She worked in a design consulting capacity and also took in student boarders ("homestays") at her rented house in an upscale Vancouver neighborhood. In addition to the boarders, she shared the house with another single mother, with whom she split the rent. Marta described living with the students as easier than sharing her space with another parent:

> That is . . . there has been some challenge, sometimes, yes. Yep. Sometimes because there is two different families and when there's small children. You want certain things, and their things are different. So there has been some challenges in that part. I don't think, like, the homestays have been a challenge. But more of a challenge has been sharing with somebody else.

Marta's relationships with her homestays, usually foreign students paying for room and board while they attended local English classes, were contractually bound. Her relationship with her roommate, while it began quite cordially, was not so well defined, and had soured over their time together. Marta described several problem spots in their relationship, including "the kitchen, because it's like, we don't have a lot of place for storage and then sometimes, things are missing," and her roommate's children, "because they throw things on the floor everywhere, don't pick up—leave it there, then [I] have to clean up, or [I] get in trouble for cleaning up." In this sense, Marta's

---

[12] Blomley 2004.

problems with her roommate were readily linked to the ways the roommate and her children interrupted Marta's everyday inhabitance of their kitchen and their shared living space. Marta described her attempts to fix the situation by, for instance, disciplining her roommate's children, as getting her "in trouble."

Many people we talked with had lived with roommates at one point or another. They often felt they aged out of these situations—with aging linked to the acquisition of new, more intimate ties. Callista Allen and her husband shared their house with roommates for many years. But then Callista became pregnant, and the roommates moved out. As Callista noted, this avoided the awkwardness she would have felt had they stayed:

> Just with family time, and running around, and you know, the middle of the night too, just—and with nursing her, and that, you know, privacy, physically I guess. Um, yeah. I can't imagine having had the roommates here and . . . like, it just felt good . . . when she came along, to have the space, just with her, you know? . . . Yeah. And just time to spend together, as a family, without constant, like, other guests, I guess, you know?

For a time, Callista and her husband served as both landlords and roommates, which was not especially unusual as a situation described within our interviews. The informal means by which they both maintained and relaxed boundaries with their roommate/tenants presented a potential problem for them as they transitioned to parenthood—a problem solved by what seemed to Callista to be a natural drifting away of former roommates at the onset of pregnancy.

Callista and her husband still maintained a tenant in a separate apartment downstairs. But he too was a friend, leading to continuously negotiated boundaries. As Callista noted, "Once all our roommates left, we kind of gained a little bit more privacy, but our tenant downstairs always, like, it's almost as if he lived up here with us in a way, so . . . sometimes that's not as private as I would like it to be, maybe." In this sense, landlord-tenant relationships, where a tenant has a nominally distinct housing unit, are not necessarily so different from landlord-roommate relationships when landlords and roommates live within the same building. Even when legal contracts are spelled out, the lack of well-defined boundaries can create a sense of intrusiveness.

Of course, from the tenant side, many people also found their landlord neighbors quite intrusive. Before moving to their current apartment, Greg and Charity Rattner lived in a basement suite, with their landlord above. They ultimately found this situation so problematic that it led to a reactive move to their current residence, a purpose-built rental building where the landlord remained off-site. Describing their former troubles, they noted:

> CHARITY: Every time we'd go out, all of our windows faced another garden, and they were kind of raised basement windows, so every time they were in their garden, they were right next to you in the living room, that sort of thing, right next to you in the kitchen.
> GREG: Like, we could reach out and touch them.
> CHARITY: Yeah. It was very awkward, very close. And every time you'd walk out, they would start talking with us, and you could never get away, they were just . . . [*chuckle*] It was horrible. That's why we left, actually, it was [a] total lack of privacy. He'd come over for a glass of wine, and never leave, and . . . he wanted to get away from his two kids upstairs.

Charity's interpretation that their landlord just wanted to get away from his own children speaks to the fluidity of household boundaries and how they relate to where people feel most at home. Roommates, tenants, family members: the categories do not always correspond to where people spend their time, but many people still use them as normative guidelines. For Greg and Charity, at least, their landlord was an unwanted addition to their home—an intrusion. Yet their interpretation of his motivations for regularly visiting them rested on his desire to escape his children, who clearly left him feeling displaced from his own living quarters. Detached houses help solidify the otherwise fluid boundaries between households, for better or for worse.

Some of the discomfort associated with boundary violation may arise from the work people do to establish household governance along justly democratic lines. Many people we spoke with seemed to want something close to egalitarianism within the household—even between parents and children.[13] Correspondingly, people actively worked to reduce the appearance of power imbalances between household intimates. Landlord/tenant relationships could easily disrupt this dynamic, as could the introduction of other legal claims. Even when residents were unlikely to directly encounter those making competing claims to control over their space, the presence of a legal claim itself represented a sort of intrusion to internal household governance that many resented. Jill Sampson put this, perhaps, the most directly. She noted of her strata council:

---

[13] Of course, the desire for egalitarianism does not necessarily lead to equity in household labor. Instead "myths" tend to develop to preserve at least the image of equity (Hochschild and Machung 1989).

They actually dictate what color the umbrellas can be on your porch. Not that I'm inclined to be buying, you know, super wazoo-colored . . . um . . . umbrellas! But there's something about someone telling me that I'm not allowed to that brings out a desire for hot pink umbrellas on the porch [*laughter*].

Janice Akers-Kearney similarly described her dislike of living in a condominium building, with policies governing the use of space set and enforced by a council. In her case, she noted the difference in lifestyle between her family and the typical council member. She made the case that such differences left the building governed in a manner that disrupted her family's daily flow of activities. As she noted:

So . . . [one] example is we have a parking spot, but we're not allowed to put a bike in our parking spot . . . which doesn't really make sense in today's environmentally friendly world. They want us to keep the bike in the bike room, which may seem you know, logical, but it's another room to have to get into, and for [my husband] it's like, another lock he has to open. And it costs a bit more money, so, like, why can't we just keep it in the parking spot? And why can't we just keep it on the patio? 'Cause they don't think it looks very nice on the patio! . . . So I guess, some of the rules . . . make it difficult [for] transportation via bikes and it's just . . . another thing you have to think about. Like, you know, if you have your own house . . . you can, pretty much, do whatever you want. I mean, you have to follow the city's rules and keep your yard neat and orderly and things like that, but yeah. Sometimes the rules don't seem logical, and overstep . . . [into] normal family [life]. . . . And they give certain people too much power, and other people not enough.

Ironically, though houses are normally associated with cars, in this case Janice saw a house as more readily enabling her partner to use his "environmentally friendly" bike to get around. While it might seem a small thing to open an extra door, Janice described her strata rules as interfering with her husband's ability to set up a problem-free network of inhabitance involving his bicycle. Such inconveniences come to matter—especially when they serve to remind people of the intrusiveness of others and their own lack of control. They challenge how lines of authority within a "normal family" should be distributed. For Janice, ownership of a house offered potential refuge from the intrusions associated with competing claims of control over space.

Like many others, Janice noted that ownership still meant adhering to municipal regulations. In other words, there is no pure form of control over space on offer. But even if it all is illusory, the house as a package still seems to maximize the control available to the household it contains, cutting off the external claims of landlords and strata councils. Relatively speaking, even duplexes add more complications. As considered by Karen and Gary Shen, negotiations with the "co-owner" of a duplex could be even more fraught than with a strata council. Asked what they might consider a housing nightmare, they suggested:

> KAREN: Being stuck in a duplex with, like, a neighbor that you can [GARY: Oh yeah]—a co-owner, not a neighbor, that you couldn't work with, live with. Um . . .
>
> GARY: That's one of the problems in this area, too, is there are so many duplexes going [in]. And, well, it can be a great arrangement if you've got a great co-owner. A nice thing [for us in our strata] is there's safety in numbers. One person can't really influence that much here. And duplexes around here are $800,000 to $1.2 million, and that's a lot of money to be sharing property, and then have stupid neighbor issues. . . . [W]hen they smoke, there's nothing you can do about it!

Because of their size, houses seem to offer a reduction in the degree that intimates living within the same household need to negotiate with one another in order to feel at home. Because of their greater detachment from other dwellings, houses also seem to offer a reduction in the degree residents need to negotiate with non-intimates in order to feel at home. Houses overlap most with ownership, and the form of ownership provided by the house seems to offer the greatest degree of independence from the whims of others. Stephanie Bryson, who experienced growing up in an adults-only apartment building and bouncing between parents, also found herself shuffled between landlords who sold their properties while she was renting, effectively terminating her tenancy. Reflecting on her lack of control relative to intimates and non-intimates alike, Stephanie noted:

> I think that's partly why I'd like a home. No one can kick you out if you own a home. That's your home, you know? Uh, I think I like the idea of a house over an apartment in that, you know, if the house burns down you've got the land. You can build another house, you know, even if it's a shack, it's yours! . . . And that may go back to having been moving between parents as a child. I just like the idea of having a home base that's yours, and no one can kick you out of it.

Having seldom lived in a house, Stephanie nevertheless concurred with many other interviewees in defining home and house interchangeably. In this she saw having a house as a solution to a persistent problem in her life—the threat of being intrusively kicked out, dislodged, cut adrift. Houses seemed to many to provide additional barriers to intrusion, both through their physical separation from their surroundings and through their frequent association with a particularly independent form of home ownership. Jackie Eberhardt, who seemed to have the most experience with intrusions, also put this most succinctly. She described her ideal living situation as "even just a small little house, where you have your own yard, you know, you take care of your own place, it's your own private place and nobody's allowed to come in there and bother you."

Control over Space Outside

Many people, like Jackie, considered the yard an additional barrier to intrusion. Similarly, yards provided greater control over noise, and extra space for people to spread out their networks of inhabitance. Yards, as part of the house package, enable and extend the ways in which houses already provide solutions for common problems people experience in making themselves at home in the city. Yet yards are also different kinds of spaces from those enclosed within walls, floors, and ceilings. Yards provide access to the outside. They enable different sorts of networks of interaction to be established and brought home. As a result, the people who spoke with us often experienced the absence of a yard as a distinct sort of problem. For Stephanie, living in an apartment in the West End, the lack of a yard challenged her understanding of who she was and how she wanted to make herself at home:

> STEPHANIE: I think of myself as a bit of a, oh you know, just kind of a[n] earthy type of person. I don't know if . . . I'm a Taurus, it's my birth sign. They're supposed to be quite earthy, and so I like gardening and stuff like that. And so I've always wanted to do that, but I've never had the space for it.
> NATHAN: Right. And the balcony gardening . . . ?
> STEPHANIE: I've tried that a few times, but it doesn't work very well. In little pots, things don't do that well. So I can, I can grow a few things, but it's not quite a garden.

Gardening represented a fundamental way Stephanie wanted to expand her sense of home. But the assembly of pots she placed on her balcony refused to cooperate. Unless she dramatically limited her ambitions to the few things she could raise in pots, Stephanie needed access to a patch of ground in order to garden.

Many other people quite explicitly included pets as members of their families and homes. As tenants and strata members they frequently ran into problems with pet restrictions. Cats, at least, tended to be stealthy pets. For those with dogs, the most visible and audible of pets, multiunit buildings—both rental and strata-governed—were more overtly hostile. Ariel Koljevic lived, during our interview, in a rented apartment with pet restrictions. She identified her desire to add a dog to her home as the biggest reason she was looking to move:

> What's motivated me to start looking into places, is, um, I'd like to be responsible for [a] dog. I'd like to have that responsibility of taking care of another human—not human being—but living being. Um . . . yeah. I think it has a huge impact, because it's my motivator.

Despite the noted importance of pets to many interviewees, and the way they often transcend the boundaries placed around what we consider "human," few researchers have studied their role in establishing people's sense of home.[14] They occupy, in some respects, yet another source of agency that might tie people to houses, and especially to their yards. Yards provide room for dogs. Yards enable the home networks of people and dogs to coexist and support one another with only limited imposition or interference. Shivani Ryan, who already lived in a house, offered perhaps the most explicit connection between her yard and her dog:

> Say we had to sell our house and move back to an apartment: I think that would be really hard for us. 'Cause . . . you see, when you have a house and a yard, you can just let your dog out. And you don't have to get dressed, and come do that last pee of the night, you know?

Shivani was very clear that she never would have brought a dog to live with her family in their old place, where they did not have a yard. Now that she had a dog, Shivani's attachment to the dog meant she did not feel she could easily readjust to life without a yard. Interestingly, and as was true for many people, the ways Shivani talked about her dog sometimes mirrored the ways she talked about her child:

> And in terms of just having the outdoors right there, I mean, I love being able to just hop outside and throw my son on a blanket in the front yard! And I can putt around in the garden and [all] that. So I find, you know, that brings a lot of relaxation. So not having your own green space would be hard.

Yards provide people access to the outdoors—a space qualitatively different from indoors. And the convenience people attached to a yard had real

---

[14] This seems to be changing; see, e.g., Haraway 2003 and E. Power 2012.

implications for their ability to feel at home. They could spend more time enacting the sorts of activities that made them feel relaxed, many of which they could perform only in a yard, and less time preparing for the more involved excursions that might be required to visit the outdoors someplace else. Samantha Lyeung, married mother of one, expressed her longing for a yard in similar terms:

> We found that it was important to have some outside space to let a child run around. And . . . we could go to the park, but I mean, it's so much easier if you just step outside right into your backyard. And let them loose for, you know, an hour. But it's such a production, you know? You have to get the child dressed, you have to put them in a stroller, and then you have to walk to a park which is not necessarily going to be close by. Or else you have to bundle them and put them into a car . . . so [I] kinda wanted . . . an accessible, ready space just outside the door.

Here, too, a yard was viewed as providing important and ready access to the outside. The "production" required for excursions farther away was deemed prohibitive for many people's routines. Still, all kinds of people felt that being outdoors was an important part of childhood. Former Hong Kong resident Enid Ngai linked direct access to the "ground" to children's development, noting, "Your creativity [comes] from . . . when you're young, your tactile experience." Sandy Harris, from the United Kingdom, similarly suggested that the outdoors provided important pedagogical benefits: "I think it's really, really important . . . for play, and just to learn about the outside as well." Others, like committed urbanist Linda Jones, believed that "children should have unstructured play, and time for where they're just them"—something, she thought, a yard might help provide. Unlike everyone else just mentioned, Annabel Marks had decided she was never going to have any children of her own. Nevertheless, evoking many parents' darkest fears, she articulated perhaps most forcefully parents' interests in finding a yard:

> Kids need that safe space to run around. And again, when I was growing up, my parents had no qualms about saying, "Go with your sister to the park." . . . These days, correctly or incorrectly, there's certainly the perception that you can't leave the kids alone for a second because they're going to get abducted. . . . And so, you know, you don't see kids in parks by themselves anymore. So if the only place your kid is safe is in your own backyard, then we better make sure all the kids have backyards.

A yard provides a safe form of access to the outside. In this sense, it offers a place to play, to try out new activities, to mess around, that still seems safe from intrusion. Condo dweller Gary Shen brought together both kinds of special household members as he summarized the importance of a yard, noting: "You just need an easy way to get outside—a safe area—[where] the dog and kid can run around, without the dog needing to be on a leash." Yards replace leashes, for both dogs and children.

As revealed in the previous chapter, the house has become an important symbol across North America, signifying the good life to many people. But it is also more than that. Detached houses offer more control over more space of more types than other forms of housing do. They provide more space for living, for playing, for working, and for storing, enabling people to protect their variously assembled projects. They offer more space for sharing, and more space for children, making it easier to negotiate over living space with intimates. They offer space indoors and out, providing access to pets, to gardens, and to the assorted backyard encounters of childhood. They offer more control over noise, offer healthier and sweeter-smelling air, work against the fear of intrusion, and better patrol the boundaries governing day-to-day interaction. In many respects, they make it easier for household members to feel that they are governing themselves in a democratic and just fashion without interference from the outside world. In short, as solutions to the problems of everyday livability in the city, houses have much to offer.

In the terms of inhabitability, the house provides on multiple fronts. It blends seamlessly with most North Americans' cognitive habits, making it easy for people to view themselves as successes, both at parenting and at life. Moreover, it provides imminently inhabitable grounds by offering stability for an expansive and diverse set of everyday routines. Both cognitive and material habits work together in enabling people to feel at home within houses. Providing more space for children to play both encourages them to develop and stabilize new routines and enables parents to feel like they are doing the job of parenting right.

But are houses really the only inhabitable form of dwelling? In comparison with alternatives, the house tends toward maximum control over maximum space. If these are the foundations of inhabitability—indeed, of home—then there seems to be little contest: detached houses offer the *most* inhabitable dwelling environments. But this logic is open to two lines of attack. First, even if houses are the *most* inhabitable form of dwelling, other types of dwellings may suffice for the making of home. Why install a maximizing lifestyle as a minimum living standard? Second, it is worth emphasizing the tentative aspects of the Douglas dictum: "Home *starts* by bringing *some* space under control." Focusing on the starting conditions of home, attention turns toward the process of outward expansion, rather than consolidation of maximum control over maximum space. One's housing can serve as a launching point for making home, rather than a neatly demarcated end point.

By enabling a firm anchor to home, houses could encourage outward exploration and broader social engagement. But it is far from clear that they do so.[15] Instead, single-family detached houses encourage residents to devote their attentions inward. By history and by design, more control over more space implies fewer distractions from and negotiations with other claimants on one's territory. The "single-family" portion of "single-family houses" comes to define and bind the ultimate ties of obligation. The desirability of the house suggests that one attractive solution to the persistent problem of how we should govern living together is to detach from the body politic, retracting our circles of engagement to people we think we will be able to agree with. "A man's house is his castle": though the feudal politics of castle life may have evolved in a more egalitarian fashion within the house, they have done so only by favoring the tiny yet spacious democracies inside the walls over the big and crowded ones beyond.[16]

And what of the house's socially exclusionary nature? Many people continue to view exclusion of the poor as a potential plus, preferring to be surrounded by the "same or better." But this leaves the poor—and cities as a whole—worse off. This is not to suggest that all people are drawn to houses for exclusionary or antisocial reasons. Quite the opposite: many are drawn toward houses to make their social lives easier and more inhabitable, to bring them home. But the spaciousness of houses, combined with the lack of surrounding spaces for shared sociability, leads to less outwardly engaged and more overtly enclosed social habits. The same is true of people's material activities. House habitat encourages people to bring their diverse projects home, enabling habits associated with private consumption while discouraging those more associated with public settings.

It does not have to be this way. In the next chapter, I look into different kinds of urban habitat. As it turns out, they have a lot to offer. Ultimately, it takes more than a house to make a home. For many people, it takes a city.

---

[15] A survey by the Vancouver Foundation (2012) on community connectedness found that people living in single-family detached houses were more likely to know and trust their neighbors than high-rise dwellers, a finding that occasioned some discussion in the City. However, the methods of the study seem questionable, and low-rise dwellings were often ignored, as in a follow-up "A Closer Look" report.

[16] See Fuller et al. 1996 for a discussion of experiences of crowding and inequality within the home.

AT HOME IN THE CITY

> For a long time we have made a sort of fetich of the house,
> and have come to believe that a man has a sense of being at home
> only when he is within four walls standing alone upon one piece of
> ground. In reality, the idea of a home reaches back so much further
> than the four walls, and is so much more deeply implanted in the
> human breast than the ownership of land that we do not need
> to fear that a new type of house will destroy it.
>
> —JANE ADDAMS, *The Housing Problem in Chicago*

The "four walls" of the house "standing alone upon one piece of ground" work to maximize control over a maximum amount of space. In so doing, houses make space eminently inhabitable. But they also cause trouble. Addams, an early North American urbanist, demonstrated admirable foresight in critiquing her contemporaries' fetishes. But it was not enough to stop them from unfolding the house into law. From there the house took over the continent.

Whereas the previous chapter took seriously the idea that houses might provide the best of homes, here I provide alternative evidence. Returning to the trouble caused by houses ultimately provides grounds for revisiting the range of social problems catalogued in Chapter 2. But there the primary metaphor for the house was as an invasive species. Here I consider the house as habitat. I demonstrate how the challenges created by the house—in destroying local and global ecosystems and fostering auto-dependence, in displacing urbanity and fostering inequality, in harming democracy and reinforcing unhealthy habits—all translate into everyday life as challenges to livability.

Many Vancouverites drew out unflattering themes concerning the maintenance needs of houses, the boredom they produced, the rigidity with which they reinforced habits, and the isolation they caused. These themes illustrate the ambivalence people often feel about houses: they make the best of homes; they make the worst of homes. More to the point, describing the unflattering aspects of houses enabled people to speak to all the things they loved about living in diverse urban alternatives. Most Vancouverites found city living quite inhabitable. And their locations outside the house habitat kept them more connected.

Katrina's View

Living in Vancouver's dense West End neighborhood, Katrina helped to establish the foundations of an integrated and grounded critique of the house through her description of making her home in the city. Her thoughts and experiences tied together many common themes. A married and highly educated mother of a newborn, Katrina actively resisted the cultural pull of the house. Her rebellion began over the idea that she would need more space for her daughter:

> So . . . that's really, like, I don't know what my expectations were so much as what . . . my intentions were. Like, I was not going to let this change our lifestyle a lot. And I wanted [my daughter] to have access to [urban] things, so . . . you know, and since we've had her, I guess . . . I'm surprised at how little space she really does need! You know, I had hoped that, as I said, I had hoped that we were right. I hoped that we didn't need that house, I hoped that we were resisting for a reason, and then now since we've had her, I'm kind of realizing that there's something to that. We didn't need to have space! We didn't need those things! So maybe my thoughts have changed . . . or they've just, uh . . . yeah. Maybe I had different—let me put it a different way. Maybe I had doubts, without realizing I had doubts, and now I realize that it's true: it's silly to need all that stuff!

Strikingly, Katrina was not even certain at first *why* she was rebelling. She hoped there was a reason for it beyond her stubbornness. After it all worked out for the best, she seemed to be in the process of building a theory: why did she rebel, and why did it work out so well? This reflexive theory building, grounded in the data of her personal experiences, might have extended from Katrina's training in the sciences. Regardless of its origins, it provided a useful window into the materials Vancouver residents draw on in assembling homes.

Speaking to why things worked out so well, Katrina gave a lot of credit to her daughter, whom she described as "very quiet, very easygoing." She noted that her daughter's temperament seemed to match well with living in the city: "There's people going around, and action, and she seems pretty happy to just hang out and watch people." Her daughter's contentment countered the prominent idea that urban environments might be bad for children. Just as Jane Jacobs famously suggested that people generally enjoy watching street life, children—even infants—may enjoy it as well.[1] What of making room for

---

[1] See Jacobs 1961.

children and their things? Asked if she felt she had enough room, Katrina responded:

> Yes. Believe it or not, yes! We were told we wouldn't. . . . She sleeps in our room. We have a little sidecar that's attached to the side of the bed. You know, we keep the toys to a minimum. We've asked for no big toys, and, like, all those, all the things that kind of take up the house. We've been pretty strict about not letting those things come into the house. Parents, our parents want to buy them all! And give us the Fisher-Price battery-operated whatever, and we've taken them back in some cases and just said "no," upfront. And for that reason . . . we haven't felt like we've outgrown our house. But she's not walking yet! . . . [S]he's not really even crawling yet!

Katrina remained opened to revising her assessment of whether or not they had enough room. Nevertheless, she and her husband had worked hard to ensure that their daughter's stock of toys remained manageable within their apartment. This meant, in many cases, saying "no" to parents and taking back toys that were deemed too large. Discipline of this sort is morally fraught, and could well cause stress within extended families. But having a small apartment can actually enable greater control over the intrusions associated with gifting practices. Parents are forced to actually govern, but are also provided a ready rationale for saying "no" that they may not possess when they live in a house.

Overall, Katrina thought of her urban home as anchoring a more expansive and exploratory form of dwelling. For her, such dwelling enabled progressive inhabitance of the world. She came to think of houses, by contrast, as promoting greater insularity, and reducing the size of the communities their residents inhabited. As a high-achieving professional, Katrina placed this assessment in the context of her experiences reading through and evaluating the scholarship applications of children on the verge of young adulthood:

> You know, in the city, you have a lot more access to, just, opportunities. I'm sitting on a scholarship committee . . . and we have to pick basically the best of the best high school kids. This was a couple of years ago, and I mean, these kids were fantastic! You know they were, these were the volunteers who were, like, straight-A students, who'd done all sorts of charitable work, and extracurricular activities, and one person jokingly said, "They're already geniuses!" You know, like, they were just fantastic kids. But . . . what would happen, what they would say to us was, you have to look at where they're from. Because if they're from a rural community, they won't have near the things

they have if they're from the city. I mean, and I think that was a really great way of, um . . . showing the difference between the rural and the urban setting. And so for me, an urban house, like, you can live in a city and still live in a suburb, and that's how you get these suburbs. [But] you know, the bigger the houses get, the smaller your communities tend to get, in my opinion. Whereas, um . . . the more you get into the actual city, the bigger the communities get.

Katrina herself grew up in a house in a small town. Asked whether or not her interest in developing an expanded community for her daughter stemmed from her own experiences, Katrina agreed. She wished she had been exposed to more diversity as a child. She noted that she learned about social class, but little else that made people different:

In the city you start throwing in things like . . . the effects of ethnicity and background . . . whether your parents were born in Canada versus whether they immigrated. . . . You have access to people who are gay or transgendered. You have access to . . . people who are poor because of mental illness, not poor because their parents grew up in a trailer so they grew up in a trailer, you know? I think that there's . . . —hopefully by seeing diversity—a better appreciation where you're lucky and where you're not . . . [e]specially if you're born with money or something like that, you know? That's maybe the worst situation: where you're born with extreme privilege but you don't have encounters regularly where you're made aware of the privilege. . . . That's a big part of it, for why [we're in] the city and probably why we're in a smaller space too . . . to hopefully have them . . . exposed to that. It might be very idealistic, but that's kind of where we're at now.

In this, Katrina's version of home emphasized exposure as a means of growth. She saw the city as a relatively safe space for exploration, both for herself and for her daughter—as well as for the next one she and her husband planned on having. Asked about whether or not the kids would need their own bedrooms eventually, she noted, "No, I think . . . kids can share a bedroom—it's fine." Pressed to further consider if it would matter if she had a son, she expanded on this theme, drawing from her experience growing up with differently gendered twins for siblings. She said of her mother, "One of the biggest regrets of her life was that she listened to people that said that twins shouldn't—boy and girl—shouldn't share a room." Her siblings "were always touching" growing up, but eventually grew more distant. Katrina's mother wished she had done more to keep them closer. As a result, Katrina saw no reason to separate kids by gender, "not until there's an obvious need to separate them: they want extra privacy or something, you know?"

Asked to articulate how she thought housing related to her ability to be a good parent, Katrina at first demurred, returning to the theme of how she did not want to judge—or be judged by—any abstract standards of parenting. Then she returned more forcefully to the theme of experience—and of teaching her children, by providing them with both intimacy and independent experiences, how to live with one another and, more broadly, with the world around them:

> I think it's important to have close proximity. You want to have a certain amount of privacy, um . . . but it goes back to this issue of independence . . . and visibility. On the one hand, you're all together. You're living together, and you're having to learn how to interact with one another. And work out difficulties and whatnot. And I think it's hard. When you're a teenager and there's all the hormones and the things you don't know how . . . to deal with and, you know, you're learning how to make decisions [with] repercussions and stuff like that. I think it's important to be around people that can support you. [But] it's just as important to be independent and you learn that independence, you know? . . . This whole issue [of] that eleven-year-old in New York who took the subway and the mom was labeled the worst mother ever—I think that's really important that you have access to staying on your own! And . . . when they're at a certain age, they take the bus somewhere and they can do that by themselves—in the protection of the big city. You know, I think the big city offers, there's a lot of people around. If they get lost, there's always someone around them.

In this, Katrina described providing her children a secure base for exploration. But her home base differed markedly from that provided by the heavy anchor of the house. The intimacy of living together in a little apartment assured Katrina that her children would always feel supported, and would come to understand how to inhabit a small, shared space. Being in the heart of the city assured her that her children would never want for the chance to explore and to develop their independence. Katrina explicitly referenced, in the "worst mother ever" anecdote, the story of "free-range kid" advocate Lenore Skenazy, who gained fame after writing about letting her child (age nine rather than eleven) ride the subway home alone in New York City. Skenazy turned the story into a media career, promoting the idea that parents need to let their children freely explore their worlds without all of the fear entailed in the worldview described so well by Annabel Marks in the previous chapter. Like Ms. Skenazy, Katrina wanted her children to both explore and learn to feel at home in the broader, shared world outside their secure apartment. Underscoring the distinctiveness of this approach to parenting, Katrina described her worst nightmare:

> A big, suburban house, I think that's my biggest fear. A minivan household, you know? I . . . don't want to have the room where kids are separate from their families . . . and where, you know, parents are watching TV in separate locations. And where I have to drive my kids everywhere . . . where they can't do anything by themselves. . . . I have to take them swimming and take them to dance, and all these things. . . . That's probably my biggest fear, that we're going to some-how end up in . . . in a house. Too much space!

Katrina saw the house as a horror show. She worried about all the space dissolving the solidarity of her family life. She worried about leaving her children unprepared for engaging with the wide world outside. She worried she would be left doing all the work of driving her children to various iso-lated activities. She worried about the habits she would fall into. The house as habitat did not appeal.

Through building a theory for why she did not want a house and why she thought city living had worked out so well for her so far, Katrina offered a window into the process of adaptation. As her experiences flashed by, she assembled them into an integrated defense of living in a compact urban dwelling. We are able to witness the emergence of a coherent alternative to the house habitat, and it seems both warmer and more welcoming. It looks like a home.

Still, Katrina's version of home was only one of many assembled by Van-couverites. Many others shared some of her experiences and concerns, but often in different combinations. Correspondingly, there is no single way that people think about living in the city and occupying denser forms of hous-ing. Where the house offers a relatively homogenized package, its alterna-tives provide diversity. Collectively they suggest there are many ways to put together a home.

I cannot address all the different paths by which people have constructed homes from the diverse materials of Vancouver's urban habitat. But I can draw from the places where their experiences and pointed observations over-lap to offer a common set of critiques of the house as habitat. These critiques relate mostly to the maintenance work, boringness, rigidity, and isolation people often associated with houses.

Maintenance

Allison Smith, in her early twenties, was the youngest person we talked to who actually owned her own place. She grew up in a townhouse with a single mother. She more or less inherited the townhouse after her mother's untimely death, but lived there for only two years before selling it and buying a much smaller apartment. As she described it, the townhouse was just too much space:

> Having the right amount of space is, like, really big in, like, housing decisions. 'Cause, like, my townhouse was just too big, you know? Like, I couldn't keep it clean, I was afraid of the basement, there were spiders. Like . . . it was just so much space, and I didn't need so much space. And now that I'm in a place that's, like, the right amount of space for me, it's just so much easier. I don't mind, like, keeping it tidy. I don't mind cleaning. It's like, it's cozy; it's my space.

Allison declared she would want something bigger again if she formed a family, but for the time being she seemed quite attached to her apartment for being just the right size, "'cause my place is nice, like, it's perfect for me." By contrast, her old townhouse was too cavernous and frightening to maintain. Like Allison, Kathy Martin and Ted Demarest described their continuing experiment—living in a one-bedroom rental apartment with their newborn—in similar terms. It was working for them, as Kathy noted, at least for the time being:

> For us right now, we love living in the location where transit is great, where the shops are nearby, where there's, like—we can walk to the library, we can walk to the . . . movie theatres nearby, and all of those sorts of things . . . and there are some things that are less important to us. We have never felt the need for a lot of space, um, or a backyard or any of those sorts of things. And we still aren't at the point where we're thinking that that will be a priority.

In fact, for Kathy, as for Allison, keeping more space under more control seemed more like a burden than a route to feeling truly at home. Neither Kathy nor Allison described feeling the strong aversion for house living that Katrina seemed to feel. Nevertheless, they felt more at home in urban alternatives. For Kathy this feeling of being at home without a house actually seemed to provide more time for family life:

> I'm not opposed to buying a house, but we . . . always sort of drive through neighborhoods on a Saturday morning and see people out, mowing their lawn. I've always sort of thought, "Oh, look at those poor suckers," right? We're on our way to go do something nice that's just what we want to do, and those people are having to mow their lawn!? And some people love mowing their lawn and . . . we have

friends who love fixing up their place, right? Love doing drywall-
ing and are so impressed with themselves 'cause they've figured out
plumbing for the toilet, and gardening and stuff. My mom loves gardening. She's a teacher and she spends her whole summer gardening,
and hours in her garden. She doesn't see that as a chore. It's what
relaxes her. . . . But neither of us are really into that sort of thing,
right? Like, we are not really into gardening or fixing things up, and
we'd rather be doing other things with our weekends and evenings,
especially now that we have a family.

As a new parent, Kathy did not want to spend all of her time looking after a
house with a yard. Even though her mother enjoyed gardening, Kathy also
expressed amazement at the maintenance required for all of the extra room
inside her parents' house. She seemed especially amazed that "they've got a
whole kind of room that's known as the Cat's Room because all that's really
there is the cat's litter box."

Echoing his wife's opinions, Ted volunteered that several of their friends
had houses that just seemed too large. Nevertheless, he still thought a yard
might be nice, especially for kids to play in. Kathy countered with a story
about friends of theirs who lived in the suburbs, with a huge yard. When Ted
complimented them on it, Kathy said, their friend responded: "Yeah, well . . .
the kids never play out here." All the work in creating a beautiful yard seemed
to go to waste, according to Kathy, following the prevailing attitude of "Don't
let your kids play outside, you know, without adult supervision!"

The work of maintaining a house and yard takes time. But the commute
involved often takes even longer. Nathalie Langdon grew up in a detached
house in the suburbs outside London, England. Asked whether or not this
influenced her thoughts about housing now, she immediately turned to a
description of her father's daily commute: "I just saw my dad commuting for
all those hours, and just being really miserable and it just seemed like such a
drain on his energy, and just seemed to age him and I just, he just hated it!"
Nathalie continued her train of thought by following another family member: "Then my eldest brother . . . he was working in London and doing the
same commute, and I saw what it was doing to him, and I just kind of went,
I'm not doing that with my life."

Nathalie described trying out alternatives until her last big move: "When
I came to Vancouver I realized this is a great place, because you can afford
to have a good quality of life and live in the city." Though she found herself
shuffled between homes for a couple of years as various landlords sold their
properties while she was renting an apartment within them, she eventually
found refuge for herself, her husband, and her child within a purpose-built
rental building just across False Creek from downtown: "This is much more
my style of living."

Many people described similar orientations toward minimizing their commute, not least Jason Laserre, whose quotes in opening this book also evoked his father's misery. Jill Sampson took these concerns full-circle, imagining everything her two children stood to lose from the longer commute to school that might be necessitated by a move to the suburbs.

> I don't like the idea, you know, of the kids being in the car for an hour a day. Like, it's just . . . and part of it, I have to say, I grew up in a really small village in Ontario, and . . . you know, we drove the car on the weekends to go into town. And so—we walked absolutely everywhere—so for me that's a big part of what makes a childhood, and that's part of how I believe people connect with their community. I don't think you can connect to your community if you're in a car, and . . . anyway. Yeah. That's not my philosophy about housing, it's more how I feel about being in a car all day.

Though Jill attempted to distinguish her feelings about cars from her philosophy about housing, it was not at all clear the difference mattered, as she quickly clarified: "Well they are, yeah, no, I think they really are connected, yeah!" By definition, homogenous residential neighborhoods tend not to be located near work, and in many cases they are not located near desirable schools, either. As Katrina noted, they are also typically far from everyday shopping and all the places kids might want to go. In this sense, the maintenance involved in keeping up the house package extends from the material upkeep of the massive structure itself, inside and out, to the yard and to the location. Time spent commuting, driving to shopping, and driving kids around should be added to time spent cleaning, mowing, gardening, and repairing as part of maintaining the suburban dream. Altogether, there is a great deal of home-making labor that goes into keeping a house as home.

Unlike Katrina and most of our other interviewees, Dina Warner held to quite traditional views of motherhood. "I'm very, very old-fashioned," she noted, following up with "I personally feel that, that society in all would be better if, you know, if kids were raised by one of their parents." She made it clear that she wanted to be that parent. In terms of housework, Dina described a textbook split: "I just do the inside stuff, and my husband does the outside stuff."[2] Overall, Dina held it important not to complain about work of any sort. A devout convert to Islam, she generally saw contentment with her lot as part of her religion.

Dina was the mother of both an infant and a teenage daughter. She had raised her older daughter largely on her own in a dense part of Toronto after

---

[2] Hochschild and Machung (1989) describe a similarly gendered and ultimately unequal split in housework as commonplace.

divorcing her first husband. Recently she had remarried to a man working on the West Coast, the father of her younger daughter. For complicated
job-related reasons, they were not yet able to live together, so she and her
daughters had moved to a rental suite in a subdivided house within a gated
suburban community south of Vancouver. Her landlords were also Muslim,
and she had found the suite through her mosque. She was happy to move
into what she saw as a quiet suburb, but also very happy about the small size
of her two-bedroom apartment. Dina noted:

> I personally grew up in a large home, and, uh, I don't really like large
> homes. I like having, you know—being able to hear if the baby . . .
> or if there's any—even if she's on the phone . . . [*nodding to teenage
> daughter*] I can pretty much hear everything.

Small size enabled easy surveillance. Perhaps unsurprisingly, Dina's teenage daughter, who remained present during the interview and occasionally
offered comments, seemed somewhat less thrilled with the recent move.
Nodding again to her daughter, Dina suggested: "This one, she's wanting to
move back to Toronto to be back with her friends—so *that* we'll see." When I
asked how long until her daughter graduated, making such a move possible,
Dina replied, "Two years—she knows how many days if you ask her." Her
daughter smiled and nodded enthusiastically. Continuing the theme of surveillance, Dina returned the conversation to the house where she grew up:

> Growing up, it was great. But . . . as a mother, I would prefer a small
> area. When you're kids, of course, you want to do anything you want
> and your parents can't hear you and things. But [it's a] completely
> different concept when you're a parent yourself!

Maintaining a house takes a lot of work, but many people assume they will
get something in return. As in the previous chapter, it seems that having a
house should make maintaining a home easier. For Dina, part of the work
of maintaining home was keeping a close watch on her daughters' activities. Leila Ferreira, who described concerns over the possible range of her
thirteen-year-old son's unsupervised interactions in Chapter 6, felt the same
way. Though, like Dina, she enjoyed living in an exclusive neighborhood, she
also liked the more confined space of her townhouse. As she noted: "We'd
probably be farther apart if we had a couple of floors in a house, 'cause, you
know, the kids would be on a different floor, whatever, [but] here, we're in
these close quarters, you know, we have to talk." Having a large house makes
it harder to keep tabs on the kids.

Of course it is also true that people enlist many allies in maintaining
both house and home. Far fewer house owners keep servants than in the

past, though many still outsource cleaning and lawn care. As Leila noted, nannies remain quite popular agents of surveillance for privileged parents with children. More strikingly, a variety of nonhuman allies have been put to work supporting the house package. Cars help get people to and from their suburban environs, while lawnmowers and vacuum cleaners take on cleanup duty. Baby monitors and web-cameras keep watch over far-flung rooms. Vast flows of energy engage with various appliances to keep the interiors of houses readily inhabitable and at constant temperatures. This is what makes the house such an energy hog. Similarly, the many "wasted hours" spent commuting contribute directly to the steady warming of the planet.[3] What is striking here is that despite all the assistance people have gathered, maintaining detached houses remains quite work intensive. Houses ask much of their keepers. Some balk, some rebel, some learn to their growing delight that there are different ways of making themselves at home and seldom look back.

Boredom

Though they ask much, detached houses offer a form of control that holds the promise of few intrusions. In many respects, houses offer ideal spaces for inhabitance. Residents can do the same things, over and over, until they form secure and comfortable habits—until they need not think through their actions. Theoretically, house dwellers need experience relatively few disruptions as they carry out their days. The routines enabled by houses mean people can come to feel very much at home within them. They also mean people can grow very, very bored.

By contrast, the disruptions of urban life mean residents often need not leave their apartments to experience novelty. Living in an older high-rise in Vancouver's West End, Kassy Aldridge provided insight into how an obvious-seeming drawback of her apartment could also become a source of its appeal. In effect, she came to appreciate the intrusions from next door.

> I mean, the soundproofing is not the best. It's great between the floors, it's not so great between the suites. Like, you can hear through the walls, kind of thing. So if people are playing their music too loud, um, that can be problematic. I'm really fortunate that I'm bounded on both sides by fantastic neighbors. One of them plays cello, or violin. So—and she is a symphony player! So it's like having the CBC [Canadian Broadcasting Corporation] on the other side of my wall. No complaints. It's fantastic!

---

[3] See Jason Laserre's comments in the introductory chapter.

Of course, not every apartment dweller will be blessed with a concert cellist as a neighbor. Nor would everyone find it a blessing to live next to a musician, as discussed in the previous chapter. But in Kassy's case, her neighbor's sonic intrusions became an ideal part of her home—beyond her control, but in a beautiful sort of way that both took her outside her own little world and ultimately enlarged it. Kassy often mentioned this sort of back-and-forth wonder about her apartment and its urban location. It provided her both a sense of familiarity and sense of exciting novelty right around the corner:

> I can walk to the end of my street and there are probably, at a minimum, thirty ethnic restaurants within three minutes of my front door. I overlook the ocean. . . . Access to transportation, to work, it's so central. It doesn't matter where I go, I'm in the middle of everything! And yet, I feel like I'm in a tiny little community. . . . I know all the shopkeepers. I know all my neighbors. It's like being in a small town, but living in the center of a huge city. I really feel like I have the best of all worlds. Really, I don't think I can get it as good [anywhere else].

Returning to a theme, people crave both the familiar comforts of home *and* the excitement of novelty. Many appreciate what political theorist Iris Marion Young described as the eroticism of the city: "the pleasure and excitement of being drawn out of one's secure routine to encounter the novel, strange, and surprising."[4] As they explore their worlds, they come to make themselves at home in new ways. Kassy experienced home as radiating out from her apartment. She described the familiar as intermingling with the new and different in a way that allowed her to constantly expand her sense of home, even as much of her environment fell outside her immediate control.

To the extent houses offer control they also often limit exploration. To be sure, bringing new things into houses can become a source of novelty. But novelty wears off, and the weight of stuff eventually accumulates to the point where even the ample space offered by houses can be filled up. Suburban house dweller Matt Ng observed, "We're the family that just keeps on buying . . . stuff!" Buying stuff only takes people so far, and seeking novelty outside, beyond the yard, remains complicated for those living in privatized and homogenous environs. House dwellers tend to find themselves surrounded by more houses, each dedicated, in many respects, to the minimization of intrusion. It may take a while to get anywhere exciting. It will very likely take a car. Matt and Cathy spoke thoughtfully to this issue as they imagined

---

[4] Young 1990, 239.

how the "Vancouver lifestyle" might differ from their own, settled down in the distant suburbs:

> MATT: [It] would be more of the biking, walking to work, [every-where] you need to get to. You get the fresh foods and stuff, like Granville Island . . .
>
> CATHY: Parks . . .
>
> MATT: Yeah. City parks, um . . . just more entertainment downtown and stuff like that that you can get to easily. And maybe take more transit and things like that.

Matt and Cathy seemed cognizant of the difficulty they faced in getting from their suburban house to all of the places in the city that might offer new experiences. They thought highly of the accessible diversity of things to do in Vancouver. Echoing this theme from a strikingly different position was Linda Jones, who lived in the very heart of Vancouver, on its downtown peninsula, with her husband and son. Like Kassy, she described enjoying the novelty provided by city living. Like Katrina, she also integrated the exposure of her son to new things into her ideal of how to be a good parent:

> I guess we're not traditional in the sense that we don't feel that, you know, we have to have a house and a yard . . . for our son. What he's exposed to here, you know, and the friends in the community that we have: I laugh 'cause my mom came from the Maritimes last summer to look after him for a month, and he went to a little day camp at the community center. And she walked down every day to pick him up and one of the little projects he did was a little sushi bento box. And she's like, "You know it's an urban child when they make sushi at [day camp]!" . . . He's exposed to so many different cultures and people, it's just, I mean, I don't think he's missing out on anything. And we actually spend more time with him, I think, 'cause when you take him to parks, and we have to go out as a family and we have to walk. And so, you know, I think we probably spend more time than if he was just, you know, in a neighborhood where he could just go play by himself all the time.

In this, Linda, like Katrina, married urban living to a version of intensive parenting, emphasizing time spent with her child and the provision of diverse opportunities. She recognized that hers was an unconventional form of parenting, insofar as she rejected suburban norms. Houses were not the best allies for Linda's form of mothering. Instead, she saw her version of intensive parenting, anchored to regular family walks through the urban landscape to her high-rise apartment, as more stimulating and ultimately better for her son.[5]

Rigidity

Ever the keen observer of early twentieth-century city life, Jane Addams noted that "quick adaptability is the great gift of the city child."[6] Exposure to newness just around the corner inculcates in urban residents both a readiness for dealing with difference and a generalized "blasé attitude" of tolerance. Adaptability guides the matching process between habits and habitats. Being possessed of a "quick adaptability" enables people to find more situations inhabitable. By contrast, the suburban house caters to a high-maintenance form of settled comfort. By reinforcing residents' abilities to form stable routines, and by providing an environment tailored to match their cultural expectations, houses can foster within their dwellers a certain rigid quality: a calcification of old habits and an aversion to forming new ones. Houses tend to ossify as they shelter, leaving people less adaptable and more intolerant. This rigidity can close residents to new experience.[7]

Many Vancouverites appreciated how city life kept them on their toes. In extolling the virtues of her urban apartment, Kassy Aldridge also described a conflicted relationship to the house and the cultural expectations surrounding ownership. In a characteristically reflexive moment, she suggested: "I'm constantly battling what society tells me I ought to have at this age versus what I really think is enough for me." Kassy's biggest ally against societal norms seemed to be her joy in trying new things:

> I've never really wanted to own a house because of the responsibility attached to it. I'm very spontaneous, so I love the thought of being able to give a month's notice, and go off and travel the world. Like . . . when I moved to Vancouver, I did it on six weeks' notice. It was just kind of a decision, you know? Tied up all the loose ends in my life, gave work six weeks' notice, and said, "Yeah, I need to make a career change; I'm going to do it!" That would have been significantly more difficult if I had a house that I needed to sell.

Kassy's spontaneous nature seemed to drive her openness to life. A house ultimately formed too strong of an anchor to facilitate exploration. Kassy saw

---

[5] Hays (1996) describes the generally pervasive logic of intensive parenting for the middle class.

[6] The quote is from Addams 1910, 241.

[7] Simmel (1903) first described the blasé attitude as associated with metropolitan life. Of note, in personality psychology, "openness" is generally associated with intellectual development and creativity (Digman 1990; McCrae 1987).

this anchoring as based, in part, in the maintenance work and contractual responsibilities of owning a house. But she also viewed houses as enabling everyday habits to get too complicated and constraining. By contrast, Kassy considered herself "a fan of simplistic living." She observed that her lifestyle was not for everyone:

> There are many people who want the trappings, and the toys, and . . . lots of space to spread out. I don't need that. . . . The more simply I live, the more happy I am. You know? It's less complicated; it's less expensive; it's less time consuming. I get to engage in the business of enjoying my life, instead of being worried about all the details. Yeah.

If Kassy's spontaneity seemed inherent, she nevertheless recognized it as constantly under threat. Not having a house helped prevent Kassy from spreading out and adopting all the trappings of a more complicated and less adaptable life. Living in a small apartment kept her from becoming too comfortable, too boring, too unreflective, and too inflexible. It reinforced her openness and gave purchase to her grappling with her cultural upbringing. While Kassy seemed to start as a free spirit, others found themselves gradually loosening as they learned to do without a house. Their transformations came as pleasant and welcome surprises to many, including apartment dwellers Gary and Karen Shen:

> GARY: I used to think I always wanted to live in a house. Like, a house was definitely the end-all, be-all. And then I look around at all the houses here, and they're run down, beaten up, and then, townhouses look pretty good. [*Laughter.*] Yeah, I'd say, definitely, living in Vancouver has changed my view on housing. Definitely. Like, living here, I'm actually happier in this place than a lot of housing that I've seen in the local area, too. Like, duplexes which are about the same size, or even that they're a little bigger. I like the place that we [are in; it's] comfortable, so it definitely has changed. Like, it's actually a lot easier to live in a small space than I thought it would be. It's been easier since we've started purging things that—throwing things away, too.
>
> KAREN: And fun!
>
> GARY: Yeah.
>
> KAREN: You know, living a—you know, paring down, it feels good, you know?

Spatial constraints reinforced the simplification of daily routines. Living a simpler life felt good and encouraged adaptability. Unlike Gary and Karen, Enid Ngai was considering buying a house in Vancouver—though mostly, she noted, as an investment, which made her unusual in this regard. Despite this possibility, she still saw countervailing benefits to apartment living:

> Living in an apartment is also good because it's easier. You actually have more time with your family, because you don't have to shovel snow, and [*laughter*] do the [eaves], and . . . it's just different ways. I may not buy a house. It's just my life is so easy right now! Just throw the garbage down the chute and I'm done, ha ha!

As my assistant tugged the conversation away from Enid's investing tips, which she was eager to share, her history and family life moved to the fore. She described growing up "poor" in Hong Kong: "I grew up in a place less than 330 square feet [for] eight of us!" Rather than reacting against this upbringing, Enid saw it as providing her certain strengths. She saw herself as a nerd, and she wanted to provide her young daughter with similar "nerd training." As she put it, "Nerd training [means] she'll say, 'Mommy, mommy, I want to watch TV' and I say, 'Why don't we just read a book?'" She also expressly wanted her daughter to experience spatial constraints, if not quite as extreme as those shaping her own childhood. Enid thought of these experiences as endowing her daughter with an adaptable orientation toward others:

> I personally don't think children should have their own room. They become so . . . um . . . isolated eventually when they grow up. . . . Too bad I only have one child. I'd like to have, like, five or six! I would gladly . . . so they can learn how to survive in a real situation. Like right now at work, how many people actually have their own office? They don't! And that's why a lot of people, they have office politics. . . . They just don't know how to deal with interaction, face to face! . . . In most countries it's quite normal. It's just in rich countries, they think, "I have my space, and in my space, I am the princess or prince." I just don't need one. I'm very lucky I have my own office, but I personally don't like it. It's just so isolated. [*Laughter.*]

Enid blended a particular sort of intensive parenting—"nerd training"—with a concern that her daughter develop social adaptability. She did not want to raise an "owner" or a "princess." She did not want a child who equated home, or work, with castle-like privileges. This sort of adaptability was one of the things urban parents, like Katrina and Linda, often attempted to instill within their children. They wanted their children to learn how to live with others, and they saw this lesson as starting at home. Put differently, parents saw learning to live with others in small spaces as allowing their children to make themselves at home more broadly, beyond the walls of their housing units.

Isolation

Enid's concern to avoid raising her child "isolated" from others spoke to a broader problem many people had with houses. More control over more space seemed to imply less development of community. Many people wanted their housing to serve as a platform for reaching out to others and making connections. This was especially important for Dana Jarvison. A young single mother living in social housing, Dana grew up a third-generation Canadian, but remained quite critical of what she thought of as Canadian culture:

> I really don't like the culture . . . that Canada has grown to have. And continues to grow to have. And from doing travels, I've seen, um, the way other communities are, in other countries. And the kids, the kids are stronger because they share. They share! Like, they don't have their own little house and their own little world. They share the whole community. Like, I don't know, it just seems like I see the kids all the time there.

For Dana, this sharing of the whole community, rather than retreating to the insular world of the single-family house, was something she wanted to experience and encourage for her own child. Just *seeing* children everywhere, rather than locked away in houses, provided Dana a greater sense of community. Asked to elaborate on her description of Canadian culture, Dana particularized her understanding as stemming from her suburban upbringing:

> Well, I'm describing what I grew up in, but, um, suburbs, where you got a big house, and you drive everywhere that you go, even to get groceries, you drive there. And, um, you buy all the food that's packaged, so . . . you go to work, you come home, and you don't, don't really talk to your neighbors that much. Like, you hide. No real connection.

For Dana, the development of community and connection related to everyday practices of sharing with others. This was a theme she returned to over and over again. Like many suburban misfits, she ultimately experienced the environs in which she grew up as alienating. For her, the alienation was intimately tied to isolation from the everyday lives of others:

> I hated suburbia, like, how everything is so private and not shared. And that's why, I don't know, I felt like there was no community. . . . It's, like, lonely sometimes.

All in all, Dana echoed many of Enid's concerns as she discussed how sharing and being around many different people kept children flexible and well equipped to deal with the world around them. But Dana also found the development of community important, and mourned its absence. In an early part of her conversation with my research assistant, Dana noted that she would love to move to a two-bedroom suite within a house. Asked if this might be her ideal, she clarified that she would really love "a whole house." But, crucially, she noted she wanted to share the house with others: "Shared with a family, like, a couple of families, like, whether they have kids or not, but, like—and sharing groceries—and, you know, that's like the ideal situation for me." Dana continued on the theme of sharing as constitutive of community:

> And it's more cost-effective. Like, it's really not cost-effective to buy your own of everything, right? Um, and it's healthier, like, you know, to share space with other people. Um . . . it's, it's good for children to be around lots of people when they're growing up, and the food that you buy would probably be healthier, because you can buy in bulk of, like, vegetables, and they won't go bad.

Dana recognized community as a healthy sort of defense, keeping both vegetables and children from going bad. Her idea of community involved ensuring that her everyday routines overlapped with those of others. Dana rejected the isolation produced by limiting houses to single families. In so doing, she directly rejected the detachment from community produced by the single-family house, with emphasis on the "single family." Somewhat strikingly, she also linked such detachment back to ownership, a key feature of the broader house package. When asked why she thought renting promoted community, Dana suggested:

> I think people who rent are more in touch with the other people. . . .
> I think that the lifestyle is different. I don't know. I don't know why. I guess it's because they're not chained to their mortgage, they're chained to their monthly rent, but, um . . . when you buy a house, you're like, chained to it, or you're chained to a job, and then you don't really have much time outside.

Despite certain notable differences—the mortgage, the high-rise—what Dana seemed to want in terms of the everyday experience of community seemed rather like what committed urbanist Linda Jones already had. Before moving into a two-bedroom condo with her husband, Linda first considered buying a house together with his parents in the suburbs. But she and her husband decided they loved the downtown too much, so instead they bought a place in a high-rise:

What's been a really big surprise in our building is the number of families that live in the building, and our floor in particular. There's five suites on the floor, and one of them is empty—for what reason I don't know why—but there's five kids who live on the floor. And . . . we have become friends with all of the people on the floor, and we literally, we leave our doors open and the kids run back and forth, and we have, we have them over for dinner. And you know, and our neighbors are from all over the world, and it's just a real sense of community, and I wasn't necessarily expecting that [downtown], and we, we've found it! And that is such a huge factor in, in where we live, is having, having that community. And what our neighbors, they're in a smaller suite, and they have two kids, and they were going to move to a bigger place but they said, you know, having . . . neighbors that our kids can play with and—it's more important to them than space, so they, they're deciding to stay where they are. And that's just made a huge difference, and having, you know, thinking back to my childhood, and running next door, and you know, playing with the kids next door, and my son's getting the same thing, yet we're getting all the benefits of living downtown, and having, having a walking lifestyle.

Linda did not anticipate finding such a family-friendly community in her high-rise. Much of the communal feel hinged on the doors to the hallway being left open, as well as the shared dinners. At the same time, unlike Dana's vision, the community within the building rested on the legal foundation of strata tenure, clearly spelling out and bounding private and public obligations.

The technology of the condominium-governed high-rise remains flexible. It allows and encourages the interpenetration of everyday living through shared space, but also enables people to close doors, controlling and demarcating their boundaries to a greater extent than would likely occur in Dana's communal house. Linda also felt her desired community extended to the shared public space outside her building. And it was a big part of why she remained committed to city-living:

It, it's the walkability. It's, you know, we definitely want to be close to the water. And it's, it's a, it's the community. It's funny how . . . as you get older you just realize how much community means, and just what you get out of it. And, you know, living in the suburbs, everybody [lives] by their driveway. And often you don't know people who live next to you, and you get in and out of your car. And we go to Edmonton, and I don't think I ever set foot outdoors. I go from a house, to a car, to a mall, to . . . [Laughter.]

Here Linda made a strong claim about what the built environment encourages, and does not encourage, in the way of interactions with others. Small privatizable spaces, along with prolific semipublic and public spaces (e.g., hallways and sidewalks) prompted her to maintain sociable habits. Large and tightly controlled spaces, including both houses and cars, foster a more entitled form of isolation.

Even those who just could not get over the cultural pull of the house often still recognized how it constrained the development of community. Jill Sampson, management professional and married mother of two, continued to dream of moving to a detached house. But she admitted she saw yards as real barriers to getting to know the neighbors. Speaking of her last move, from a house-dominated suburban neighborhood to a dense townhouse complex near shared park space, she noted:

> We wanted a place [where] we would also be in more of a community, and closer to other people with families . . . that definitely influenced our decisions about wanting to move. [The old neighborhood] is really terrific. But, um, it's, it's not, um . . . it's not necessarily easy—or it wasn't for us anyway—to connect with other people. In part because one of the neat things about here is that no one has a backyard. So everybody has to go to the park, everyone has to leave their own [space] in order to give their kids a place to run around. And that whole process means that you meet people and you make a community much more quickly. Whereas in [the suburbs], of course, people have backyards, and so they don't necessarily leave the house. . . . Whereas here, they do.

Jill contrasted her trajectory, from low-density to high-density living within Vancouver, to that of friends in the United States: "They moved to the suburbs in Seattle, and they used to live right . . . downtown." Despite their different starting and end points, Jill noted, the two had discovered the same insight: big yards lead to empty parks.

> And so, like here, absolutely everybody went to the parks, and it was really easy to make friends, and really easy to meet people. But in the suburbs, [my friend] was saying, "No one leaves their house! I never see anyone! We go to these huge empty parks, and there's no one there because the families have all of their equipment in their backyards."

As Jill described it, even when public spaces like parks are sprinkled liberally around house-dominated neighborhoods, they tend to remain unused.

Houses and their yards make it too easy to stay at home, rather than getting out and mingling. When asked to describe what she thought good family housing looked like, retiree Emma Miller emphasized much the same point. Getting children and dogs and people more generally out and walking around was especially important:

> EMMA: Good family housing? Well, I think it should have all the elements of community that I talked about. And again, probably some I can't quite remember right now. Um . . . I think it should be, in the kinds of . . . settings that are conducive for children and pets and parents to participate in community life. Just in how they live their lives. So, again, with the little handkerchief park half a block away, a lot of the parents of little kids, right from the time that they're in the strollers, and, you know, if you'd come down the hall you would've seen the stroller [of] my next-door neighbor. . . . I mean, they get out, they wander the street, they go over and meet at the playground, and the moms get to chat with each other, right from the time when the kids are . . . just born. Um, so they . . . begin to know each other and to know their neighbors in a way they probably didn't when they didn't have a kid, and didn't have that. Or the dog owners, they all go and stand in the middle of the park and chat, and throw balls for their dogs, and the dogs get to socialize and the people get to socialize. And corner stores, I think, are important, because again, the people go to the corner stores and going in and out of them, the newer generation of corner stores is really working to include, or encourage people to be more social. Because of course that means people will hang out more, they'll have another coffee, they'll buy a sandwich. So they get more customers that way, but it does mean that people are mingling a bit more in that way.
>
> MIA: Like the little shop that's down the street?
>
> EMMA: Mmhmm. Yeah. And, um . . . so. Uh, community gardens, especially in areas where people can't have their own plot. I used to be a member of the [local community garden], and then had to stop for a while, but now I'm going back to it again. And, uh, you meet people by gardening beside each other and saying, "Oh, what are you growing?" And it . . . those interactions where you have something in common, whether it be a baby, a dog, a garden, uh . . . a cup of coffee or whatever, that can allow for the conversation to be casual. And over time you keep connecting in the same place, again and again and again. That's really what I think makes a community.

Good family housing for Emma—good housing in general—was housing that actively promoted community. For both Jill and Emma, community remained somewhat less interpenetrating than for either Dana or Linda. Doors remained closed. Private spaces remained private. But daily lives, by necessity, extended beyond these private spaces, drawing people into one another's orbits. For Emma, this extended to sharing tasks with the other members of her small and self-managed condo building: "Because it's only got twelve units we can't really afford a management company so we have to do some of the stuff ourselves . . . so I mean, in a sense it's all our home, for all of us, and we have that sense of communal responsibility." It is perhaps no coincidence that the dream of a house remained strong for both Jill and Emma. But they recognized the limitations such a dream placed on their sense of community. They did not want to be surrounded by a sea of other houses. Emma, in particular, spoke to the importance of having diverse facilities around, to support people carrying out their everyday lives in a local fashion where they were likely to run into one another again and again:

> Those [facilities] are all really essential because it gets people out into the community mingling with each other. Being able to afford food and housing and, and, um, uh, getting to know each other a little bit and, um, doing things that keep them healthy, like going to exercise classes or language classes or . . . uh, art classes or whatever. To the gym! And all of these are ways that people connect in the community. And if you're all doing it in the same community—rather than going, you know, downtown to the gym at the Y, or off to Superstore to buy your groceries; [in those cases] you don't keep meeting the same people— . . . [if you're all doing it in the same community], even if I don't know these people intimately, I begin to say hello to them in the street. I mean, to me, that's pretty normal in that, in this neighborhood, um, even when I realize that it might be an individual who doesn't speak my language. I say "hi," and they say "hi" back in their own language! . . . It's really important that way, and to me it was also important to have a mix of cultures. Um . . . it doesn't always lead to easy relations, but it, it can be enlivening, enriching, and, um, and a big piece of community. What I hadn't even thought about when I came here was that because the Chinese Canadians use the streets every morning, they're out there early in the morning, going out for walks. They take their kids to the little handkerchief park, half a block away. By using the streets, by being there, um . . . that . . . that everybody is aware of what's going on around them, as well as meeting each other socially, they're also observing if there's anything that isn't where it should be, all those things.

Emma discussed both how community worked for her, and why it struck her as important. Ultimately, she settled on quite sociological insights. The more diverse attractions and services in a neighborhood, the more likely residents are to repeatedly run into one another during their daily rounds, creating bonds of solidarity. This kind of community solidarity didn't require demographic homogeneity. Indeed the daily ballet of diverse urban neighborhoods, where people's networks of inhabitance overlap one another and many eyes keep watch over the streets, can be joined or simply observed without the requirement of a common language.[8]

As discussed in Chapter 5, acquiring a house constitutes an important cultural goal for many people, part of a well-ingrained cognitive habit defining success as an adult. Chapter 6 reveals that detached-house living also provides ready solutions to many problems of everyday life. But Vancouver continues to grow in population and reputation as a particularly "livable" city despite placing houses out of reach for most of its residents. Most Vancouverites manage to make themselves at home without houses. In fact, many people we spoke to described feeling more at home without a house than they would with one. What is more, urban living is not just for free-floating young hipsters. Diverse families with children of all ages continue to find Vancouver quite inhabitable, along with people from many other kinds of households.

Yet it is worth drawing attention to the ways in which inhabitability works differently in Vancouver than elsewhere across North America. To make it work, residents need to be open to reconfiguring their cognitive habits, to deemphasizing the cultural importance of a house as a symbol of success in life. Residents also need to be open to adapting to new and different sorts of everyday routines. In many cases, this means adjusting their daily habits to fit into smaller, more intimate spaces but also expanding their daily rounds to carry them outside into a shared public realm.

To be certain, these adjustments can be hard for Vancouverites. But the metro area tends to support an open-minded and reflective (some would say flaky) attitude. There is plenty of the cultural scaffolding required for renovating people's ideas about how housing matters. Vancouver also provides a great deal of infrastructure for supporting alternative routines. In its more urban parts, a mixture of walkable pathways, accessible shopping, parks and gardens, and a varied streetscape all encourage people to share the public realm. Vancouver makes adaptation easy.

This is what makes it a very livable and inhabitable city. As a habitat, Vancouver provides a poor match for the habits of living and thinking of

---

[8] Here Emma echoes Jane Jacobs's (1961) observations about mixed uses keeping eyes on the streets.

most of its newcomers. But on the whole, the region encourages and supports the formation of new habits. Learning new ways of thinking and living can be fun. This kind of learning also sustains a reflective critique of the old ways of thinking and living that characterize most of North America. Though the house seems to solve many everyday urban problems by maximizing control over space, it does so only by creating new problems in the maintenance work, the boredom, the rigidity, and the isolation that attend to houses as habitats. To relieve these problems, giving up a little bit of control over a little bit of space seems entirely sensible to the many who have tried it.

The everyday problems of maintenance, boredom, rigidity, and isolation ultimately return us to the larger-scale problems of habitat loss and change chronicled in Chapter 2. The construction of houses destroys alternative habitat all by itself. But it is the maintenance needs of houses that consume so much energy and entail so much driving. The greenhouse gases that result from this activity produce climate change, which in turn destroys habitat at a whole new level. The boredom of house life speaks directly to the loss of habitat for urbanity; houses leave little room for urban amenity and adventure. The isolation and rigidity often identified with houses above speak to a host of problems. As house dwellers withdraw, their engagement with the broader body politic suffers. They may lose touch with the diversity of human experience. Their tolerance for difference sometimes dims. Their habits ossify, and they often quit walking to get around. These patterns can undermine the grounds for democracy, constrain family life, erode empathy for the poor, and challenge human health.

In short, it might be a good idea to encourage more people to try living without a house. The easiest way to do this is to stop setting aside so much metropolitan land as house habitat. By limiting the further spread of the Great House Reserve and removing the protections put in place around it, we can encourage a more diverse regulatory ecology to form. Why not open up some room for different kinds of life to bloom? As it turns out, there are many different ways for people to find themselves at home in the city, just as there are many different ways to make a home without a house.

HABITAT FOR DIVERSITY

> Governments will stand or fall by the evidence they
> give their citizens that they are dealing imaginatively,
> vigorously, and realistically with the greatest need of the
> people, second only to food: a satisfying place to live.
>
> —CHARLES ASCHER, "WHAT ARE CITIES FOR?"

House habitat: I have approached the subject matter of this book from two angles. What do we get by treating houses as alive, as having habitats of their own? What do we get by considering the kinds of habitat houses create for people? Along the way I have wandered increasingly into the realm of social justice. In this chapter, I more explicitly bring together habitat thinking and social justice thinking. As it turns out, building a bridge between the two has much to say about how and why we should rebuild our cities.

Habitat Thinking

Let's begin by thinking more about habitat. People are not pine beetles, and houses are not fungi. So why center a book on a concept most often reserved for understanding wildlife?[1] To start with, ecological thinking was foundational for urban sociology. Early sociologists of the Chicago School borrowed freely from plant and wildlife ecology as they studied urban growth. One of the most important observations they made was about neighborhood succession—the "natural" transition from one urban habitat to another that accompanied outwardly invasive urban growth.

As noted by critics of the Chicago School, describing urban growth in terms of "nature" hid many of the important dynamics at work. Shifting

---

[1] Though as an exception, see Duneier's (1999) discussion of the sidewalk as a sustaining habitat.

metaphors, one prominent group of detractors argued that cities acted more like growth machines than organic ecologies. After all, what really drove neighborhood succession was political economy, and the attempt to govern urban land by market. Dividing the city up into parcels for sale represented nature commodified rather than nature in action.[2]

But history demonstrates that the free market in land sales was short-lived, at best. Speculation and succession accompanied rapid fluctuation in prices. Chaos in land uses turned cities uninhabitable—especially for the middle class. So a strong set of regulations grew up around attempts to govern by market. Licensing regimes and enclave formation provided temporary solutions. Then the house was unfolded into a zoning bylaw, walling off the maelstrom at the heart of the city.

Zoning bylaw maps wrote the single-family house simultaneously into law and across the urban landscape, protecting the Great House Reserve. From there, like an invasive species, the house in code continued to spread, both out into the suburban hinterland and into new realms, like mortgage finance regulations and complex housing investment instruments. Habitat reserved for houses displaced alternative habitats, both directly and indirectly. Habitat thinking, in returning from "machine" imagery back to the ecological roots of urban sociology, provides an important conceptual tool for seeing both what it is that houses are doing to the environment and what we are doing for houses when we reserve land for them.

What about what houses are doing for us? If we can think of houses as *having* habitats, we can also acknowledge that they *provide* habitats. Here the term offers a new conceptual grasp on how people relate to houses as living environments. The conceptual strength of a habitat approach arises from the unexceptional and well-documented tendency of people to form habits, both in mind and body, that guide their cognition and material interactions. Learned habits match people to habitats, unless they are prevented from forming by lack of cultural scaffolding or lack of support for everyday routines.

As cultural habitat, houses are most commonly associated with success and belonging. But both the strength and direction of these kinds of cognitive associations are malleable and negotiable for most people, and Vancouver offers plenty of support for learning new associations. As physical habitat, houses tend to be differentiated from alternatives by their maximization of control and space. Their claim to being the most inhabitable of habitats rests on this distinction. When people living in urban alternatives look to houses to solve important problems of daily life, they are normally conceptualizing their problems in terms of space and control. Here it is important to recognize how the house really does offer solutions to many everyday dilemmas.

---

[2] See Molotch 1976 and Wachsmuth 2012.

But are houses really the most livable of habitats? Home only *starts* by exerting control over space—and only *some* control and *some* space seem necessary. By virtue of maximizing these qualities, houses demand a great deal of maintenance work. In replicating across the urban landscape, houses erode people's ability to extend their sense of home beyond the moats of their own yards, often producing isolation and boredom. They also encourage the formation of more rigid sets of habits than alternative dwellings do, altogether diminishing residents' adaptability. Nevertheless, most people can readily adapt to multiple habitats. Houses offer just one of many possible lifestyles, different from others, but no more fundamentally livable.

In considering human nature, habitat thinking is useful for putting us in our place as creatures of habit and as habitually engaged with our environments. The concept helps level the playing field for the ways we might approach agency, directing attention toward how different environments enable and support actors: both human and nonhuman, living and built. Habitat thinking helps us understand both how houses have spread and how their spread might be halted. But what does it have to do with social justice? Where is the careful articulation for *why* we should let the house die?

Social Justice Thinking

Maybe houses are not the most livable of habitats, but they are certainly not uninhabitable. What makes them bad habitats? To adequately answer this question requires moving away from the language of ecology, which at least aspires to value neutrality, and toward the language of social justice. To define what is bad, let's start with what is good.

Political theorist Iris Marion Young makes the case for a focus on justice. But there is more than one way of understanding justice. In Young's theory of justice, the city provides the ideal. Other visions of justice valorize either the atomized individual or the small, homogenous community as the foundational sites of just democracy. Young's city is neither atomized nor homogenous. Instead it celebrates the diversity of social groups. Diversity is both good in its own right and necessary for justice. Social groups simultaneously produce difference and identification. They also merit representation in democratic deliberations—especially to the degree they have encountered oppression. Correspondingly, the ideal city fosters an inclusive form of social differentiation, celebrates variety, promotes the emotional charge of discovering the unexpected in others, and creates space for public encounters—all providing for a "being together of strangers in openness to group difference." In this, the city can provide the most fertile ground for democratic governance to produce socially just arrangements. It does this by encouraging a broadly egalitarian form of diversity. This ideal seems especially salient within multicultural democracies, as in Canada and the United States.[3]

In many respects, Young's vision of the city retains home as a foundation. But Young adopts a feminist stance in rejecting narrow definitions of home as a separate and excluded realm, where people may be exiled from broader public participation. No one should be deprived of participation within the public by relegation to home. Instead, Young notes, "the positive idea of home I have advocated is attached to a particular locale as an extension and expression of bodily routines." This fits quite well with a home as habitat, as does Young's aspirational notion "that certain values associated with home, among them control over access to one's person and personal space, be made available to everyone." For Young, home as an ideal complements the city as an ideal. If city living shakes people up, having a home enables them to settle back down again. A good habitat is one that provides safe refuge but also encourages outward exploration, supports diversity, and creates space for intergroup contact.[4]

Young's ideal versions of city and home are thoughtfully explored, powerful, and humane. But in the last of these qualities, the humanity of Young's vision, we can see both the strength of her approach and a somewhat problematic blind spot. Her ideal city looks like a particularly malleable social contract, always open to and encouraging of direct renegotiation. In this, Young's vision of the social is very human oriented, which is to say that her discussion of the other diverse entities that populate and surround cities remains somewhat limited. Three implications of this blind spot follow.

First, though Young very clearly sees the city working through and for the people, and also for the social groups that inform those people, she does not quite see the city for the buildings or the trees. That is to say, the nonhuman entities within and surrounding the city receive little, if any, weight in the democratic deliberations she promotes. Many of these entities, including the trees, are still quite alive in a biological sense. As living entities, even though inhuman, they make ethical and practical claims on our attention. Loss of habitat for the plants and animals around us should matter in our deliberations. It seems at least plausible within Young's vision that the interests of other species should be incorporated within a definition of social justice that expands the notion of "social" beyond humanity.[5]

---

[3] See Young 1990, 256, for the quote. See also Kymlicka 1995 on social groups and multiculturalism and Sennett 1970 on the "uses of disorder."

[4] The quotes are from Young 2002, 340–341 and 343.

[5] See, e.g., meditations by Hinchliffe et al. 2005 concerning the water vole and Jerolmack 2013 on the pigeon. Donaldson and Kymlicka (2011) articulate the ethics involved in their book *Zoopolis: A Political Theory of Animal Rights*. The City of Vancouver actually does protect its trees with local bylaws.

Second, different sorts of nonhuman actors also seem relevant, including regulatory creatures like the house that nevertheless lack breath or DNA in any but a metaphorical sense. Such actors demonstrate that cities are something more than malleable social contracts between their human residents. Instead, cities are diversely built things, actively haunted by the creations of the past. Most obviously, they are physical presences, constructed in load upon load of concrete, wood, and reinforced steel. Less obviously, they are also regulatory agglomerations, layered with bylaws and codes. These govern where the newer buildings go, how the older ones get used, and when structures might be torn down. It is far from clear that such constructed entities are owed any ethical due, though a conservative position, or a more general respect for the law, might be mobilized to suggest such. Regardless of what they are *owed*, they nevertheless *receive* deference. Buildings acquire "heritage" value. Legal decisions set precedents. Both become subject to habituation, gathering a certain agency unto themselves to the degree they become taken for granted.

The return of habits via habituation sets the stage for the third blind spot in Young's humanism. If people are really creatures of habit, not so different from other life forms in this regard, then they might not find the malleable social contract implied by Young's vision of how a just democracy should operate to be especially livable on a day-to-day basis. In place of Polanyi's world, where self-governing markets undermine the social fabric people seek to inhabit, Young substitutes a broader, continuously churning people's governance that might conceivably have the same effect.

Ultimately, social justice thinking provides a signpost for what constitutes a good habitat. In turn, habitat thinking provides remedies to the blind spots associated with too humanistic a focus on social justice. In the process, habitat thinking calls attention to the fundamental stability of environments as an important feature of what makes them inhabitable for people. Quite often, it is the nonhuman entities—especially the built entities constructed as a regulatory response to the damage wrought by self-governing markets— that produce stability for cities. Unfortunately, not all of these nonhuman entities are really our friends.

The complementary tools of habitat thinking and social justice thinking provide us a guide for good city building. What is the biggest stumbling block we are likely to encounter along the way? My answer: the house, of course.[6]

The house represents a direct threat to enacting Young's vision of the city. The house works against diversity, legislating homogeneity throughout the

---

[6] I do not think Young (1990) would be entirely opposed to this interpretation. While she avoids suggesting that human creations have agency, she devotes a substantial part of her work to problems with bureaucracy and technocratic governance, where she at least edges around some of the same issues. She also argues against those who would dismantle cities in favor of rewriting history.

Great House Reserve. In similar fashion, the house works to reduce the number and range of encounters with difference, with otherness. It produces an isolating environment, reducing the variety of places people could run into one another as much as it reduces the variety of places they could be coming from. In this, a house-dominated landscape diminishes the publicity Young wishes to see in the city. In addition, the enormous costs associated with the purchase and maintenance of houses exclude many people from them altogether. The house as regulatory creature tends to divide in an unjust fashion, marginalizing some while valorizing others. It works against more egalitarian forms of social differentiation, diminishes the public sphere, and encourages rigidity and withdrawal, fostering the dangerous illusion of disentanglement. At best, the fundamental demand of democracy—that we figure out how to live with one another—becomes tightly bounded and miniaturized. At worst it disappears altogether.

To these sins against a humanely just democracy we may add sins against other species. Young's city may be interpreted as providing the basis for valuing ecological diversity as a fundamental otherness. It enables us to consider our world as a city from which we may not withdraw. We can envision a broader public, a greater appreciation for variety. Our encounters with diverse other species remain important in their own right. The living, but nonhuman, deserve some representation. As detailed in Chapter 2, the house displaces habitat for other forms of life, eats energy, fosters car dependence, and spews out climate-altering greenhouse gases. The proliferation of houses tends toward the marginalization and at times outright slaughter of other species. In turn, it takes its ecological toll on the diversity all of us may come to encounter.

To be clear, I do not believe this is at all the intent of most house dwellers.[7] To get right to the point, they are seldom the ones building houses. When it comes to the implications of house habitat, *building*, rather than *dwelling*, is mostly what matters. But since so many of us encounter the house primarily as dwellers, the implications of building for justice disappear, swimming somewhere beneath our reflections. Drawing deliberative attention to the processes by which our worlds are created—to building—becomes imperative for doing the job better.

Building for Diversity

How do urban habitats get built? Relatively few people participate in this process. The construction workers, the carpenters, the brick layers and masons, electricians, plumbers, and painters: these are the people who build

---

[7] As Rome (2001) notes, suburbanites are often sympathetic to environmentalist causes and opposed to most development occurring after their own arrival.

our dwellings. Yet they take their directions from elsewhere, and are most commonly viewed as the more or less willing tools of "those who count" within the growth machine.[8] The developers, the politicians, the planners, the regulators, the architects themselves all direct what is built. The chain of command takes us to a smaller and smaller subset of people.[9] But as I argue throughout this book, supply has also been harnessed to a number of nonhuman actors.

Bylaws specify what can be built where and the uses to which it can be put. Building codes specify how things must be built. These nonhuman entities were themselves at one time constructed, and then set free to do their work. As a decreasing proportion of human actors participate in the direction of building, nonhuman entities, like the house, rise up to fill in the gaps. They necessarily shape the markets that so many assume govern the city. From five types of zones in 1927, the City of Vancouver now supports well over seventy, a fourteen-fold increase accomplished without even counting all of the hundreds of site-tailored comprehensive dwelling (CD) districts. There are ten types of single-family residential (RS) standards alone, even though none of them in Vancouver now effectively limit lots to only single-family detached houses.

Should we get rid of the regulatory creatures governing our cities? I am not at all certain we can do without them. They provide much of the stability that makes the city inhabitable. But if we cannot get rid of them, then I propose another strategy. We need to build more of them, and build them in a more inclusive fashion. Build enough of these entities and they will produce a complex urban regulatory ecology, ideally a good habitat for a diverse democracy.

Vancouver holds some lessons here, both positive and negative. Certainly it has succeeded in diversifying its landscape beyond a strict monoculture of houses. But rather than tearing down the house and completely deregulating its Great House Reserve, Vancouver has gradually reenabled a controlled form of *urban* succession while severely limiting outward *suburban* succession. Where it has been most effective, it has succeeded by building new regulatory creatures. Returning to the themes of Chapter 4, Vancouver has done well by (1) building around the house, (2) building over the house, and (3) renovating the house.

Building around the House

Building around the house includes halting the spread of houses across the rural landscape. In Vancouver's case, I have discussed how this was

[8] Logan and Molotch 2007, 50. See R. Harris 2004 on the decline of self-building.

[9] As Young (2002) notes, women are especially left out.

accomplished most dramatically via construction of the Agricultural Land Reserve, locking away the fertile lands remaining in agriculture within the Fraser Valley. Along the mountains, other regulations, like West Vancouver's twelve-hundred-foot-elevation restrictions, played a role in preventing further expansion, in conjunction with parks and reservoirs. So diverse built entities were at work there as well. Of course, Vancouver also borders a substantial body of water in the Salish Sea, and has a large river running along its southern edge. Much discussion of the city's revitalization has been linked to the opening of its shores to the public—enabled in many cases by cleaning up former industrial lands. Excepting the ports, relatively little of Vancouver's shoreline remains inaccessible, and privatization via, for instance, the extension of docks for the mooring of boats and float homes, has become tightly regulated. Finally, parks were a significant part of planning throughout the city's history; Vancouver remains especially blessed in this regard, with the wilds of Stanley Park sitting right alongside the downtown core.

However it is accomplished, some combination of Agricultural Land Reserves, parks, wildlife reserves, and other barriers to outward sprawl should be set up around other North American cities. These should be relatively durable in nature and also facilitate public access (e.g., via trails, bicycle paths, u-pick farms). The regulatory creatures protecting the rural lands around cities should be durable enough to facilitate a reorganization of the growth machine. Expectations should change. In particular, the prominence of large-tract greenfield developers should diminish, as they transform themselves into more urban developers or find new lines of work. The lands protected should be publicly accessible and reach far enough into the city itself to ensure that urban dwellers can experience diverse cross-species encounters, ideally within their everyday lives.

The other place to build around the house is within the Urban Core. Continuing to increase diversity here is the order of the day. Vancouver's condos and cooperatives, low-rises and high-rises, townhouses and mixed-uses, mortgage shares and lease-holds, communes and co-housing arrangements, rental protections and social housing experiments all introduce variation in how much control over how much space they provide. More variation should be enabled and encouraged here, as elsewhere. Let a thousand little living experiments commence, tempered by an awareness of social justice that I discuss more below.

Building over the House

Building around the house without reenabling urban succession can lead to gentrification pressures. A conservative solution to this problem is to gradually annex land from the Great House Reserve, rezoning it into nearby

Urban Core zones, lot by lot and parcel by parcel. This enables building over houses by adding to the existing urban fabric nearby. As a regulatory entity, the house is not so much destroyed as severely weakened by the persistent threat of annexation. This weakening is important. We need houses that remain flexible parts of the urban fabric, instead of completely removed and protected from it. When the house is opened to annexation, it becomes just one of many possible zoning standards, adjustable and subject to change. In effect, neighborhoods dominated by houses join the rest of the Urban Core, directly engaged in negotiations over the shape of the city.

Within Vancouver, the pace of annexation has historically been quite limited. Even after the transformative decades of the 1960s and 1970s, relatively few houses within the Reserve were built over and thereby shifted into the Urban Core. Nevertheless, the pace of annexation seems to be picking up. As one example, the area surrounding Oakridge Mall, the very first comprehensively zoned (CD-1) site in the city, is undergoing extensive rezoning. Single-family designations (mostly RS-1) are being replaced by site-tailored expansions of CD-1 classification. The Mall itself is also undergoing redevelopment, with the proposal including relatively tall towers. In this sense, the Mall will likely become a dense, towering node of Urban Core land use. Rezoning of surrounding sites, especially along the major arterials (41st Avenue and Cambie Street), will enable approved higher-density developments to move outward from this core. There are drawbacks to this pattern, insofar as arterial traffic creates noisier, more polluted living environs for those excluded from more protected single-family residential neighborhoods. But at least planners are working directly with developers, and in sometimes contentious consultation with neighbors, to negotiate a form in which succession can take place.

Renovating the House

Finally, of course, the house as a regulatory creature has undergone some serious renovation in Vancouver. Vancouver has not gone as far as to drop its use-based zoning restrictions. But it has come part of the way within the Great House Reserve, enabling at least a limited form of internal subdivision. The RS-1 district description, for instance, has been modified so that it now begins with a short and contradictory-seeming passage, with character subtly undermined by substance: "The intent of this Schedule is generally to maintain the single-family residential character of the RS-1 District, but also to permit conditionally one-family dwellings with secondary suites and laneway houses."[10] The maximum lot use conditionally permitted here is no longer the single-unit detached house of yore. It has been both expanded in

---

[10] City of Vancouver 2011, 1.

size and subdivided, containing up to three separate kitchens and supporting up to three separate households.[11]

This is, in some ways, the sneakiest of paths to reenabling a controlled form of urban succession. It is also the easiest for residents to direct: although few people engage in building, many engage in renovation.[12] Lifting the use restrictions in zoning offers a ready path for reform. Without building over the house, we can retain the form and shape of houses, as they currently exist, while enabling residents to fashion new uses. This, indeed, is the broader goal promoted by many advocates of Smart Growth: form-based code.[13] Excepting nuisances that might be characterized as directly harming or inhibiting the rights and capacities of others, why restrict the *use* of buildings at all? Too noisy? Target and identify appropriate noise levels. Too smelly? Target noxious odors directly. Ironically, and as noted by Richard Babcock all the way back in the mid-1960s, in some cases the minimum "performance standards" governing noise and pollution as applied to industrial zones are more restrictive than those in place in residential areas.[14] Gas-powered lawnmowers and leaf blowers regularly and noisily pollute the suburban air, even setting aside the outright toxicity associated with many lawn-related chemicals.[15] Renovating and subdividing old houses offers a low-impact way to diversify cities.

Building for Justice

Vancouver's successful diversification of its housing stock is not making the city uninhabitable. Far from it. But distributing housing almost entirely through the market might be, especially under circumstances of increasing inequality.[16] Many people—poor people—still find themselves in uninhabitable living situations, like Joanie with mold in her walls, and Jackie with strangers threatening her in the laundry room. Many people—poor people—sleep on the streets or in shelters, some 2,777 in a recent count.[17] Proportionally speaking, at a little over one in a thousand, this

---

[11] The expansion arises in part because the development of laneway housing does not count against floor space in the maximum floor space ratio (FSR) calculations. It remains unclear how census workers might classify laneway houses.

[12] See R. Harris 2012.

[13] Talen 2012. See also Grant 2006, which offers a critique of implementation.

[14] Babcock 1966, 59.

[15] Robbins 2007.

[16] Saez 2005.

[17] Vancouver Homeless Count 2014 figures are from Greater Vancouver Regional Steering Committee on Homelessness 2014.

is lower than homeless counts in nearby Calgary and Edmonton, as well as south in Seattle and Portland, but it is still too high. Many more people—still poor people—experience what the Canada Mortgage and Housing Corporation (CMHC) considers "Core Housing Need." This includes about 20 percent of households, a higher figure than in any other large Canadian metropolitan area.[18] In short, Vancouver is a hard city for poor people to inhabit.

In many respects, this is unsurprising. Vancouver seems especially expensive, perhaps a consequence of relying too strongly on building around the Great House Reserve while enabling too little expansion of the Urban Core. But the poor have a hard time finding housing just about everywhere. Polanyi wrote of a centuries-old balancing equation: "The poor man shall be satisfied in his end: Habitation; and the gentleman not hindered in his desire: Improvement."[19] But all across North America, both the process of turning housing over to the market and the subsequent reactionary creation of single-family residential zones upended this formula. Both habitation and improvement became reserved for the gentry. So what should Vancouver and other cities be doing to bring habitation and improvement to the poor?

One approach would be to replace the market distribution of housing entirely. If turning housing into a commodity is leaving the city uninhabitable for the poor, then maybe housing should be taken back from the market. Such a drastic move might be warranted by inequality, but the inevitable upheaval that would result risks making the city less rather than more inhabitable.[20]

Another approach, taking the risks of disruptions to the existing habitat into account, would be to start building new regulatory entities with a focus on making the city more inhabitable for those most oppressed by market-led development and distribution. Build new things, and build them well! Three construction projects could readily make cities both more just and more inhabitable: (1) build a better set of legal rights, providing more protections for those disempowered by the market and market-led change; (2) build more inclusive and empowering governance, providing voice and opportunity to the oppressed; and (3) build better dams against too much change occurring too quickly, thus keeping the city inhabitable.

---

[18] Canada Mortgage and Housing Corporation 2013, fig. 6.10, combining census and panel survey estimates. Toronto remains a notably close rival.

[19] Polanyi (1957, 34), quoting an official document from 1607 prepared for the Lords of the Realm.

[20] See, e.g., Forrest and Izuhara 2012 for a discussion of the overall decline in housing quality accompanying the Communist revolution and turn away from markets in Shanghai.

Building Better Legal Rights

Making market-oriented cities inhabitable for everyone means providing the poor, in particular, with the means of preserving a stable living environment. Two components are especially important to establish: a right to a living and a right to housing. Vancouver has neither.

A right to a living and a right to housing would provide a comprehensive response to broader efforts to turn both labor and land into commodities.[21] Securing these rights would fill the gaps that remain in the long history of policy-based protections against the disruptions associated with market governance. Single-family residential zoning produced inhabitable urban space for the middle classes. Organizational bureaucracies produced protected careers for the salaried. Unions and more progressive governments have often established similar protections for working classes. Those securing jobs earned various benefits accruing with tenure. A minimum wage was installed, and has recently been renegotiated upward in places like Seattle. Minimum living standards were required of lodging houses. More recently, those renting their housing were provided with residential contract protections, including rent control.

Minimum standards (in wages and living conditions) and contract protections (in jobs and rental contracts) are good starts at making Vancouver an inhabitable city. When enforced, they work relatively well for large swathes of the metropolitan area's residents. But they still leave excluded those unable to secure contracts to begin with: the unemployed, insecurely employed, and informally employed, as well as the unhoused, insecurely housed, and informally housed.[22] Establishing a right to a living and a right to housing would address those currently left unprotected by an otherwise expansive set of policies. But as Polanyi notes, "No mere declaration of rights can suffice; institutions are required to make the rights effective." So it was with the building of a minimum wage, minimum living standards, and rent control. So it has been when versions of the right to a living have been tried elsewhere, as with the small town of Dauphin, Manitoba's federally supported experiment with installing a guaranteed minimum income.[23]

What should a guaranteed minimum housing standard look like? Though imperfect, the Canadian measure of Core Housing Need provides a

---

[21] As noted by Polanyi (1957), labor and land can only ever be constructed as fictional commodities by policy intervention, since neither people nor nature are produced for the market. Polanyi also argued for a right to a job as one remedy.

[22] Burawoy (2015) labels this ex-commodification, or precarity.

[23] Polanyi 1957, 264. See Forget 2011 on the history of the MINCOME program. See also Block and Somers 2003 on how Polanyi wrongly interpreted the evidence of Speenhamland as suggesting that guaranteed minimum incomes might be a problematic approach.

start, incorporating consideration of affordability, repair, and crowding.[24] As currently used, Core Housing Need measures help direct policy discussions but play only a limited role in the provision of direct assistance to households. But with a bit of care, similar measures could be used to establish the minimum housing owed. Incorporating some of the same standards once developed to regulate lodging houses as measurements of crowding, together with affordability and repair standards, Core Housing Need could mandate state protection for qualifying individuals and households.[25] This could come in the form of direct housing provision, as in Hong Kong, where the public housing sector dwarfs anything in North America. Or it could come in the form of housing subsidy, as in U.S. voucher programs, or within a revitalized cooperative housing program, as discussed below. In many cases, establishing a right to housing can also tear down barriers to housing diversification, as when single-family residential zoning is overturned on the basis of its exclusionary nature and promotion of de facto discrimination against protected groups. Such a movement is now occurring across New England.[26]

Building More Inclusive and Empowering Governance

As argued eloquently by Young, justice means more than ensuring more equal distribution of things. It also means providing more empowerment to the oppressed, more access to creativity and decision making. It is important to create a context where people from marginalized groups can earn a voice and learn to develop new capacities. Inviting the disempowered to take part in the city-building process, as well as in governance over their own housing, can accomplish both of these goals.

How would this work? One solution would be to form a social justice panel reviewing new development projects. The City of Vancouver already has a much-lauded urban design panel.[27] Architects and planners review projects, vote on their worthiness, and provide advice on making them better. Their reports, in turn, are taken into advisement both by city staff in reporting to council and by City Council in deciding to approve new projects. A social justice panel could do much the same thing, reviewing new

---

[24] The crowding measure (the Canadian National Occupancy Standard) remains somewhat problematic (Lauster and Tester 2010, 2014), and appears to be based on old lodging house regulations. See also its punitive applications in Australia (Batten 1999) and similarly in the United Kingdom (Gentleman 2013).

[25] See Bratt 2002 for a similar perspective based on guaranteeing access to housing in the United States.

[26] See, e.g., Bratt and Vladeck 2014 on a comparison of efforts to overturn exclusionary zoning across four states.

[27] See, e.g., Punter 2002 and 2003.

projects for how well they meet the needs of those left out and providing crucial advice for making them better. Members of the panel could be selected from marginalized groups, especially those whose rights to a living and/or to housing have been violated. What better way to motivate developers to pay attention to the poor than to have their projects approved by the poor?

In addition to providing the oppressed with a voice and developing their capacities to engage in shaping projects, the institution of a social justice panel would also considerably broaden the range of experiences drawn on in the building process. Developers, politicians, planners, regulators, and architects comprise too narrow and too privileged a slice of humanity to entrust with building our cities.[28] Adding to the mix should help diversify the outcomes and provide a larger bulwark against all the nonhuman entities working to crowd out human actors entirely. Finally, a social justice panel could help overcome neighborhood resistance to change, providing broad political legitimacy to projects that diversify more exclusive local enclaves. Justice means that groups placed lower in social hierarchies must always be capable of overruling those voices insisting that their neighbors should come from "same or better" social groups within the city.

Another solution, targeted toward ensuring self-governance in housing, would be to encourage more cooperative housing projects. Various forms of cooperative housing—especially non-equity forms—have long offered an alternative to market housing, providing people with mixed incomes a way to live together.[29] As discussed in Chapter 4, cooperatives were supported by the federal government of Canada as part of reforms in the 1970s meant to deconcentrate the poor gathered within public housing projects. Government assistance to cooperatives helped structure mortgage financing, ensure maintenance, and provide subsidies for low-income members. Unfortunately, government support since then has been haphazard at best. Reinvigorating the cooperative sector with targeted provisions for supporting low-income households would go a long way toward addressing housing as a human right and providing the marginalized with real experience in cooperative governance.

Building Better Dams

Delving into the development processes she saw at work ripping apart the fabric of the city around her, Jane Jacobs wrote of the dangers associated

---

[28] The deputy mayor of Toronto recently provided an example of this kind of narrow privilege in opposing family housing downtown on the basis that it was a terrible place to raise children. See Church 2012.

[29] See Lasner 2012 for more on the history of cooperatives, as well as their governance challenges.

with "cataclysmic money" pouring into neighborhoods.[30] Though Vancouver planning has taken on board much of the wisdom of Jacobs (nicknamed the "Mother of Vancouverism"), it has also often welcomed the flood of money pouring into the kind of transformative, high-stakes, high-rise developments she opposed.[31] Today many residents of the old Urban Core consider change inevitable, and even welcome it. But often they do not welcome the spread of expensive "tower and podium" projects.[32] Too much money brings too large a scale to redevelopment efforts, changing neighborhoods too fast. Ironically, the high-stakes nature associated with big money also often leads to a failure to experiment, meaning that the changes wrought on neighborhoods can be homogenizing rather than diversifying.

It seems a bit of a paradox, but better integrating the Great House Reserve and the Urban Core means treating them differently in the process. The pace and scale of change need to be picked up across the Great House Reserve just as they need to be constrained within the Urban Core. Keeping the pace of change slower within the Urban Core makes it more inhabitable there. Keeping the scale of change smaller encourages experimentation by keeping the stakes lower. Smaller building footprints also promote more walkable, human-scaled, and diverse streetscapes.

As Jacobs so accurately observed, money, with the change it brings to cities, can roar in like a raging river. Then it can pull out again, leaving nary a drop behind. In general, the job of good city administrators is to tame the river and make it both sustainable and inhabitable. The regulations they build should operate something like beaver dams: slowing down the money, channeling it into ponds and pools on its way through, making it last, and diversifying the local environment in the process. The job of city builders is to make a nice place for many different creatures to live.

How to translate this insight into policy instruments? Municipalities across Metro Vancouver tend to have many of the tools already at their disposal to keep lots small, thus preserving a check on their assembly into larger mega-projects, and to maintain limits on heights and massing. They should use these powers more effectively to promote diversity and soften the force of change. Vancouver could also work to establish more careful limits on approving new building permits, paying close attention to regulating the volume of applications within a given neighborhood in order to keep the neighborhood inhabitable. To its credit, the city has enacted these kinds of

---

[30] Jacobs 1961, 291.

[31] The quote is from D. Wood 2012; see also Wickens 2011. A defense of Vancouverism's high-rise towers is that they tend to keep commercial, social, and outwardly oriented townhouse residential facilities located on the first floor, preserving a mixture of uses and contributing to eyes on the street.

[32] Bula 2013; Campbell 2013, n.p.

limits on development applications associated with tearing down existing rental buildings, especially those preserving low-income rentals. Finally, and perhaps most crucially, municipalities could work toward encouraging a stable stream of financing for small and midsize projects. Local lending institutions (like VanCity Credit Union, in the case of Vancouver) could offer ready partners for local builders who demonstrate a commitment to social responsibility. Something like Denver's Urban Land Conservancy could be constructed to acquire land for small and nonprofit developments. On the other side of the equation, instituting progressively structured permitting fees for larger projects might go a long way toward reducing their footprint.[33]

Conclusion

What kind of animal are we? As it turns out, we are probably not pine beetles. We are more like beavers. We build.[34] And we inhabit the buildings that get built. But then we take it a step or two further, building things to build for us, reserving habitat for habitats. Here is where the trouble starts—but it does not have to.

Our ancestors built the house, bringing it to life as they wrote it down in the technical details of local bylaws. From there it spread, a standard on the loose across the urban landscape, building our cities for us and squeezing in the Urban Core. The house in law keeps plenty of habitat preserved for the house in concrete. In turn, the house in concrete makes a seductive habitat for people. But inhabiting the house means adopting a particular set of habits: high-maintenance, boring, isolationist, and rigid. Not the stuff of a vibrant democracy, nor the stuff of a sustainably green coexistence on the Earth. We can do better.

What is the solution? Keep building. Build a habitat for justice. Build dams to slow down the dynamic forces of the market, taming them to make our cities more inhabitable. Build experimentally and incrementally. Build in a way that encourages co-inhabitance and encounters with otherness. Build in a way that promotes diversity and provides for a more inclusive democracy. Build in a way that recognizes the relationship between our building activities and the Earth around us. It is still the only one we have. At least until we build another.

---

[33] Existing use of "community amenity contributions" may be modified to produce more progressive permitting fees, making the process more transparent along the way.

[34] Ferraro and Reid (2013) argue that broader acceptance of building as a defining feature of humanity (*homo faber*) could help reorient how we think about pressing issues like sustainability.

APPENDIX

Data and Methods

The weight of this book rests on a solid body of research evidence. As I recount below, the assembly of this evidence began with a somewhat different investigative purpose in mind, but bread crumb by bread crumb, the information I collected led me here. Along the way, data were analyzed and reanalyzed as part of the process leading from one crumb to the next, then analyzed all over again with the aim of synthesis. In this Appendix, I recount some of the history of the research project that led to this book and provide further detail regarding the evidence marshaled here.

The types of data collected and compiled for this book, and the methods of analyzing that data, have largely flowed from a series of research questions I began asking around 2007. I was interested in better understanding the cultural and moral underpinnings of people's expressed and revealed housing preferences, especially as these preferences related to the formation of families. Based on analyses of historical census data, I started theorizing about parents' changing relationships to housing (e.g., Lauster 2010a, 2010b, 2012). It seemed the next step was to actually talk to people to find out what they were thinking. Vancouver provided a great place to recruit people to talk about housing, given local obsessions with the tight, exceptionally expensive real estate market.

With the support of a grant from Canada's Social Science and Humanities Research Council (SSHRC), I hired a research assistant (first Amanda Watson, who helped me start the project, and then Mia Chung, who actively joined me in interviewing participants). Together we attempted to recruit Metro Vancouverites who were in the process of looking for housing or undergoing recent family changes. We sought to collect information from them, including what their present housing situations looked like, what their past housing experiences were, why they had moved in the past and were thinking of moving

now, what their ideal housing looked like, their hopes and fears about their future housing, where they thought those hopes and fears might have come from, what their family
situations and plans were, and the connections they drew between their family plans and
their housing plans. We broached all of these topics through a series of open-ended questions written up in an interview guide. We frequently followed up on the answers people
offered with more probing questions, and also asked whether or not they felt there were
important and relevant things we were missing with our line of questions.

Roughly 40 percent of those we interviewed found us through our first recruitment
effort, from 2008 to 2009, which involved advertisements placed in various housing listings and in community centers. In a second phase of recruitment, from 2009 to 2010,
we actively looked for Metro Vancouverites who had undergone recent changes in their
family situations to see whether or not this influenced how they felt about their housing
situations. We advertised our study in libraries and similar community centers, as well as
in baby stores, and provided gift certificates to encourage participation. This brought in
approximately another 40 percent of our sample. The remaining 20 percent of our sample
were generally people who had contacted us after hearing about the study from a friend
during both recruitment efforts. In addition, we interviewed a small collection of realtors
and a social worker to get more insight into how families related to housing in Vancouver.

The sampling strategy was designed to bring us people who were actively involved
in negotiating the fit between housing and family. Perhaps not too surprisingly, those
who came to us were overwhelmingly women, but we also talked with men, and we
interviewed five couples where both members were present. All in all, we talked with
forty-three women and eight men. In age they ranged from a teenager to a recently
retired woman in her fifties, but nearly half of our interviewees were in their thirties,
with the rest scattered across their twenties or their forties. Locations, housing circumstances, household configurations, education levels, and incomes all varied widely. Most
of our interviewees came from the City of Vancouver, with a smaller contingent from
the suburban municipalities (outside the City of Vancouver, we advertised most intensively in Surrey). More rented than owned. Few lived in detached houses. We talked to
people living alone, people in couples, single parents, couples with children, and those
in more complicated and unusual households. About a quarter of the households clearly
included pets.

Participants included those with graduate degrees, those with undergraduate degrees, those who attended some college, and those who never attended any postsecond-
ary education at all. Reported annual household incomes ranged from under C$7,500 to
over C$200,000, with a median of just under C$60,000. Most people grew up in detached
houses. About a quarter were immigrants, and our interviewees reported a wide variety
of cultural and ethnic backgrounds. In all of these ways, we managed to recruit a fairly diverse sample that reflected a cross-section of Metro Vancouverites in our target age range
(centering on family formation) relatively well. Nevertheless, it is important to bear in
mind that the sample was self-selected by situation, rather than randomly selected across
the area. Most of the people attracted to the study were actively sorting through their fit
with their family and housing situations. For related reasons, we definitely reached more
women and slightly fewer immigrants than would be suggested by a demographic profile
of Metro Vancouver as a whole. Our English-language advertising probably contributed,
as did a pattern noted by other researchers whereby women tend to be both more interested in housing and family issues and more influential in determining housing outcomes

(e.g., Rabe and Taylor 2010). Many women approached us to talk while on maternity or family leave, which provided them partially paid time off from work (up to a year) in which they were especially open to chatting. This also left us interviewing more parents of young children than parents of older children, which might also be expected, since parents of younger children are generally more likely to move (Long 1992).

In the material of our interviews, I found what seemed like compelling evidence that many people connected a normative, suburban vision of house ownership to achieving adulthood and being a good parent, as recounted mostly in Chapter 5. This confirmed my starting suspicions. But I also found some surprises, effectively engaging in abductive analysis along the way (Timmermans and Tavory 2012). First, there were many contradictions in people's narratives and gaps in their logic. These were often accompanied by outright admissions that interviewees had not thought through much of their relationship to housing. Frequently they described using the interview process as a chance to do so. Among other things, this suggested that the rational choice models on which I had sometimes relied in the past (e.g., Lauster and Fransson 2006) were severely flawed, as suggested by a variety of critiques (e.g., Joas 1996; Swidler 1986). It also suggested that cultural norms were going to take me only so far in understanding people's relationships to housing. Most people could identify cultural influences at work around them—the very same ones I was attempting to document through my initial research plans—but many people nevertheless seemed to shrug off or actively resist these influences, as discussed in Chapter 5 and explored more through later chapters.

As I attempted to wade through how people accounted for their thinking and reported their actions, my attention was increasingly drawn to the alternately acknowledged and downplayed roles of habits and habitats in the stories I heard. Tracing lines of action backward tended to result in accounts of things—particularly those relating to housing situations—producing human responses. I began to incorporate things as actors by drawing on how they showed up within people's accounts of their own thinking and actions, bringing back Bruno Latour's "missing masses" (1992). As a result, I gradually worked out a model of habits and habitats that offered an alternative to rational choice models while ultimately incorporating culturally driven models. The situations and problems people reported responding to in their past moves and future plans left them oriented differently toward the house, as recounted in Chapters 6 and 7.

It became clear throughout my interviews, as in my own living situation, that the iconic, single-family house that many (but not all) of my participants idealized was no longer deemed achievable in and around Vancouver. As I began to conceptualize things as actors, the single-family house began to occupy center stage in my analysis. I redirected my efforts outside my interviews toward understanding how the single-family house became an actor, and where its actions mattered. Vancouver's history provided a ready case study for investigating these issues. The more I investigated the matter, the more it seemed clear that there were multiple forms the house could take. It also seemed increasingly clear that the history of local planning was enormously influential in shaping the house when and where it mattered as an actor. This sent me to the archives (both online and off) in order to learn more.

Drawing from the work of authors like Thomas Gieryn (2002) and Mariana Valverde (2011, 2012) helped me make sense of the different legal entities produced to govern the use of land across the city and broader metropolitan area. Much of the material in Chapters 1, 3, and 4 came from my attempts to reconstruct Vancouver's history in terms of the making of these regulatory creatures. I gradually realized that my interviews were really engaged in documenting the ways in which people responded to this thing that had taken over North American city-building efforts. People and houses were positioned vis-à-vis one another within a broader heterogeneous network of relationships: an actor-network. Moreover, the constitution of people and of houses as actors varied by the form they took within actor-networks.

Better understanding how all of this worked meant adopting the kinds of research methods amenable to exposing actor-networks. I looked to my own experiences, and those of my family members, as a helpful guide, but I also pursued a close reading of texts, as suggested by Nimmo (2011), including bylaws, media accounts, and statistics, as well as the transcripts of the qualitative interviews we had collected. I reviewed, coded, organized, and recoded transcripts multiple times, ultimately focusing on the problems that people encountered in their housing and how these related to their attempts at dwelling there. I also paid close attention to what could be learned from the contradictions in people's narratives and the gaps in their logic (recognizing, in the process, that an interview with me would no doubt elicit similar contradictions and gaps in my own logic).

Where possible in quoting from interviews, I have attempted to preserve people's speech patterns. At times, I have inserted text in brackets to provide the contexts that would make their speech intelligible. I have also imposed sentence structures and shortened sentences (e.g., removed certain repetitions of words and mumbling) in some places, inserting ellipses to indicate either lengthy pauses or the elision of intervening text that effectively worked like lengthy pauses, just keeping the conversation going. Overall I have attempted to keep my editing as minimal as possible, in order to let people speak for themselves. I have also attempted to preserve enough of their quotes to provide them a more embodied and integrated voice.

When describing interviewees, I have worked to provide enough detail to offer a sense of the perspectives they were likely to bring to our interviews. At the same time, I have attempted to ensure that people's identities remain confidential. Pseudonyms were generally chosen to correspond with the ethnic identities people described for us. While it does not include all of the people interviewed for the present study, the guide in Table A.1 provides a way to track down where introduced participants appear in the book. The many interviewees left out of the book generally provided perspectives in line with those included, offering valuable evidence that we had achieved some form of saturation in our data-collection efforts.

As a baseline, and because as a demographer I was intimately familiar with the data, I began the project by examining census numbers. Both for emphasis and reassurance, I found myself returning, again and again, to census and related forms of survey data. I take these to be generally representative of populations of actors (e.g., people, households, and dwelling units) of interest to me, even if the form each actor takes often remains ambiguous. Everyone counted in the census or survey at hand received a vote of sorts in what I wrote, ultimately weighted to reflect the North American population—though it should be noted that I almost always subdivided North America into a variety of what I think of as electoral districts (e.g., by country, by metropolis, by age, by occupation, by dwelling type, by geography). All of this more or less corresponds to standard statistical practice.

The census and survey datasets I drew on came primarily from three sources. First,

TABLE A.1 INTERVIEW PARTICIPANTS BY PAGES OF APPEARANCE

Pseudonym	Pages
Janice Akers-Kearney	133–134, 168–169
Kassy Aldridge	185–186, 188–189
Callista Allen	144, 166
Stephanie Bryson	129–131, 169–170
Sadie Carter	128–129
Vicky Chenowith	33–34, 131, 155
Christina Chu	162–163
Marlene Darcy	127–128, 157
Jackie Eberhardt	145–147, 156–157, 170
Scott Engeman	131, 153
Leila Ferreira	163–164, 184, 185
Joanie Folsom	142–143, 157
Amanda Garrison	124–125
Katrina Gower	134–135, 136, 176–180
Janine Harmon	161–162
Sandy Harris	172
Dana Jarvison	191–192
Linda Jones	135–136, 172, 187, 192–194
Ariel Koljevic	171
Lada Kurochkin	137
Cathy Kwan and Matt Ng	136–137, 142, 186–187
Nathalie Langdon	182
Jason Laserre	1–2, 183
Samantha Lyeung	126–127, 172
Annabel Marks	159–161, 172
Kathy Martin and Ted Demarest	31–32, 132, 154, 161, 181–182
Emma Miller	140–142, 195–197
Enid Ngai	172, 189–190
Mark Patterson	158
Marta Perez	165–166
Greg and Charity Rattner	138, 166–167
Shivani Ryan	153, 158–159, 164, 171
Jill Sampson	150–151, 167–168, 183, 194–195
Karen and Gary Shen	154, 169, 173, 189
Allison Smith	180–181
Risako Tagami	29
Tina Tremaine	151–152
Dina Warner	183–184

I drew on data published directly by census and related survey organizations, both in the United States (www.census.gov) and Canada (http://www.statcan.gc.ca/start-debut -eng.html). These data were frequently useful in their reported form, and I often simply reported these data as I found them, though fitted into slightly different categories (usually simplified) or plotted in slightly different ways (e.g., Tables 2.1, 2.2, and 3.1 and Figures 2.1, 2.3, and 4.8). Unfortunately, this data was frequently limited by the form within which it was published. Many of the comparisons or tabulations I wanted to see were not provided. To expand the array of data I could get, I drew on microdata derived from the census but published by academic researchers. For U.S. data (and occasional international comparisons), I drew on data published by the Minnesota Population Center

through the IPUMS (Integrated Public-Use Microdata Series) project, accessible at www
.ipums.org (Ruggles et al. 2010). A postdoctoral fellowship provided me close familiarity
with this dataset, and I contributed to its construction. Here I used the data mostly in a
very descriptive fashion, and often generated tables from the IPUMS database through
online data analysis. For Canadian data, I drew from the Data Centre maintained by the
CHASS (Computing in the Humanities and Social Sciences) project (http://datacentre
.chass.utoronto.ca/census/), housed at the University of Toronto. The online data analysis programs were quite similar between CHASS and IPUMS, making comparisons relatively easy. That said, there were numerous occasions, as documented in my descriptions
of tables and charts and figures throughout the book, when the methods by which data
were generated were not entirely the same between census or survey organizations in
Canada and the United States.

For contemporary data, I used both 2006 and 2011 census (or National Household
Survey) data for Canada. There were differences in sampling strategy and content between the two census years (the Canadian long-form census was replaced in 2011 with
the voluntary National Household Survey), as well as differences in data availability.
These generally provide explanations for why I jumped back and forth between the two
census years. In order to ensure comparability, I often used the American Community
Survey data (which has replaced the long-form census in the United States) from years
corresponding to the Canadian Census years to compare countries (e.g., Table 1.2 and
Figures 1.2, 1.3, and 2.2).

The use of 2006 and more recent 2011 data also brackets both the time period during which I collected my interviews and the intervening impact of the Great Recession
on housing patterns. For my overarching argument, the differences between 2006 data
and the most recent data available are unlikely to change the general patterns laid out
here. Nevertheless, readers should carefully check the source data in each table before
assuming it represents the latest estimate and/or takes into account the effects of the
Great Recession. In some places, especially where I was less worried about establishing comparability (e.g., Figure 1.4), I attempted to work with data directly covering the
period in which my interviews occurred. I combined both 2006 and 2011 census data in
establishing net migration estimates, and here the data were derived from short-form,
full-count estimates, making them readily comparable (Figure 5.1).

For historical data, I also worked with the sources available to me. I intensively
used 1961 data to describe a particular moment in Vancouver's history, both because
the data were available (via CHASS) and because the 1960s led to a major turning point
in Vancouver's trajectory (e.g., Figures 3.4, 4.1, and 4.3), but other moments sometimes
had better data and were also key (e.g., Figure 5.2). Nevertheless, I also drew on a variety of other historical data. Some maps are borrowed directly from archival resources
(Figures 3.1, 3.3, 4.4, and 4.5). Other maps (e.g., Figures 3.4 and 4.6) were drawn with
the assistance of both archival documents (often providing a base) and a simple, open-
source graphics program (GIMP). I also had help from a research assistant in assembling
Figure 4.6 from GIS software. All told, all findings of a quantitative nature, presented in
both figures and tables, should be easily replicable. Estimates were weighted, either by
household or individual, in line with suggestions by IPUMS and CHASS. Most estimates
were descriptive in nature, requiring few assumptions about causality and little, if any,
in the way of complicated statistical modeling.

REFERENCES

Abbott, Andrew. 1997. Of Time and Space: The Contemporary Relevance of the Chicago School. *Social Forces* 75 (4): 1149–1182.

Abu-Lughod, Janet, and Mary Mix Foley. 1960. Consumer Strategies. In *Housing Choices and Housing Constraints*, ed. Nelson Foote, Janet Abu-Lughod, Mary Mix Foley, and Louis Winnick, 71–271. New York: McGraw-Hill.

An Act to Incorporate the City of Vancouver. 1886. In *Statutes of the Province of British Columbia*, 4th Parl., 4th Sess, chap. 32, 161–256. Victoria: British Columbia.

Adams, Thomas. 1911. The British Point of View. In *Proceedings of the Third National Conference on City Planning*, 27–37. Boston: National Conference on City Planning. Available at http://www.library.cornell.edu/Reps/DOCS/adams_t.htm.

Addams, Jane. 1902. The Housing Problem in Chicago. *Annals of the American Academy of Political and Social Science* 20 (July): 99–107.

———. 1910. *Twenty Years at Hull House.* New York: Macmillan.

Anderson, Kay. 1991. *Vancouver's Chinatown: Racial Discourse in Canada, 1875–1980.* Montreal: McGill-Queen's University Press.

Archer, John. 2005. *Architecture and Suburbia: From English Villa to American Dream House, 1690–2000.* Minneapolis: University of Minnesota Press.

Ascher, Charles. 1945. What Are Cities For? *Annals of the American Academy of Political and Social Science* 242:1–6.

Baar, Kenneth. 1992. The National Movement to Halt the Spread of Multifamily Housing, 1890–1926. *Journal of the American Planning Association* 58 (1): 39–48.

Babcock, Richard. 1966. *The Zoning Game: Municipal Practices and Policies.* Madison: University of Wisconsin Press.

Baldassare, Mark. 1978. Human Spatial Behavior. *Annual Review of Sociology* 4:29–56.

Ball, Michael. 2003. Markets and the Structure of the Housebuilding Industry: An International Perspective. *Urban Studies* 40 (5–6): 897–916.

Barman, Jean. 1986. Neighbourhood and Community in Interwar Vancouver: Residential Differentiation and Civic Voting Behavior. *BC Studies* 69–70:97–141.

———. 1997. Whatever Happened to the Kanakas? *The Beaver: Exploring Canada's History* 77 (6): 12–19.

Barry, Lynda. 2002. *One Hundred Demons*. Seattle: Sasquatch Books.

Bartholomew, Harland. 1930. *A Plan for the City of Vancouver, British Columbia*. Vancouver: Vancouver Town Planning Commission. Available at http://archive.org/details/planforcityofvan00vanc.

———. 1944. *A Preliminary Report upon the Economic Background and Population (Revision of a Plan for the City of Vancouver)*. Vancouver: Vancouver Town Planning Commission. Available at http://archive.org/details/econbackground00vanc.

———. 1946. *A Preliminary Report upon Zoning Vancouver, British Columbia*. Vancouver: Vancouver Town Planning Commission. Available at http://archive.org/stream/reportzoning00vanc.

Batten, David. 1999. The Housing Mismatch Argument: The Construction of a Housing Orthodoxy in Australia. *Urban Studies* 36 (1): 137–151.

Bauer, Catherine. 1945. Good Neighborhoods. *Annals of the American Academy of Political and Social Science* 242:104–115.

Beauregard, Robert. 2006. *When America Became Suburban*. Minneapolis: University of Minnesota Press.

Becker, Gary. 1992. Habits, Addictions, and Traditions. *Kyklos* 45 (3): 327–345.

Belden, Russonello, and Stewart [consulting firm]. 2011. *The 2011 Community Preference Survey: What Americans Are Looking for When Deciding Where to Live*. Conducted for the National Association of Realtors. Available at http://www.brspoll.com/uploads/files/2011%20Community%20Preference%20Survey.pdf.

Bellett, Gerry. 2013. In the City, Single-Family Homes Are a Dying Breed. *Vancouver Sun*, November 5. Available at http://www.vancouversun.com/business/city+single+family+homes+dying+breed/9128287/story.html.

Berelowitz, Lance. 2005. *Dream City: Vancouver and the Global Imagination*. Vancouver: Douglas and McIntyre.

Bertaud, Alain. 2010. Land Markets, Government Interventions, and Housing Affordability. *Wolfensohn Center for Development Working Paper* 18. Brookings Institute.

Beyer, Kristin, Anne Baber Wallis, and L. Kevin Hamberger. 2015. Neighborhood Environment and Intimate Partner Violence: A Systematic Review. *Trauma, Violence, and Abuse* 16 (1): 16–47.

Bickford, Susan. 2000. Constructing Inequality: City Spaces and the Architecture of Citizenship. *Political Theory* 28 (3): 355–376.

Black, Jennifer, Richard Carpiano, Stuart Fleming, and Nathanael Lauster. 2011. Exploring the Distribution of Food Stores in British Columbia: Associations with Neighbourhood Socio-demographic Factors and Urban Form. *Health and Place* 17 (4): 961–970.

Block, Fred, and Margaret Somers. 2003. In the Shadow of Speenhamland: Social Policy and the Old Poor Law. *Politics and Society* 31 (2): 283–323.

Blomley, Nicholas. 2004. *Unsettling the City: Urban Land and the Politics of Property*. London: Routledge Chapman and Hall.

Blunt, Alison, and Robyn Dowling. 2006. *Home*. New York: Routledge.

Boddy, Trevor. 2003. New Urbanism: "The Vancouver Model." *Places* 16 (2): 14–21.

———. 2005. Vancouverism and Its Discontents. *Vancouver Review* 5 (Spring). Available at http://www.vancouverreview.com/past_articles/vancouverism.htm.

Booth, Alan, and John Edwards. 1976. Crowding and Family Relations. *American Sociological Review* 41 (2): 308–321.

Booth, Alan, David Johnson, and John Edwards. 1980. In Pursuit of Pathology: The Effects of Human Crowding. *American Sociological Review* 45 (5): 873–878.

Bourdieu, Pierre. 1973. The Berber House. In *Rules and Meanings: The Anthropology of Everyday Knowledge*, ed. M. Douglas, 98–110. Harmondsworth, UK: Penguin Education.

———. 1990. *The Logic of Practice.* Cambridge, UK: Polity Press.

———. 2005. *The Social Structures of the Economy.* Trans. Chris Turner. Cambridge, UK: Polity Press.

Bowker, Geoffrey, and Susan Star. 1999. *Sorting Things Out: Classification and Its Consequences.* Cambridge, MA: MIT Press.

Bratt, Rachel. 2002. Housing and Family Well-Being. *Housing Studies* 17 (1): 13–26.

Bratt, Rachel, and Abigail Vladeck. 2014. Addressing Restrictive Zoning for Affordable Housing: Experiences in Four States. *Housing Policy Debate* 24 (3): 594–636.

Bridge, Tyee. 2011. Going Gone. *Vancouver Magazine*, November 1. Available at http://www.vanmag.com/News_and_Features/Gone?page=0%2C0.

Brooks, David. 2002. Patio Man and the Sprawl People. *Weekly Standard* 7 (46). Available at http://www.weeklystandard.com/Content/Public/Articles/000/000/001/531wlvng.asp. Accessed July 30, 2013.

Brown, Daniel, Kenneth Johnson, Thomas Loveland, and David Theobald. 2005. Rural Land-Use Trends in the Coterminous United States, 1950–2000. *Ecological Applications* 15 (6): 1851–1863.

Brueckner, Jan. 2000. Urban Sprawl: Diagnosis and Remedies. *International Regional Science Review* 23 (2): 160–171.

Bruegmann, Robert. 2005. *Sprawl: A Compact History.* Chicago: University of Chicago Press.

Buitelaar, Edwin. 2009. Zoning, More than Just a Tool: Explaining Houston's Regulatory Practice. *European Planning Studies* 17 (7): 1049–1065.

Bula, Frances. 2012. Should You Sell Your Vancouver Condo Today? *Vancouver Magazine*, March 1. Available at http://www.vanmag.com/Real_Estate/Should_You_Sell_Your_Vancouver_Condo_Today.

———. 2013. Vancouver Planning Manager Faces Anger over Community Plans. *Globe and Mail*, July 14. Available at http://www.theglobeandmail.com/news/british-colum bia/city-planning-manager-faces-anger-over-community-plans/article132 14670/?cmpid=rss1.

———. 2014. The Challenge of Vancouver's Appeal to Foreign Investors. *Globe and Mail*, April 9. Available at http://www.theglobeandmail.com/news/british-columbia/the-challenge-of-vancouvers-appeal-to-foreign-investors/article17910691/.

Burawoy, Michael. 2015. Facing an Unequal World. *Current Sociology* 63 (1): 5–34.

Burgess, Ernest. 1925. The Growth of the City: An Introduction to a Research Project. *Trend of Population* 18:85–97. Publication of the American Sociological Society.

———. 1928. Residential Segregation in American Cities. *Annals of the American Academy of Political and Social Science* 140:105–115.

Buzzelli, Michael. 2001. Firm Size Structure in North American Housebuilding: Persistent Deconcentration, 1945–98. *Environment and Planning A* 33:533–550.

Buzzelli, Michael, and Richard Harris. 2006. Cities as the Industrial Districts of House-building. *International Journal of Urban and Regional Research* 30 (4): 894–917.

Calhoun, John. 1962. Population Density and Social Pathology. *Scientific American* 206:139–150.

Callon, Michel, and John Law. 2005. On Qualculation, Agency and Otherness. *Environment and Planning D: Society and Space* 23 (5): 717–733.

Camic, Charles. 1986. The Matter of Habit. *American Journal of Sociology* 91:1039–1087.

Campbell, Charles. 2013. At Ground Zero for Vancouver's Towering Debate. *The Tyee*, June 25. Available at http://thetyee.ca/Opinion/2013/06/25/Vancouver-Tower-Debate/.

Canada Mortgage and Housing Corporation (CMHC). 2006. *Canadian Housing Observer 2006*. Ottawa: CMHC.

———. 2007. *The Newcomer's Guide to Canadian Housing.* Ottawa: CMHC.

———. 2013. *Canadian Housing Observer 2013.* Ottawa: CMHC.

Canadian Home Builder's Association (CHBA). 2013. *Pulse—The CHBA Poll: Winter 2013.* Available at http://chba.ca/uploads/pulse%20survey%20results/main%20report2013.pdf. Accessed July 25, 2013.

Canadian Institute of Planners. 2013. *History of CIP.* Available at http://www.cip-icu.ca/web/la/en/pa/9ab7d1e80d2a48bd915c86479fbfcb92/template.asp. Accessed August 1, 2013.

Canadian Press. 1981. Houses Only for the Rich: NDP. *Globe and Mail*, September 14.

———. 2011. Vancouver No Longer World's Most Livable City. *Canadian Broadcasting Corporation*, August 30. Available at http://www.cbc.ca/news/canada/british-columbia/story/2011/08/30/bc-vancouver-livability.html.

Cheng, Lai-Sum Lisa. 1980. Secondary Suites: Housing Resource or Problem, the Vancouver Case. Master's thesis, University of British Columbia, Vancouver.

Church, Elizabeth. 2012. Toronto's Deputy Mayor Faces Backlash over Disparaging Downtown Living. *Globe and Mail*, July 12. Available at http://www.theglobeandmail.com/news/toronto/torontos-deputy-mayor-says-he-wouldnt-want-to-raise-his-children-downtown/article4411595/.

City of Hong Kong. 2007. The Survey on Waiting List Applicants for Public Rental Housing. *Hong Kong Monthly Digest of Statistics* (February): FB1–FB15. Available at http://www.censtatd.gov.hk/hkstat/sub/sp100.jsp?productCode=FA100102.

City of Vancouver. 2010. *City of Vancouver Rental Housing Strategy Research and Policy Development—Synthesis Report Final.* Vancouver: City of Vancouver. Available at http://vancouver.ca/docs/policy/housing-rental-housing-strategy-synthesis.pdf.

———. 2011. *RS-1 District Schedule.* May version. Vancouver: City of Vancouver. Available at http://former.vancouver.ca/commsvcs/BYLAWS/zoning/RS-1.PDF.

———. 2013. *Non-market Housing Inventory.* Vancouver: City of Vancouver. Available at http://app.vancouver.ca/NonMarketHousing_NET/ProjectSearch.aspx.

Collins, Randall. 2004. *Interaction Ritual Chains.* Princeton, NJ: Princeton University Press.

Coltrane, Scott. 2000. Research on Household Labor: Modeling and Measuring the Social Embeddedness of Routine Family Work. *Journal of Marriage and Family* 62 (4): 1208–1233.

Coolen, Henny, and J. Hoekstra. 2001. Values as Determinants of Preferences for Housing Attributes. *Journal of Housing and the Built Environment* 16 (3–4): 285–306.

Coontz, Stephanie. 2005. *Marriage, a History: From Obedience to Intimacy, or How Love Conquered Marriage.* Toronto: Penguin.

Co-operative Housing Federation of BC (CHFBC). 2013. Co-op Programs: Non-profit Co-operative Housing Funding Programs. Available at http://www.chf.bc.ca/what -co-op-housing/co-op-programs. Accessed August 1, 2013.

Coupland, Gary. 1991. The Point Grey Site: A Marpole Spring Village Component. *Canadian Journal of Archaeology* 15:73–96.

Cowan, Micki. 2012. Dunbar Residents Take "Densification" Fight to Steps of City Hall. *Vancouver Courier,* November 16. Available at http://www.vancourier.com/news/ Dunbar+residents+take+densification+fight+steps+city+hall/7562526/story.html.

DBRS. 2011. *Methodology: Rating Canadian Residential Mortgage-Backed Securities (RMBS) Transactions.* Available at http://www.dbrs.com/research/243240/rating -canadian-residential-mortgage-backed-securities-rmbs-transactions.pdf. Accessed July 23, 2013.

Demographia. 2013. *Ninth Annual Demographia International Housing Affordability Survey: 2013 Ratings for Metropolitan Markets.* Demographia. Available at http:// www.demographia.com/dhi.pdf.

Digman, John. 1990. Personality Structure: Emergence of the Five-Factor Model. *Annual Review of Psychology* 41:417–440.

District of West Vancouver. 2001. *Upper Lands Report.* Available at http://westvancou ver.ca/sites/default/files/dwv/assets/gov/docs/Committees-Groups/working-groups/ upper-lands/additional-documents/upper_lands_report_2001.pdf%208.55%20MB .pdf. Accessed July 25, 2015.

———. 2014. *Upper Lands Study, Map 7: Environmentally Sensitive Areas Synthesis.* Available at http://westvancouver.ca/sites/default/files/dwv/assets/gov/docs/Committees -Groups/working-groups/upper-lands/2014/Map%207%20Environmentally% 20Sensitive%20Area%20Synthesis.pdf. Accessed July 25, 2015.

———. 2015. *Upper Lands Working Group Final Report, June 22, 2015.* Available at http:// westvancouver.ca/sites/default/files/dwv/council-agendas/2015/jun/22/15jun22-5 .pdf. Accessed July 25, 2015.

Donaldson, Sue, and Will Kymlicka. 2011. *Zoopolis: A Political Theory of Animal Rights.* Oxford: Oxford University Press.

Doucet, Michael, and John Weaver. 1990. *Housing the North American City.* Montreal: McGill-Queen's University Press.

Douglas, Mary. 1991. The Idea of a Home: A Kind of Space. *Social Research* 58 (1): 287–307.

Dowling, Robyn. 1998. Neotraditionalism in the Suburban Landscape: Cultural Geographies of Exclusion in Vancouver, Canada. *Urban Geography* 19 (2): 105–122.

———. 2000. Cultures of Mothering and Car Use in Suburban Sydney: A Preliminary Investigation. *Geoforum* 31:345–353.

Downing, A. J. 1842. *Cottage Residences; or, A Series of Designs for Rural Cottages and Cottage Villas and their Gardens and Grounds. Adapted to North America.* New York: Wiley and Putnam.

Dunbar Resident's Association. 2011. Spring Newsletter. Available at http://dunbar-van couver.org/wp-content/uploads/2011/02/DRA-Feb-2011-Final-web.pdf. Accessed August 1, 2013.

Duneier, Mitchell. 1999. *Sidewalk.* New York: Farrar, Straus and Giroux.

Dunn, Kris, and Shane Singh. 2014. Pluralistic Conditioning: Social Tolerance and Effective Democracy. *Democratization* 21 (1): 1–28.

Dunski, Laura. 2005. Zoning after *Lawrence v. Texas*. *University of Illinois Law Review* 2005 (3): 847–872.

The Economist Intelligence Unit. 2015. *A Summary of the Liveability Ranking and Overview: August 2015*. Available at http://www.eiu.com/public/topical_report.aspx?campaignid=Liveability2015. Accessed December 1, 2015.

Environment Canada. 2013. *National Inventory Report 1990–2011: Greenhouse Gas Sources and Sinks in Canada (The Canadian Government's Submission to the UN Framework Convention on Climate Change: Part 1)*. Ottawa: Minister of the Environment. Available at http://unfccc.int/national_reports/annex_i_ghg_inventories/national_inventories_submissions/items/7383.php.

Evans, Jonathan St. B. T. 2008. Dual-Processing Accounts of Reasoning, Judgment, and Social Cognition. *Annual Review of Psychology* 59:255–278.

Ezzy, Douglas. 1998. Theorizing Narrative Identity: Symbolic Interactionism and Hermeneutics. *Sociological Quarterly* 39 (2): 239–252.

False Creek Co-op. 2013. About False Creek Co-operative. False Creek Co-op. Available at https://falsecreekco-op.com/about-our-co-op. Accessed August 1, 2013.

Fava, Sylvia. 1975. Beyond Suburbia. *Annals of the American Academy of Political and Social Science* 422:10–24.

Ferraro, Emilia, and Louise Reid. 2013. On Sustainability and Materiality: Homo Faber, a New Approach. *Ecological Economics* 96:125–131.

Ferree, Myra Marx. 1990. Beyond Separate Spheres: Feminism and Family Research. *Journal of Marriage and Family* 52 (4): 866–884.

Fischer, Claude. 1981. The Public and Private Worlds of City Life. *American Sociological Review* 46 (3): 306–316.

———. 1995. The Subcultural Theory of Urbanism: A Twentieth-Year Assessment. *American Journal of Sociology* 101 (3): 543–577.

Fleischmann, Arnold, and Carol Pierannunzi. 1990. Citizens, Development Interests, and Local Land-Use Regulation. *Journal of Politics* 52 (3): 838–853.

Florida, Richard. 2002. *The Rise of the Creative Class: And How It's Transforming Work, Leisure and Everyday Life*. New York: Basic Books.

Fogelson, Robert. 2005. *Bourgeois Nightmares: Suburbia, 1870–1930*. New Haven, CT: Yale University Press.

Foote, Nelson, Janet Abu-Lughod, Mary Mix Foley, and Louis Winnick. 1960. *Housing Choices and Housing Constraints*. New York: McGraw-Hill.

Forget, Evelyn. 2011. The Town with No Poverty: The Health Effects of a Canadian Guaranteed Annual Income Field Experiment. *Canadian Public Policy* 37 (3): 283–305.

Form, William. 1954. The Place of Social Structure in the Determination of Land Use: Some Implications for a Theory of Urban Ecology. *Social Forces* 32 (4): 317–323.

Forrest, Ray, and Misa Izuhara. 2012. The Shaping of Housing Histories in Shanghai. *Housing Studies* 27 (1): 27–44.

Frank, Lawrence, Martin Andresen, and Thomas Schmid. 2004. Obesity Relationships with Community Design, Physical Activity, and Time Spent in Cars. *American Journal of Preventive Medicine* 27 (2): 87–96.

Frank, Lawrence, James Sallis, Terry Conway, James Chapman, Brian Saelens, and William Bachman. 2006. Many Pathways from Land Use to Health: Associations between

Neighborhood Walkability and Active Transportation, Body Mass Index, and Air Quality. *Journal of the American Planning Association* 72 (1): 75–87.

Freeman, Lance, and Frank Braconi. 2004. Gentrification and Displacement: New York City in the 1990s. *Journal of the American Planning Association* 70 (1): 39–52.

Frykman, Jonas, and Orvar Löfgren. 1987. *Culture Builders: A Historical Anthropology of Middle-Class Life.* New Brunswick, NJ: Rutgers University Press.

Fuller, Theodore, John Edwards, Sairudee Vorakitphokatorn, and Santhat Sermsri. 1996. Chronic Stress and Psychological Well-Being: Evidence from Thailand on Household Crowding. *Social Science and Medicine* 42 (2): 265–280.

Galois, Robert. 1980. Social Structure in Space: The Making of Vancouver, 1886–1901. Ph.D. diss. Simon Fraser University, Burnaby.

Gans, Herbert. 1967. *The Levittowners: Ways of Life and Politics in a New Suburban Community.* New York: Vintage Books.

Garey, Anita. 1999. *Weaving Work and Motherhood.* Philadelphia: Temple University Press.

Garrish, Christopher. 2002. Unscrambling the Omelette: Understanding British Columbia's Agricultural Land Reserve. *BC Studies* 136:25–55.

Gentleman, Amelia. 2013. The Human Cost of the Bedroom Tax. *Guardian*, March 8, 2013. Available at http://www.theguardian.com/society/2013/mar/08/human-cost-of-bedroom-tax.

Gieryn, Thomas. 2002. What Buildings Do. *Theory and Society* 31 (1): 35–74.

Gill, Allison. 2000. From Growth Machine to Growth Management: The Dynamics of Resort Development in Whistler, British Columbia. *Environment and Planning A* 32:1083–1103.

Gillis, John. 1996. *A World of Their Own Making: Myth, Ritual, and the Quest for Family Values.* Cambridge, MA: Harvard University Press.

Glaeser, Edward. 2011. *Triumph of the City: How Our Greatest Invention Makes Us Richer, Smarter, Greener, Healthier and Happier.* New York: Penguin Press.

Glaeser, Edward, and Matthew Kahn. 2010. The Greenness of Cities: Carbon Dioxide Emissions and Urban Development. *Journal of Urban Economics* 67 (3): 404–418.

Glaeser, Edward, and Hedi Kallal. 1997. Thin Markets, Asymmetric Information, and Mortgage-Backed Securities. *Journal of Financial Intermediation* 6:64–86.

Glaeser, Edward, and Bryce Ward. 2009. The Causes and Consequences of Land Use Regulation: Evidence from Greater Boston. *Journal of Urban Economics* 65 (3): 265–278.

Glenn, Evelyn Nakano. 1992. From Servitude to Service Work: Historical Continuities in the Racial Division of Paid Reproductive Labor. *Signs* 18 (1): 1–43.

Grabb, Edward, and James Curtis. 2005. *Regions Apart: The Four Societies of Canada and the United States.* Don Mills, ON: Oxford University Press.

Grant, Jill. 2006. *Planning the Good Community: New Urbanism in Theory and Practice.* New York: Routledge.

Grant, Jill, and Daniel Scott. 2011. Redefining the Canadian Dream? Household Life Cycles, Housing Costs, and Aspirations for Suburban Housing. *Working Paper: Preliminary Findings from the Trends in the Suburbs Project.* Halifax: School of Planning, Dalhousie University. Available at http://theoryandpractice.planning.dal.ca/html/suburbs_project/suburbs_working.html.

Gray, Rowan, Brendan Gleeson, and Matthew Burke. 2010. Urban Consolidation, Household Greenhouse Emissions, and the Role of Planning. *Urban Policy and Research* 28 (3): 335–346.

Greater Vancouver Regional District. 1975. *The Livable Region 1976/1986: Proposals to Man-age the Growth of Greater Vancouver.* Vancouver: Greater Vancouver Regional District.

Greater Vancouver Regional Steering Committee on Homelessness. 2014. *Results of the 2014 Homeless Count in the Metro Vancouver Region.* Available at http://www.metro vancouver.org/services/regional-planning/homelessness/HomelessnessPublications/2014MVHomelessCountJuly31-14Results.pdf.

Green, Brian, and Yda Schreuder. 1991. Growth, Zoning, and Neighborhood Organizations: Land Use Conflict in Wilmington, Delaware. *Journal of Urban Affairs* 13 (1): 97–110.

Gross, Neil. 2009. A Pragmatist Theory of Mechanisms. *American Sociological Review* 74:358–379.

Gutstein, Donald. 1975. *Vancouver Ltd.* Toronto: Lorimer.

Gyourko, Joseph. 2009. Housing Supply. *Annual Review of Economics* 1:295–318.

Haaf, Angela, and Hilary Meredith. 2011. *Frank E. Buck Fonds.* Vancouver: University of British Columbia Archives. Available at http://www.library.ubc.ca/archives/u_arch/buck_frank.pdf.

Haan, Michael. 2005. The Decline of the Immigrant Home-Ownership Advantage: Life Cycle, Declining Fortunes and Changing Housing Careers in Montreal, Toronto, and Vancouver, 1981–2001. *Urban Studies* 42 (12): 2191–2212.

Hanna, Kevin. 1997. Regulation and Land-Use Conservation: A Case Study of the British Columbia Agricultural Land Reserve. *Journal of Soil and Water Conservation* 52 (3): 166–170.

Haraway, Donna. 2003. *The Companion Species Manifesto: Dogs, People, and Significant Otherness.* Chicago: Prickly Paradigm Press.

Harcourt, Mike, Ken Cameron, and Sean Rossiter. 2007. *City Making in Paradise: Nine Decisions That Saved Vancouver.* Vancouver: Douglas and McIntyre.

Harris, Douglas. 2011. Condominium and the City: The Rise of Property in Vancouver. *Law and Social Inquiry* 36 (3): 694–726.

Harris, Richard. 2000. More American than the United States: Housing in Urban Canada in the Twentieth Century. *Journal of Urban History* 26 (4): 456–478.

———. 2004. *Creeping Conformity: How Canada Became Suburban, 1900–1960.* Toronto: University of Toronto Press.

———. 2012. *Building a Market: The Rise of the Home Improvement Industry, 1914–1960.* Chicago: University of Chicago Press.

Harris, Richard, and Doris Forrester. 2003. The Suburban Origins of Redlining: A Canadian Case Study, 1935–54. *Urban Studies* 40 (13): 2661–2686.

Hartmann, Heidi. 1981. The Family as the Locus of Gender, Class, and Political Struggle: The Example of Housework. *Signs* 6 (3): 366–394.

Harvey, David. 1973. *Social Justice and the City.* London: Edward Arnold.

Hayden, Dolores. 2002. *Redesigning the American Dream: Gender, Housing, and Family Life.* New York: W. W. Norton.

Hayes, Derek. 2005. *Historical Atlas of Vancouver and the Lower Fraser Valley.* Vancouver: Douglas and McIntyre.

Hays, Sharon. 1996. *The Cultural Contradictions of Motherhood.* New Haven, CT: Yale University Press.

Heidegger, Martin. 1971. *Poetry, Language, Thought.* Trans. and with introd. by Albert Hofstadter. Repr., New York: Harper and Row, 2001.

Hess, Paul. 2005. Rediscovering the Logic of Garden Apartments. *Places* 17 (2): 30–35.

Hiebert, Daniel. 2009. Newcomers in the Canadian Housing Market: A Longitudinal Study, 2001–2005. *Canadian Geographer* 53 (3): 268–287.

Hiebert, Daniel, and Pablo Mendez. 2008. Settling In: Newcomers in the Canadian Housing Market 2001–2005. *Metropolis BC Working Paper* 08-04. Vancouver: Metropolis BC.

Hinchliffe, Steve, Matthew Kearnes, Monica Degen, and Sarah Whatmore. 2005. Urban Wild Thing: A Cosmopolitical Experiment. *Environment and Planning D: Society and Space* 23 (5): 643–658.

Hirt, Sonia. 2014. *Zoned in the USA: The Origins and Implications of American Land-Use Regulation.* Ithaca, NY: Cornell University Press.

Hochschild, Arlie, and Anne Machung. 1989. *The Second Shift.* New York: Viking Penguin.

Holden, Erling, and Ingrid Norland. 2005. Three Challenges for the Compact City as a Sustainable Urban Form: Household Consumption of Energy and Transport in Eight Residential Areas in the Greater Oslo Region. *Urban Studies* 42:2145–2166.

Holdsworth, Deryck. 1986. Cottages and Castles for Vancouver Home-Seekers. *BC Studies* 69–70:11–32.

Hulchanski, David. 1993. New Forms of Owning and Renting. In *House, Home, and Community: Progress in Housing Canadians 1945–1986,* ed. John Miron, 64–75. Montreal: McGill-Queen's University Press.

Jackson, Kenneth. 1985. *Crabgrass Frontier: The Suburbanization of the United States.* New York: Oxford University Press.

Jacobs, Jane. 1961. *The Death and Life of Great American Cities.* New York: Random House.

Jacques, D. H. 1859. *The House: A Pocket Manual of Rural Architecture: Or, How to Build Country Houses and Out-Buildings.* New York: Fowler and Wells.

Jerolmack, Colin. 2013. *The Global Pigeon.* Chicago: University of Chicago Press.

Joas, Hans. 1996. *The Creativity of Action.* Chicago: University of Chicago Press.

Johnson, Steven. 2006. *The Ghost Map: The Story of London's Most Terrifying Epidemic— and How It Changed Science, Cities, and the Modern World.* New York: Riverhead Books.

Jonathan Rose Companies. 2011. *Location Efficiency and Housing Type: Boiling It Down to BTUs.* Environmental Protection Agency Working Paper. Available at http://epa .gov/dced/pdf/location_efficiency_BTU.pdf.

Kemeny, Jim. 1992. *Housing and Social Theory.* London: Routledge.

Kenworthy, Jeffrey, and Felix Laub. 1996. Automobile Dependence in Cities: An International Comparison of Urban Transport and Land Use Patterns with Implications for Sustainability. *Environmental Impact Assessment Review* 16:279–308.

———. 1999. Patterns of Automobile Dependence in Cities: An International Overview of Key Physical and Economic Dimensions with Some Implications for Urban Policy. *Transportation Research Part A* 33:691–723.

Kimelberg, Shelley McDonough. 2010. "Can We Seal the Deal?" An Examination of Uncertainty in the Development Process. *Economic Development Quarterly* 24 (1): 87–96.

———. 2011. Inside the Growth Machine: Real Estate Professionals on the Perceived Challenges of Urban Development. *City and Community* 10 (1): 76–99.

Kirby, Jason. 2011. The Real Problem with Vancouver's Outrageous House Prices. *Maclean's*, July 1. Available at http://www2.macleans.ca/2011/06/01/the-real-problem-with-vancouvers-outrageous-house-prices/.

Kochanek, Kenneth, Jiaquan Xu, Sherry Murphy, Arialdi Miniño, and Hsiang-Ching Kung. 2011. Deaths: Final Data for 2009. *National Vital Statistics Reports* 60 (3): 1–117.

Kotkin, Joel. 2012. Let L.A. Be L.A. *City Journal* 22 (3). Available at http://www.city-journal.org/2012/22_3_snd-los-angeles.html.

Kripner, Greta. 2011. *Capitalizing on Crisis: The Political Origins of the Rise of Finance.* Cambridge, MA: Harvard University Press.

Kusenbach, Margarethe. 2013. Place Feelings and Life Stories in Florida Mobile Home Communities. In *Home: International Perspectives on Culture, Identity, and Belonging*, ed. Margarethe Kusenbach and Krista Paulsen, 199–224. Frankfurt am Main, Germany: Peter Lang.

Kymlicka, Will. 1995. *Multicultural Citizenship: A Liberal Theory of Minority Rights.* Oxford: Oxford University Press.

Lamb, W. Kaye, ed. 2007. *The Letters and Journals of Simon Fraser 1806–1808.* Toronto: Dundurn Press.

Lanier, Christina, and Michael Maume. 2009. Intimate Partner Violence and Social Isolation across the Rural/Urban Divide. *Violence against Women* 15 (11): 1311–1330.

Laslett, Barbara, and Johanna Brenner. 1989. Gender and Social Reproduction: Historical Perspectives. *Annual Review of Sociology* 15:381–404.

Lasner, Matthew. 2012. *High Life: Condo Living in the Suburban Century.* New Haven, CT: Yale University Press.

Latour, Bruno. 1992. Where Are the Missing Masses? The Sociology of a Few Mundane Artifacts. In *In Shaping Technology/Building Society: Studies in Sociotechnical Change*, ed. Wiebe E. Bijker and John Law, 225–258. Cambridge, MA: MIT Press.

———. 1993. *We Have Never Been Modern.* Trans. Catherine Porter. Cambridge, MA: Harvard University Press.

Lauster, Nathanael. 2008. Better Homes and Families: Housing Markets and Young Couple Stability in Sweden. *Journal of Marriage and Family* 70 (4): 891–903.

———. 2010a. Housing and the Proper Performance of American Motherhood. *Housing Studies* 25 (4): 543–557.

———. 2010b. A Room to Grow: The Residential Density-Dependence of Childbearing in Europe and the United States. In *Low Fertility in Comparative Perspective*, ed. B. Ram, special issue, *Canadian Studies in Population* 37 (3–4): 475–496.

———. 2012. The Performance of Motherhood and Fertility Decline: A Stage Props Approach. In *The End of Children? Changing Trends in Childbearing and Childhood*, ed. Nathanael Lauster and Graham Allan, 70–91. Vancouver: University of British Columbia Press.

Lauster, Nathanael, and Adam Easterbrook. 2011. No Room for New Families? A Field Experiment Measuring Rental Discrimination against Same-Sex Couples and Single Parents. *Social Problems* 58 (3): 389–409.

Lauster, Nathanael, and Urban Fransson. 2006. Of Marriages and Mortgages: The Second Demographic Transition and the Relationship between Marriage and Home Ownership in Sweden. *Housing Studies* 21 (6): 911–929.

Lauster, Nathanael, and Frank Tester. 2010. Culture as a Problem in Linking Material Inequality to Health: On Residential Crowding in the Arctic. *Health and Place* 16:523–530.

———. 2014. Homelessness and Health in the Canadian East Arctic. In *Homelessness and Health*, ed. M. Guirguis-Younger, S. Hwang, and R. McNeil, 87–110. Ottawa: University of Ottawa Press.

Law, John, and Vicky Singleton. 2005. Object Lessons. *Organization* 12 (3): 331–355.

Lazaruk, Susan. 2012. Will Young Homebuyers Say Goodbye to Vancouver for Good? *The Province*, January 22. Available at http://www2.canada.com/health/asian+investors+looking /6025444/story.html?id=6033342.

Lazzarin, Celia. 1990. Rent Control and Rent Decontrol in British Columbia: A Case Study of the Vancouver Rental Market, 1974 to 1989. Master's thesis, University of British Columbia.

Lees, Loretta. 2000. A Reappraisal of Gentrification: Towards a "Geography of Gentrification." *Progress in Human Geography* 24 (3): 389–408.

Levine, Jonathan. 2006. *Zoned Out: Regulation, Market, and Choice in Transportation and Metropolitan Land-Use*. Washington, DC: Resources for the Future.

Levine, Jonathan, and Anseem Inam. 2004. The Market for Transportation–Land Use Integration: Do Developers Want Smarter Growth than Regulations Allow? *Transportation* 31 (4): 409–427.

Ley, David. 1987. Styles of the Times: Liberal and Neo-conservative Landscapes in Inner Vancouver, 1968–1986. *Journal of Historical Geography* 13 (1): 40–56.

———. 1996. *The New Middle Class and the Remaking of the Central City*. Oxford: Oxford University Press.

———. 2010. *Millionaire Migrants: Trans-Pacific Life Lines*. Oxford: Blackwell-Wiley.

Ley, David, and John Mercer. 1980. Locational Conflict and the Politics of Consumption. *Economic Geography* 56 (2): 89–109.

Lindberg, Erik, Tommy Gärling, and Henry Montgomery. 1989. Belief-Value Structures as Determinants of Consumer Behaviour: A Study of Housing Preferences and Choices. *Journal of Consumer Policy* 12 (2): 119–137.

Lizardo, Omar. 2004. The Cognitive Origins of Bourdieu's *Habitus*. *Journal for the Theory of Social Behaviour* 34:375–401.

Lizardo, Omar, and Michael Strand. 2010. Skills, Toolkits, Contexts, and Institutions: Clarifying the Relationship between Different Approaches to Cognition in Cultural Sociology. *Poetics* 38:204–227.

Logan, Gordon. 1988. Toward an Instance Theory of Automatization. *Psychological Review* 95 (4): 492–527.

Logan, John, and Harvey Molotch. 2007. *Urban Fortunes: The Political Economy of Place*. Berkeley: University of California Press.

Long, Larry. 1992. Changing Residence: Comparative Perspectives on Its Relationship to Age, Sex, and Marital Status. *Population Studies* 46 (1): 141–158.

Loudon, J. C. 1846. *An Encyclopaedia of Cottage, Farm, and Villa Architecture and Furniture*. London: Longman, Brown, Green, and Longmans.

MacDonald, Norbert. 1973. A Critical Growth Cycle for Vancouver, 1900–1914. *BC Studies* 17:26–42.

Maitland, Andrea. 1981. NDP Ghosts Come to Haunt SoCreds. *Globe and Mail*, July 11.

Mallett, Shelley. 2004. Understanding Home: A Critical Review of the Literature. *Sociological Review* 52 (1): 62–89.

Mankiw, N. Gregory, and David Weil. 1989. The Baby Boom, the Baby Bust, and the Housing Market. *Regional Science and Urban Economics* 19:235–258.

Mann, Bill. 2012. High-Priced Vancouver Losing Residents. *MarketWatch*, August 21. Available at http://www.marketwatch.com/story/high-priced-vancouver-losing-residents-2012-08-21.

Manzo, Lynne. 2003. Beyond House and Haven: Toward a Revisioning of Emotional Relationships with Places. *Journal of Environmental Psychology* 23:47–61.

Martin, Isaac, and Christopher Niedt. 2015. *Foreclosed America*. Redwood City, CA: Stanford University Press.

Mason, Gary. 2014. Vancouver's Election Just Got Interesting. *Globe and Mail*, November 11. Available at http://www.theglobeandmail.com/news/british-columbia/vancouvers-election-just-got-interesting/article21544863/.

Mawani, Renisa. 2009. *Colonial Proximities: Crossracial Encounters and Juridical Truths in British Columbia, 1871–1921*. Vancouver: University of British Columbia Press.

McCrae, Robert. 1987. Creativity, Divergent Thinking, and Openness to Experience. *Journal of Personality and Social Psychology* 52 (6): 1258–1265.

McDonald, Robert. 1996. *Making Vancouver: Class, Status, and Social Boundaries, 1863–1913*. Vancouver: University of British Columbia Press.

McKay, Sherry. 2003–2004. "Urban Housekeeping" and Keeping the Modern House. *BC Studies* 140:11–40.

McKenzie, Evan. 1994. Privatopia: Homeowner Associations and the Rise of Residential Private Government. New Haven, CT: Yale University Press.

———. 2005. Planning through Residential Clubs: Homeowners' Associations. *Economic Affairs* 25 (4): 28–31.

Metro Vancouver Policy and Planning Department. 2008. *Metro Vancouver's 2006 Generalized Land Use by Municipality*. Burnaby: Metro Vancouver.

Michelson, William. 1967. Potential Candidates for the Designers' Paradise, a Social Analysis from a Nationwide Survey. *Social Forces* 46 (2): 190–196.

Milan, Ann. 2011. *Report on the Demographic Situation in Canada: Fertility; Overview, 2008*. Ottawa: Statistics Canada.

Mitchell, Katharyne. 2004. *Crossing the Neoliberal Line: Pacific Rim Migration and the Metropolis*. Philadelphia: Temple University Press.

Modell, John, and Tamara Hareven. 1973. Urbanization and the Malleable Household: An Examination of Boarding and Lodging in American Families. *Journal of Marriage and Family* 35 (3): 467–479.

Mohamed, Rayman. 2006. The Psychology of Residential Developers: Lessons from Behavioral Economics and Additional Explanations for Satisficing. *Journal of Planning Education and Research* 26:28–37.

Molotch, Harvey. 1976. The City as a Growth Machine: Toward a Political Economy of Place. *American Journal of Sociology* 82 (2): 309–322.

Morris, Earl, Sue Crull, and Mary Winter. 1976. Housing Norms, Housing Satisfaction and the Propensity to Move. *Journal of Marriage and Family* 38 (2): 309–320.

Moss, Madonna, and John Erlandson. 1995. Reflections on North American Pacific Coast Prehistory. *Journal of World Prehistory* 9 (1): 1–45.

Mulder, Clara. 1996. Housing Choice: Assumptions and Approaches. *Journal of Housing and the Built Environment* 11 (3): 209–232.

Mulder, Clara, and Francesco Billari. 2010. Home-Ownership Regimes and Low Fertility. *Housing Studies* 25 (4): 527–541.

Murray, Karen. 2011. Making Space in Vancouver's East End: From Leonard Marsh to the Vancouver Agreement. *BC Studies* 169:7–49.

Myers, Dowell, William Baer, and Seong-Youn Choi. 1996. The Changing Problem of Overcrowded Housing. *Journal of the American Planning Association* 62 (1): 66–84.

Natural Resources Canada. 2010. *Survey of Household Energy Use 2007*. Ottawa: Public Works and Government Services Canada.

———. 2013. *Energy Use Data Handbook: 1990–2010*. Ottawa: Public Works and Government Services Canada.

Navarro, Mireya. 2013. U.S. Rules Bar Aid to Co-ops Hit by Sandy. *New York Times*, May 1. Available at http://www.nytimes.com/2013/05/02/nyregion/fema-policy-keeps-co-ops-from-disaster-aid.html?hp&_r=3&.

Newman, Kathe, and Elvin Wyly. 2006. The Right to Stay Put, Revisited: Gentrification and Resistance to Displacement in New York City. *Urban Studies* 43 (1): 23–57.

Newman, Peter, and Jeffrey Kenworthy. 1989. *Cities and Automobile Dependence: An International Sourcebook*. Aldershot, UK: Gower Publishing.

Nimmo, Richie. 2011. Actor-Network Theory and Methodology: Social Research in a More-than-Human World. *Methodological Innovations Online* 6 (3): 108–119.

Northwest Environment Watch. 2002. *Sprawl and Smart Growth in Greater Vancouver: A Comparison of Vancouver, British Columbia with Seattle, Washington*. Seattle: Sightline Institute.

Owen, David. 2004. Green Manhattan: Everywhere Should Be More like New York. *New Yorker*, October 18, pp. 111–123.

Parks, S. E., R. A. Housemann, and R. C. Brownson. 2003. Differential Correlates of Physical Activity in Urban and Rural Adults of Various Socioeconomic Backgrounds in the United States. *Journal of Epidemiology and Community Health* 57:29–35.

Paulsen, Krista. 2013. Modeling Home: Ideals of Residential Life in Builders' Show Houses. In *Home: International Perspectives on Culture, Identity, and Belonging*, ed. Margarethe Kusenbach and Krista Paulsen, 25–48. Frankfurt am Main, Germany: Peter Lang.

Peck, Jamie. 2005. Struggling with the Creative Class. *International Journal of Urban and Regional Research* 29 (4): 740–770.

Peck, Jamie, and Nik Theodore. 2010. Mobilizing Policy: Models, Methods, and Mutations. *Geoforum* 41:169–174.

Pemberly, F. 1911. Vancouver, a City of Beautiful Homes. *British Columbia Magazine* 7 (12): 1313–1315.

Perin, Constance. 1977. *Everything in Its Place: Social Order and Land Use in America*. Princeton, NJ: Princeton University Press.

Peterson, M. Nils, Tarla Rai Peterson, and Jianguo Liu. 2013. *The Housing Bomb: Why Our Addiction to Houses Is Destroying the Environment and Threatening Our Society*. Baltimore: Johns Hopkins University Press.

Polanyi, Karl. 1957. *The Great Transformation: The Political and Economic Origins of Our Time*. Boston: Beacon Press.

Power, Emma. 2012. Domestication and the Dog: Embodying Home. *Area* 44 (3): 371–378.

Power, Garrett. 1989. The Advent of Zoning. *Planning Perspectives* 4:1–13.

Pratt, Geraldine. 1986. Housing Tenure and Social Cleavages in Urban Canada. *Annals of the Association of American Geographers* 76 (3): 366–380.

———. 2012. *Families Apart: Migrant Mothers and the Conflicts of Labor and Love*. Minneapolis: University of Minnesota Press.

Price, Gordon. 2012. Density in a City of Neighbourhoods. *Carbon Talks*, June 5. Vancouver: City of Vancouver. Available at http://www.carbontalks.ca/documents/Discus sion%20guides/CarbonTalks-DensityDialogue-DiscussionGuide.pdf.

Pugh, Allison. 2009. *Longing and Belonging: Parents, Children, and Consumer Culture.* Berkeley: University of California Press.

Punter, John. 2002. Urban Design as Public Policy: Evaluating the Design Dimension of Vancouver's Planning System. *International Planning Studies* 7 (4): 265–282.

——. 2003. *The Vancouver Achievement: Urban Planning and Design.* Vancouver: University of British Columbia Press.

Pyke, Karen. 2000. "The Normal American Family" as an Interpretive Structure of Family Life among Grown Children of Korean and Vietnamese Immigrants. *Journal of Marriage and Family* 62 (1): 240–255.

Quigley, John, and Steven Raphael. 2004. Is Housing Unaffordable? Why Isn't It More Affordable? *Journal of Economic Perspectives* 18 (1): 191–214.

Quinn, Stephen. 2012. For Homeowners, Skinny-Street Strategy Is Thin on Logic. *Globe and Mail*, August 10. Available at http://www.theglobeandmail.com/news/ british-columbia/for-homeowners-skinny-street-strategy-is-thin-on-logic/ article4476305/.

Rabe, Birgitta, and Mark Taylor. 2010. Residential Mobility, Quality of Neighbourhood and Life Course Events. *Journal of the Royal Statistical Society* 173 (3): 531–555.

Radeloff, V. C., R. B. Hammer, S. I. Stewart, J. S. Fried, S. S. Holcomb, and J. F. McKeefry. 2005. The Wildland-Urban Interface in the United States. *Ecological Applications* 15 (3): 799–805.

Ramage-Morin, Pamela. 2008. Motor Vehicle Accident Deaths, 1979–2004. *Health Reports* 19 (3): 1–7. Statistics Canada.

Real Estate Board of Greater Vancouver (REBGV). 2016. *MLS Home Price Index.* Vancouver: REBGV. Available at http://www.rebgv.org/home-price-index. Accessed April 4, 2016.

Redish, A. D., S. Jensen, and A. Johnson. 2008. A Unified Framework for Addiction: Vulnerabilities in the Decision Process. *Behavioral and Brain Sciences* 31: 415–437.

Rice, A. V., and D. W. Langor. 2009. Mountain Pine Beetle–Associated Blue-Stain Fungi in Lodgepole × Jack Pine Hybrids near Grande Prairie, Alberta (Canada). *Forest Pathology* 39:323–334.

Rickwood, Peter, Garry Glazebrook, and Glen Searle. 2007. Urban Structure and Energy—A Review. *Urban Policy and Research* 26 (1): 57–81.

Robbins, Paul. 2007. *Lawn People: How Grasses, Weeds, and Chemicals Make Us Who We Are.* Philadelphia: Temple University Press.

Robertson, Leslie. 2007. Taming Space: Drug Use, HIV, and Homemaking in Downtown Eastside Vancouver. *Gender, Place and Culture* 14 (5): 527–549.

Rome, Adam. 2001. *The Bulldozer in the Countryside: Suburban Sprawl and the Rise of American Environmentalism.* New York: Cambridge University Press.

Ross, Becki. 2010. Sex and (Evacuation from) the City: The Moral and Legal Regulation of Sex Workers in Vancouver's West End, 1975–1985. *Sexualities* 13 (2): 197–218.

Rossi, Peter. 1980. *Why Families Move.* 2nd ed. Beverly Hills: Sage.

Royal Bank of Canada. 2013. *Housing Trends and Affordability—February 2013.* RBC Economics. Available at http://www.rbc.com/newsroom/pdf/HA-0225-2013.pdf. Accessed July 26, 2013.

Ruggles, Steven, J. Trent Alexander, Katie Genadek, Ronald Goeken, Matthew B. Schroeder, and Matthew Sobek. 2010. *Integrated Public Use Microdata Series: Version 5.0* [machine-readable database]. Minneapolis: University of Minnesota.

Runka, G. Gary. 2006. BC's Agricultural Land Reserve—Its Historical Roots. Presentation at Planning for Food, the Post World Planners Congress Seminar, June 21. Available at http://smartgrowth.bc.ca/Portals/0/Downloads/ALRHistoryRunka.pdf. Accessed August 28, 2013.

Rybczynski, Witold. 1987. *Home: A Short History of an Idea.* New York: Penguin Books.

Saelens, Brian, James Sallis, Jennifer Black, and Diana Chen. 2003. Neighborhood-Based Differences in Physical Activity: An Environment Scale Evaluation. *American Journal of Public Health: Research and Practice* 93 (9): 1551–1558.

Saez, Emmanuel. 2005. Top Incomes in the United States and Canada over the Twentieth Century. *Journal of the European Economic Association, Papers and Proceedings* 3 (2–3): 402–411.

Savage, Howard. 2009. Who Could Afford to Buy a Home in 2004? *Current Housing Reports* H121/09-1. U.S. Census Bureau.

Sennett, Richard. 1970. *The Uses of Disorder: Personal Identity and City Life.* New York: Alfred K. Knopf.

Sewell, John. 1993. *The Shape of the City: Toronto Struggles with Modern Planning.* Toronto: University of Toronto Press.

———. 1994. *Houses and Homes: Housing for Canadians.* Toronto: James Lorimer.

———. 2009. *The Shape of the Suburbs: Understanding Toronto's Sprawl.* Toronto: University of Toronto Press.

Shaughnessy Property Owners Association (SHPOA). 2013. *History of SHPOA.* Vancouver: SHPOA. Available at http://www.shpoa.ca/history_of_SHPOA?scroll=124. Accessed August 1, 2013.

Shiller, Robert. 2000. *Irrational Exuberance.* Princeton, NJ: Princeton University Press.

Shlay, Anne B. 1984. Regulating Scarcity: The Effects of Zoning on Urban Land Market Changes. *Journal of Urban Affairs* 6 (3): 19–35.

———. 1995. Housing in the Broader Context in the United States. *Housing Policy Debate* 6:695–720.

Shlay, Anne B., and Peter Rossi. 1981. Keeping Up the Neighborhood: Estimating Net Effects of Zoning. *American Sociological Review* 46:703–719.

Silver, Daniel, and Terry Nicholas Clark. 2015. The Power of Scenes. *Cultural Studies* 29 (3): 425–449.

Simkovic, Michael. 2013. Competition and Crisis in Mortgage Securitization. *Indiana Law Journal* 88 (1): 213–271.

Simmel, Georg. 1903. The Metropolis and Mental Life. In *The Sociology of Georg Simmel,* ed. and trans. Kurt H. Wolff, 409–424. Repr., New York: Free Press, 1950.

Six, Diana L., and B. J. Bentz. 2007. Temperature Determines Symbiont Abundance in a Multipartite Bark Beetle–Fungus Ectosymbiosis. *Microbial Ecology* 54 (1): 112–118.

Skaburskis, Andrejs. 1989. Inversions in Urban Density Gradients: A Brief Look at the Vancouver Metropolitan Area's Density Profile. *Urban Studies* 26:397–401.

Smith, Dorothy. 1993. The Standard North American Family: SNAF as an Ideological Code. *Journal of Family Issues* 14 (1): 50–65.

Somerville, Tsuriel. 1999. The Industrial Organization of Housing Supply: Market Activity, Land Supply and the Size of Homebuilder Firms. *Real Estate Economics* 27 (4): 669–694.

Statistics Canada. 2012. *Energy Statistics Handbook: First Quarter 2012*. Ottawa: Minister of Industry. Available at http://www.statcan.gc.ca/pub/57-601-x/57-601-x2012001 -eng.htm. Accessed August 1, 2013.

———. 2013. *Human Activity and the Environment: Measuring Ecosystem Goods and Services in Canada*. Ottawa: Statistics Canada.

Steele, Eric. 1987. Community Participation and the Function of Rules: The Case of Urban Zoning Boards. *Law and Policy* 9 (3): 279–303.

Storper, Michael, and Michael Manville. 2006. Behaviour, Preferences and Cities: Urban Theory and Urban Resurgence. *Urban Studies* 43 (8): 1247–1274.

Strack, Fritz, and Roland Deutsch. 2004. Reflective and Impulsive Determinants of Social Behavior. *Personality and Social Psychology Review* 8 (3): 220–247.

Ström, Sara. 2010. Housing and First Births in Sweden, 1972–2005. *Housing Studies* 25 (4): 509–526.

Stueck, Wendy. 2012. What Does It Mean to Have the World's Best Reputation? Vancouver Will Soon Find Out. *Globe and Mail*, September 27. Available at http://www.the globeandmail.com/news/british-columbia/what-does-it-mean-to-have-the-worlds -best-reputation-vancouver-will-soon-find-out/article4572459/.

Sullivan, Esther. 2014. Halfway Homeowners: Eviction and Forced Relocation among Homeowners in Manufactured Home Parks in Florida. *Law and Social Inquiry* 39 (2): 474–497.

Surborg, Björn, Rob VanWynsberghe, and Elvin Wyly. 2008. Mapping the Olympic Growth Machine: Transnational Urbanism and the Growth Machine Diaspora. *City* 12 (3): 341–355.

Swidler, Ann. 1986. Culture in Action: Symbols and Strategies. *American Sociological Review* 51 (2): 273–286.

Tafler, Sid. 1984. Tenancy Law Ignores Old, MLA Says. *Globe and Mail*, April 11.

Talen, Emily. 2012. *City Rules: How Regulations Affect Urban Form*. Washington, DC: Island Press.

Taylor, Dorceta. 2009. *The Environment and the People in American Cities, 1600s–1900s: Disorder, Inequality, and Social Change*. Durham, NC: Duke University Press.

Terriss, Kenneth. 2008. Stucco. In *Vancouver Matters*, ed. James Eidse, Mari Fujita, Joey Giaimo, and Christa Min, 115–129. Vancouver: Blueimprint.

Theobald, David. 2005. Landscape Patterns of Exurban Growth in the USA from 1980 to 2020. *Ecology and Society* 10 (1): 32.

Timmermans, Stefan, and Iddo Tavory. 2012. Theory Construction in Qualitative Research: From Grounded Theory to Abductive Analysis. *Sociological Theory* 30 (3): 167–186.

Tomas, Annabel, and Helga Dittmar. 1995. The Experience of Homeless Women: An Exploration of Housing Histories and the Meaning of Home. *Housing Studies* 10 (4): 493–516.

Townsend, Nicholas. 2002. *The Package Deal: Marriage, Work, and Fatherhood in Men's Lives*. Philadelphia: Temple University Press.

Tuan, Yi Fu. 1971. Geography, Phenomenology and the Study of Human Nature. *Canadian Geographer* 15:181–192.

Tversky, Amos, and Daniel Kahneman. 1986. Rational Choice and the Framing of Decisions. *Journal of Business* 59 (4): II:S521–S278.

UN Framework Convention on Climate Change. 2005. *Sixth Compilation and Synthesis of Initial National Communications from Parties Not Included in Annex I to the*

Convention: Addendum—Inventories of Anthropogenic Emissions by Sources and Removals by Sinks of Greenhouse Gases. Available at http://unfccc.int/resource/docs/2005/sbi/eng/18a02.pdf. Accessed August 1, 2013.

U.S. Department of Energy. 2012. *2011 Buildings Energy Data Book.* Available at http://buildingsdatabook.eren.doe.gov/docs%5CDataBooks%5C2010_BEDB.pdf. Accessed July 23, 2013.

U.S. Environmental Protection Agency. 2013. *Inventory of U.S. Greenhouse Gas Emissions and Sinks: 1990–2011.* Washington, DC: U.S. Environmental Protection Agency. Available at http://unfccc.int/national_reports/annex_i_ghg_inventories/national_inventories_submissions/items/7383.php. Accessed April 4, 2015.

Vaisey, Stephen. 2009. Motivation and Justification: A Dual-Process Model of Culture in Action. *American Journal of Sociology* 114 (6): 1675–1715.

Valverde, Mariana. 2011. Seeing like a City: The Dialectic of Modern and Premodern Ways of Seeing in Urban Governance. *Law and Society Review* 45 (2): 277–312.

———. 2012. *Everyday Law on the Street: City Governance in an Age of Diversity.* Chicago: University of Chicago Press.

Vancouver Foundation. 2012. *Connections and Engagement: A Survey of Metro Vancouver.* Vancouver: Vancouver Foundation. Available at https://www.vancouverfoundation.ca/sites/default/files/documents/VanFdn-SurveyResults-Report.pdf. Accessed January 15, 2013.

Vancouver Sun. 1974. Public Meeting Reveals Split on Legalizing Suites. March 1, p. 7.

Vancouver Town Planning Commission. 1931. *City of Vancouver, British Columbia, Zoning Diagram.* Vancouver: Vancouver Town Planning Commission.

———. 1942. *Vancouver, B.C. Zoning Diagram.* Vancouver: Vancouver Town Planning Commission.

Van Weesep, Jan. 1987. The Creation of a New Housing Sector: Condominiums in the United States. *Housing Studies* 2 (2): 122–133.

Wachsmuth, David. 2012. Three Ecologies: Urban Metabolism and the Society-Nature Opposition. *Sociological Quarterly* 53:506–523.

Wade, Jill. 1994. *Houses for All: The Struggle for Social Housing in Vancouver, 1919–1950.* Vancouver: University of British Columbia Press.

Walker, Richard, and Robert Lewis. 2001. Beyond the Crabgrass Frontier: Industry and the Spread of North American Cities, 1850–1950. *Journal of Historical Geography* 27 (1): 3–19.

Ward, Peter. 1999. *A History of Domestic Space: Privacy and the Canadian Home.* Vancouver: University of British Columbia Press.

Wardhaugh, Julia. 1999. The Unaccommodated Woman: Home, Homelessness and Identity. *Sociological Review* 47 (1): 91–109.

Warner, Kee, and Harvey Molotch. 2000. *Building Rules: How Local Controls Shape Community Environments and Economies.* Boulder, CO: Westview Press.

Warren, Samuel, and Louis Brandeis. 1890. The Right to Privacy. *Harvard Law Review* 4 (5): 193–220.

Weaver, John. 1979. The Property Industry and Land Use Controls: The Vancouver Experience, 1910–1945. *Plan Canada* 19 (3): 211–225.

Wickens, Stephen. 2011. Jane Jacobs: Honoured in the Breach. *Globe and Mail,* May 6.

Williamson, Robert. 1980. Hard to Get off Rent-Control Tiger. *Globe and Mail,* April 2.

Williamson, Thad. 2008. Sprawl, Spatial Location, and Politics: How Ideological Identification Tracks the Built Environment. *American Politics Research* 36 (6): 903–933.

———. 2010. *Sprawl, Justice, and Citizenship: The Civic Costs of the American Way of Life.* New York: Oxford University Press.

Wilson, Ellen, and Robert Callis. 2013. Who Could Afford to Buy a Home in 2009? *Current Housing Reports* H121/13-02. U.S. Census Bureau.

Wilson, Thomas. 1985. Urbanism and Tolerance: A Test of Some Hypotheses Drawn from Wirth and Stouffer. *American Sociological Review* 50 (1): 117–123.

Wirth, Louis. 1938. Urbanism as a Way of Life. *American Journal of Sociology* 44:3–24.

Wood, Daniel. 2012. Vancouver's Density Debate Pits Sullivanism versus the Ideas of Jane Jacobs. *Georgia Straight*, June 6. Available at http://www.straight.com/news/vancouvers-density-debate-pits-sullivanism-versus-ideas-jane-jacobs.

Wood, Wendy, and David Neal. 2007. A New Look at Habits and the Habit-Goal Interface. *Psychological Review* 114 (4): 843–863.

Wright, Gwendolyn. 1981. *Building the Dream: A Social History of Housing in America.* New York: Pantheon Books.

Yin, Henry, and Barbara Knowlton. 2006. The Role of the Basal Ganglia in Habit Formation. *Nature Reviews: Neuroscience* 7:464–476.

Young, Iris Marion. 1990. *Justice and the Politics of Difference.* Princeton, NJ: Princeton University Press.

———. 2002. House and Home: Feminist Variations on a Theme. In *Gender Struggles: Practical Approaches to Contemporary Feminism*, ed. Constance Mui and Julien Murphy, 314–346. Lanham, MD: Rowan and Littlefield.

Zavisca, Jane. 2012. *Housing the New Russia.* Ithaca, NY: Cornell University Press.

Zhang, Yin, Bert Guindon, and Krista Sun. 2010. Measuring Canadian Urban Expansion and Impacts on Work-Related Travel Distance: 1966–2001. *Journal of Land Use Science* 5 (3): 217–235.

Nathanael Lauster is an Associate Professor of Sociology at the University of British Columbia. He is the co-editor (with Graham Allan) of *The End of Children? Changing Trends in Childbearing and Childhood.*